Accession no.
D1394575

# Managing the Future

WARRINGTO

## Additional praise for *Managing the Future*

"This is a fascinating book, placing contemporary techniques for managerial foresight within a rich and challenging theoretical context. It is recommended equally for thinking practitioners and for practice-sensitive teachers and researchers."
*Richard Whittington, Saïd Business School*

"This timely book adds a new dimension to the strategy debate and sources of competitive advantage. The authors show that strategic foresight differentiates successful firms from failing firms as much, if not more than, a superior vision, appropriate plan, generic strategy, innovative culture, or a unique resource-pool."
*Professor Henk W. Volberda, Rotterdam School of Management,*
*Erasmus University*

"Hari Tsoukas, Jill Shepherd, and the other contributors of this book provide a compelling vision as to why the 'future could be ours to manage.' This is a thought-provoking book that offers ways by which individuals can develop foresight."
*Raghu Garud, New York University*

"This is really good material, from good scholars, on this emerging field. It will attract a wide audience."
*Colin Eden, University of Strathclyde*

# Managing
## the
# Future

Foresight in the Knowledge Economy

*Edited by Haridimos Tsoukas*
*and Jill Shepherd*

CHESTER COLLEGE

ACC. No.   DEPT. pbs
01102365

CLASS No.

WARRINGTON LIBRARY

RECEIVED
1 6 AUG 2004

**Blackwell**
Publishing

© 2004 by Blackwell Publishing Ltd
except for editorial material and organization
© 2004 by Haridimos Tsoukas and Jill Shepherd

350 Main Street, Malden, MA 02148-5020, USA
108 Cowley Road, Oxford OX4 1JF, UK
550 Swanston Street, Carlton, Victoria 3053, Australia

The right of Haridimos Tsoukas and Jill Shepherd to be identified as the Authors of the
Editorial Material in this Work has been asserted in accordance with the UK
Copyright, Designs, and Patents Act 1988.

All rights reserved. No part of this publication may be reproduced, stored in
a retrieval system, or transmitted, in any form or by any means, electronic,
mechanical, photocopying, recording or otherwise, except as permitted by
the UK Copyright, Designs, and Patents Act 1988, without the prior
permission of the publisher.

First published 2004 by Blackwell Publishing Ltd

*Library of Congress Cataloging-in-Publication Data*

Managing the future : foresight in the knowledge economy/edited by Haridimos
Tsoukas and Jill Shepherd.
p. cm.
Includes bibliographical references (p. ) and index.
ISBN 1-4051-1614-5 (hardcover : alk. paper)–
ISBN 1-4051-1615-3 (paperback : alk. paper)
1. Organizational learning. 2. Knowledge management. 3. Intellectual capital.
4. Organizational change. I. Tsoukas, Haridimos. II. Shepherd, Jill, 1965-

HD58.82.M362 2004
658.4′0355-dc22
2003016912

A catalogue record for this title is available from the British Library.

Set in 10 on 12.5pt Galliard
by Kolam Information Services Pvt. Ltd, Pondicherry, India
Printed and bound in the United Kingdom
by MPG Books Ltd, Bodmin, Cornwall

For further information on
Blackwell Publishing, visit our website:
http://www.blackwellpublishing.com

# Contents

# Figures

# Tables

# Notes on the Contributors

**Paul Argyle** is Owner and Chief Executive of Flight Directors Scheduled Services Ltd. established 1984. The 100-employee business provides a general sales agency and complementary call center facilities for several well-known airlines. Paul developed his interests in complexity, which he applies to his own business strategy, during his Masters degree studies at the University of Durham in 1999–2000.

**Deborah A. Blackman** is Senior Lecturer in Organizational Studies, University of Western Sydney. After working in the hospitality industry Deborah moved into academia teaching, researching, and consulting in organizational studies, human resources management, knowledge and learning, and change management. Her particular interests are in the areas of organizational learning and the impacts of shared mental models upon organizational and team effectiveness. Abiding interests in travel and sailing led to a recent move to Australia where visitors are welcome.

**Robert Chia** is Professor of Strategy and Organization and Director of Research, Centre for Leadership Studies, University of Exeter. Robert has consulted extensively with well-known international organizations and institutions. His research interests revolve around the issues of strategic foresight and leadership, complexity, and creative thinking, contrasting East–West metaphysical mindsets and critical cultural studies. He is the author of three books and several international journal articles as well as book chapters in a variety of management sub-fields.

**Miguel Pina E. Cunha** earned his PhD from Tilburg University and is an assistant professor at the Universidade Nova de Lisboa, in Lisbon, Portugal. His research is mainly devoted to the combination of planning and emergence in organizations, and has appeared in such outlets as the *Academy of Management Review*, *Organization Studies*, *Human Relations* and *Journal of Management Studies*, among others. He is a member of the editorial board of the *European Management Review*, EURAM's new journal.

**T. K. Das** is Professor of Strategic Management and Area Coordinator (Strategic Management and Business & Society) at the Zicklin School of Business, Baruch College, City University of New York, New York. He was a senior business executive before entering academic life. He holds degrees in physics, mathematics, and management and has a professional certification in banking. His PhD in Organization and Strategic Studies is from the Anderson Graduate School of Management at the University of California, Los Angeles. He is the author of over 120 publications in the areas of strategy making, strategic alliances, and temporal studies.

**Rodolphe Durand** is Professor of Strategic Management at EM Lyon (France). He earned his PhD in Management at HEC Business School (France), and his Master degree in Philosophy from La Sorbonne. His research interests deal with the conditions of organizational performance from evolutionary perspectives. His research has been published in academic journals (*Strategic Management Journal, American Journal of Sociology, Organization Studies,* and *Journal of Business Venturing among others*).

**Liam Fahey** is Adjunct Professor of Strategic Management at Babson College and a founding partner of Leadership Forum, Inc. Previously he taught at Kellogg School of Management at Northwestern University and at Boston University's School of Management. He is author or editor of eight books and over 40 articles or book chapters. He has published in the *Strategic Management Journal, Academy of Management Review, Journal of Management,* and the *Journal of Marketing,* among others. He has received awards for his research, teaching and professional activity.

**Ted Fuller** is Professor of Entrepreneurship and Strategic Foresight at Teesside Business School, University of Teesside. His research and publications are mainly in the field of entrepreneurship and small business and often take a futures perspective. Current research includes the sustainability of enterprises and the role enterprise plays in the futures of society. He advises a number of corporate and public sector organizations.

**Margaret Gorman** is the executive director of Center for the Study of Learning and the Executive Leadership Doctoral Program at the George Washington University. This innovative doctoral program format and research center explores phenomena relative to human and organizational studies in a wide range of organizational settings. Margaret's research areas of interest include creating organizational knowledge during transformation change, use of mix methodologies in applied research, organizational learning and leadership, chaos theory, and sociological approaches to organizational change and development. Her teaching areas of interest include consulting skills, organization development, organizational assesment, managerial and organization cognition, and organizational learning.

**Steven Henderson** is a Reader in Management, specializing in strategy. He has worked in finance, consumer research and other stuff that he mostly found dreary. He now has an exciting life, writing chapters like this with people like Debbie.

**Raanan Lipshitz** is an Associate Professor in the Department of Psychology, University of Haifa, Israel. His research interests are organizational learning, where he developed a multi-facet model of organizational learning in collaboration with Drs Micha Popper and Victor Frieman, and naturalistic decision making, with emphasis on how decision makers cope with uncertainty and the role of substantive knowledge in real-world decision making.

**Paul Moran** is a Chartered Psychologist and specialist in small and medium enterprise development. He is currently running his own consulting and human resource development business, operating primarily in China and the Far East. He was previously Senior Tutor with the Foundation for SME Development, University of Durham, UK.

**V. K. Narayanan** is Stubbs Professor of Strategy and Entrepreneurship at the LeBow College of Business, Drexel University. He is currently the chair of the Strategy Process Interest Group at the Strategic Management Society. He has published numerous journal articles, and his most recent book, *Managing Technology and Innovation for Competitive Advantage* was published by Prentice-Hall.

**Micha Popper** has a PhD from Tel-Aviv University and was a Commanding Officer of the School for Leadership Development of the Israel Defence Forces. Presently, Micha is a Senior Lecturer in the Department of Psychology and Education within the University of Haifa, Israel and a Co-Director of the Center for Outstanding Leadership in Zikhron Yaakov, Israel. His research involves organizational learning, the dynamics of the leader–follower relationship and developmental aspects of leaders. Author of three books on leadership, Micha has also written numerous articles in journals such as *The Leadership Quarterly*, *Political Psychology*, *Academy of Management Journal* and *Military Psychology*.

**Neta Ron** is a PhD candidate in the Department of Psychology at the University of Haifa. In addition to her studies she works as an OD consultant specializing in helping organizations appreciate and realize their own conceptions of excellence.

**David R. Schwandt** is Professor of Human and Organizational Studies at The George Washington University in Washington, DC and Director of the Executive Leadership Doctoral Program and the Center for the Study of Learning. His current research centers on organizational issues that relate to collective cognition. Specific areas of inquiry include organizational learning, strategy development and implementation, collective sensemaking and culture, and organizational development.

**David Seidl** is Assistant Professor of Organization and Strategy at the Ludwig-Maximilians-Universität in Munich. He studied Management and Sociology in Munich, London, Witten/Herdecke and Cambridge. He earned his PhD at the Judge Institute of Management Studies, University of Cambridge. His current research focuses on sociological approaches to strategy and change. Together with

Dr Paula Jarzabkowski he hosts an academic website on strategy as social practice (www.strategy-as-practice.org).

**Jill Shepherd** is an Assistant Professor at Simon Fraser University, Canada. After a career as a scientist, manager, entrepreneur and management consultant she is now trying her hand at academic life having obtained her PhD. Her research interests center around the use of evolutionary theory, particularly a branch called memetics, to investigate knowledge creation and innovation within corporates, high tech firms and clusters. Unusually for this area, her work is non-normative.

**Haridimos Tsoukas** is the George D. Mavros Research Professor of Organization and Management at the Athens Laboratory of Business Administration (ALBA), Greece and a Professor of Organization Theory and Behaviour at Warwick Business School. He has published widely in several leading academic journals, is the Editor-in-Chief of *Organization Studies*, and serves on the Editorial Board of several journals. His research interests include knowledge-based perspectives on organizations, the management of organizational change and social reforms, the epistemology of practice, and epistemological issues in organization science.

**Kees van der Heijden** is Emeritus Professor of General and Strategic Management at Strathclyde University, Graduate School of Business, Glasgow, Visiting Professor at Nijenrode University, Holland, Director of the Centre for Scenario Planning and Future Studies at Strathclyde University and author of the award-winning book, *Scenarios: The Art of Strategic Conversation* as well as many other publications (http://www.gbn.org). Prior to joining the Strathclyde faculty, Kees was head of Business Environment Planning at Royal Dutch/Shell, London (development and application of Shell's scenario planning, monitoring and analysing the business environment and communicating with top management on outlook and strategic implications).

# Foreword: Foresight Matters

*Spyros Makridakis*

On October 27, 1986 the cover story of *Fortune* magazine was about Ken Olsen, the founder and CEO of DEC. The story, with his photo on the front page, named Olsen *"America's Most Successful Entrepreneur."* DEC had become the major competitor of IBM at that time and had grown from zero in 1957, when founded by Olsen, to a multi billion dollar company at the time the cover story was written (DEC's revenues were close to $12 billion, with $1.3 billion in profits, in 1988). Yet ten years later, in 1998, Dec was bought by Compaq after incurring heavy losses and having to fire tens of thousands of people. Olsen's famous, or better infamous, statement *"There is no reason for any individual to have a computer in their home"* prevented DEC from entering the booming PC market which was fully exploited by the likes of Microsoft, Compaq and Intel who had the foresight to aggressively pursue the PC market and, in the process, dominate the market.

The rapid rate of technological and other changes that affect the business environment has increased the need for correct foresight. Today, there is overcapacity and keen competition in nearly all industries. Thus, the big winners are those that can accurately predict forthcoming changes and effectively implement a series of steps/actions to exploit them *before* their competitors. Doing the same as many others, or waiting for confirming evidence before acting, can lead to disaster as the telecom industry, which correctly predicted the need for broadband, has found out. Accurate prediction must also be unique, as the expectation of large future profits inevitably attracts competition and results in oversupply, as has been the case in the telecom industry, which experienced major bankruptcies and big losses by practically all players in the last few years. But there is no such a thing as a free lunch. Profiting from foresight requires taking risks, since there is always the chance that the predicted events/technologies may not materialize as planned, or their timing may be different than predicted.

The industrial revolution reversed established trends that had prevailed, often, for thousands of years and brought material abundance while also raising the standards of living of Western societies, as well as other parts of the world, while also almost doubling life expectancy during the past 150 years. Technological innovation has been the engine behind the industrial revolution, which has, consequently, affected all aspects of our personal lives and business firms. The information revolution currently developing will equally affect all aspects of our lives and business. Those able to exploit its technological advantages in order to provide new, useful products and services for both consumers and businesses will greatly benefit, as will be those who benefit from using new technologies to run their internal operations more efficiently and effectively. Foremost, new technologies require an open mind if they are to be used, not as extensions of the old ones, but in brand new ways that exploit, in the highest possible degree, the availing technological capabilities ensuing from new technology.

The role of foresight is to provide business executives and government policy makers with ways of seeing the future with different eyes and fully understanding the possible implications of alternative technological/societal paths. The most critical element in succeeding is not the correct prediction of when new technologies will arrive but rather the implications of such emerging technologies and their abilities to offer new products/services that consumers would be willing to pay for. Nothing, however, is certain. Thus, the purpose of foresight is neither to provide recipes nor specific forecasts. Its aim is to enhance an organization's ability to consider various future scenarios without any preconceptions, debate their implications, examine the risks involved, estimate potential benefits, predict the costs/investments involved to arrive with practical alternatives that can be translated into executable actions.

In order to improve the chances that foresight can be as valuable as possible, organizations must create a group consisting of the right people (mostly young high flyers with one or two seasoned executives who know the industry and firm) and provide them with ample time and resources for their deliberations. This group should not hesitate to ask the most threatening questions such as: will our industry exist five or ten years from now? Will the Internet make our business model obsolete? How easy will it be for new competitors to enter the industry? How can our firm grow and prosper in the face of keen competition from existing players and pressures from new entrants? Can our firm provide products/services that add extra value to our present and potential customers? etc. The recommendations of the group should be presented directly to the Board of Directors and must, in their majority, be implemented unless the Board, and not the Management, decides otherwise. Implementing bold changes is neither easy nor risk free. At the same time organizations must recognize threatening changes and adapt to them as technology and competition continuously affect business firms. Tomorrow's winners will not obtain leverage by being operationally efficient and effective (such abilities are fast becoming competitive requirements), instead they will need to recognize forthcoming changes and be proactive in implementing them before competitors, fully realizing the risks involved, so that they can lead their industry and make above-average profits, before others follow creating overcapacity and reduced profit margins. Finally, executives must realize that as the pace of technological change becomes faster so does the failure rate of once stellar firms (the fact that Compaq was obliged to merge with HP is a vivid example of a great company getting, in a short period of time, into serious financial trouble) that see their business model becoming obsolete because a start-up devised a brand new model.

# Chapter One

# Introduction: Organizations and the Future, From Forecasting to Foresight

## Haridimos Tsoukas and Jill Shepherd

*Deliberation is irrational in the degree in which an end is so fixed, a passion or interest so absorbing, that the foresight of consequences is warped to include only what furthers execution of its predetermined bias. Deliberation is rational in the degree in which forethought flexibly remakes old aims and habits, institutes perception and love of new ends and acts.*

John Dewey (1988, p. 138)

*The dominance of retrospect in sensemaking is a major reason why students of sensemaking find forecasting, contingency planning, strategic planning, and other magical probes into the future wasteful and misleading if they are decoupled from reflective action and history.*

Karl E. Weick (1995, p. 30)

Several leading social theorists have pointed out that one of the most significant features of modernity is its attitude to time in general and the future in particular. As Giddens (1990, 1991) has repeatedly argued, whereas for pre-modern societies the future is something that just happens, with individuals exercising only a limited influence over it, for modern societies the future is something to be carefully thought about, influenced and, ideally, planned. Nowhere is this modern tendency better manifested than in the field of strategy. Companies are advised to plan meticulously ahead and several techniques have been on offer to that effect.

However, research has shown the limits of the planning-cum-design approach to strategy (Mintzberg, 1994; Mintzberg et al., 1998), as well as the inherent limits to the ability of organizations to forecast, especially discontinuities and radically new developments (Hogarth and Makridakis, 1981; Makridakis, 1990; Makridakis and Hibon, 1979). Popper (1988) famously remarked that, for radically new innovation to occur at all, the future must be *unknowable*, for otherwise an innovation would, in principle, be already known and would have occurred in the present and not in the future. As MacIntyre (1985, p. 93) observed, commenting approvingly on Popper's claim:

any invention, any discovery, which consists essentially in the elaboration of a radically new concept cannot be predicted, for a necessary part of the prediction is the present elaboration of the very concept whose discovery or invention was to take place only in the future. The notion of the prediction of radical conceptual innovation is itself conceptually incoherent.

If we are to take the idea of the future seriously, we must accept that the future is inherently open-ended – it will always surprise us (Rorty, 1989).

While such an agnostic attitude towards the future points out the limits of a purely cognitive attitude to it (namely, it highlights the limits of trying to forecast and plan for what lies ahead), it makes it possible, at the same time, to emphasize an *active* attitude to the future: the latter may not be known ex ante, but it is useful to remind ourselves that the future is *created* by human beings and, insofar as this happens, the question of foresightful action – action that aims at influencing what will be – becomes relevant and important to explore. The main questions, therefore, in an organizational context at least, are: what does an active stance towards the future imply for organizations? What is organizational foresight and how can it be developed?

## Organizations and the Future

In a celebrated lecture given at the Harvard Business School in 1931, Alfred North Whitehead (1967) posed similar questions. The distinguished philosopher identified *foresight* as the crucial feature of the competent business mind. Anticipating contemporary notions of "sensemaking," "double-loop learning," and "scenario planning," Whitehead perspicuously saw that business organizations need to cultivate foresight in order to cope with the relentless change that modernity generates. Foresight is rooted in deep understanding, he remarked. It marks the ability to see through the apparent confusion, to spot developments before they become trends, to see patterns before they fully emerge, and to grasp the relevant features of social currents that are likely to shape the direction of future events. While Whitehead (and other philosophers, such as Dewey and Popper, who also addressed the question of foresight) had individual actors (entrepreneurs) in mind, his remarks can be extended to organizations as well. But to appreciate what foresight may mean in an organizational context, we need to revisit some key properties of organizations.

It has been suggested that organizing is about reducing equivocality between actors and generating recurrent patterns of behavior over time (Weick, 1979). Another way of putting this is to point out that organizing is a process for institutionalizing cognitive representations, routines and sequences of predictable behavior. Strictly speaking, when a social system is organized it creates the conditions for a standardization of time, whereby events and processes are placed in a patterned chronological order. Take, for example, the case of a university. Classes are scheduled, meetings are planned, office hours are announced, events are put on the calendar – university life has its own patterned rhythms. Chronological time is superimposed over the subjective time of individuals so that the synchronized carrying out of organizational tasks is possible (see Das, this volume; Hassard, 2002). Or, to use Giddens' (1991) language, experienced (subjective) time is "disembedded" – it is lifted out of its subjective individual context and placed in an abstract (organizational) context (Tsoukas, 2001). Insofar as this happens, an organized social system creates quasi-predictability: its internal life is structured along standardized routines sequenced over time.

That predictability, however, is never complete. Partly this is because of the, ultimately, non-programmable human nature: the "disruptive" student, the "awkward" academic, the "indifferent" administrator conspire to make university life more interesting than it would otherwise have been. Predictability, moreover, is mainly limited by the changes in the external environment. Although this is more difficult to see in a regulated academic environment, it is clearly visible in the case of business organizations operating in the market place. Changes in competition, legislation, customer tastes, and technology are some of the most important changes that make a market-based business environment truly unpredictable in the long term. And if those researchers who have studied "high-velocity" environments (Brown and Eisenhardt, 1998; Ilinitch et al., 1998) are to be believed, such changes are faster and more frequent than ever in the history of capitalism.

The environment is thus a source of uncertainty for business organizations much more so than human behavior within organizations is. The reason for this is not difficult to see. Human behavior in organizations is regularized and normalized to some extent (but never completely) through the authority relationship. The latter standardizes expectations, homogenizes to some degree individual cognitive maps and, through management control systems, elicits certain intended behaviors. The environment, however, is, to a large degree, beyond an organization's control, hence it is not clear how it will change over time. Think of how disruptive technologies have reshaped the semiconductor and the watch industries (Glasmeier, 1997; Tushman et al., 1997), or how legislation has influenced the activities of accounting firms, in the aftermath of corporate scandals in the USA in 2002. Precisely because of the uncertainty of the environment – that is to say, the uncertainty generated by the interactions of all those factors that make up the business environment over time – strategy making is important: it represents senior managers' wish to steer a distinctive and coherent course of organizational action over time (Mintzberg, 1994, p. 239). But how do organizations do that? How do they deal with the uncertainty of the future? (See Narayanan and Fahey in this volume.)

How organizations deal with the future depends on how they answer the following two questions: first, to what extent is there a knowledge base for anticipating important events? And second, to what extent is there a stock of knowledge on which to draw for undertaking action? How these two questions are answered, gives four different ways organizations attempt to deal with the future (see Figure 1.1). When important events are anticipated (that is, when we have knowledge of forthcoming events) and there is a stock of knowledge as to how to deal with them, organizations use forecasting methods. Seasonal demand, for example, is such an event that may be anticipated, which, say, a beverages company knows how to deal

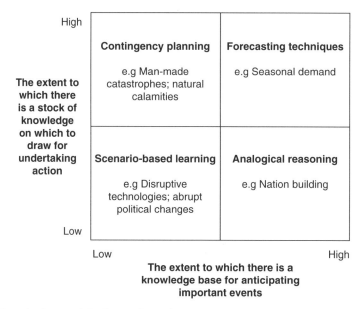

**Figure 1.1**   Organizations and the future: A typology

with. Such events are typically extrapolations from the past and a relevant knowledge base has been developed over time. The future in this case is not qualitatively different from the past; it rather is a pattern that is being repeated over time (Makridakis, 1990).

When, however, certain events may be anticipated, but a knowledge base on how to deal with them does not yet exist, forecasting is of limited utility. In such cases, *analogies* is the method most often used for drawing conclusions. In politics, nation building is a good example. Overthrowing a government and disrupting the political and institutional status quo in a country leads, typically, to a power vacuum, lawlessness and a breakdown of institutions (at least initially). Such events may be anticipated but how to deal with them – how, in other words, to create new institutions, which will command the loyalty of the local people – is far from clear. The case of Iraq is a good case in point. Building institutions, especially democratic ones, which will, at the same time, reflect the values and culture of the indigenous population for post-Saddam Iraq is fraught with huge difficulties and uncertainty. As is seen in the debate about the future of Iraq, drawing analogies with similar situations concerning nation-building in post-War Japan and Germany, as well as more contemporary ones in Bosnia, Kosovo, and Afghanistan, is the most feasible way for policy makers to figure out what to do. The same applies to policy making at large. How to create a functioning market economy and a liberal democracy in former communist countries is far from clear (Elster et al., 1998). Analogies with the development of capitalism in other parts of the world help to derive lessons of what to do.

Cases in which knowledge about the extent to which certain events and processes may be anticipated is limited leads typically to the use of "what if" contingency planning and scenarios. Forecasting in this case is inadequate, since forecasting relies heavily on the established patterns of past behaviors and/or a good understanding of cause–effect relationships in order to predict what may happen in the future. Some events, however, may be novel or rare, about which there is very little prior knowledge, hence they cannot be predicted. There are, however, certain events, for which, although uncommon, should they occur, there is a stock of knowledge of how to deal with them. For example, a biological terrorist attack on the London underground is an event no policy maker knows will happen, but, if it does, hospitals need to be ready to treat the patients in certain ways. The same applies to some environmental catastrophes. There is now a certain know-how concerning, for example, the treatment of oil leaks in the sea or earthquakes. Policy makers know, broadly, how to respond to such events, although they do not know if and when they will happen.

It is far more difficult for managers and policy makers to respond to events about which (a) they know very little about the probability of their happening, or even cannot imagine what form they will take (think, for example, of the terrorist attack on the Twin Towers – who would have imagined it?), and (b) managers and policy makers have very little knowledge about how to deal with them. Such events represent discontinuities—they are rare events that happen on an ad hoc basis (Mintzberg, 1994, p. 228). Rapid price increases, draconian legislation, dramatic political changes, disruptive technologies, and abrupt shifts in consumer attitudes are discontinuities, whose occurrence and/or timing are difficult to predict and there is no developed knowledge base as to how to deal with them.

Currently, scenario-based organizational learning (SBOL) is the most widely used method to deal with such discontinuities. Notice that the use of scenarios is not an attempt to attach probabilities to a set of events, but a *process* to prepare the organization to see such discontinuities "soon enough ... and to do so earlier or at least better than anyone else" (Mintzberg, 1994, p. 233; see also van der Heijden et al., 2002, p. 176). SBOL does not attempt to eliminate uncertainty; it rather recognizes its irreducible character and, consequently, the fundamentally unpredictable changes in the environment (van der Heijden, 1996, p. 103). Uncertainty now is not so much a threat to be eliminated as an opportunity to be taken up and given form (Tsoukas, 1999). The burden is on the organization: how clearly and quickly it can see developments in its environment, how sensitive it is to environmental changes, how quickly it can spot differences both within and outside the organization.

SBOL is not so much about the future per se as about sharpening the organizational ability of perceiving in the present. As van der Heijden (1996, p. 118) remarks:

> The language of scenarios is about the future, but they should make a difference in what is happening now. If it is successful in embedding different models of the business environment in the consciousness of the organization, it will make the organization more aware of environmental change. Through early conceptualization and effective internal communication scenario planning can make the organization a more skilful observer of its business environment. By seeing change earlier the organization has the potential to become more responsive.

In this view, a foresightful organization is an organization that has sharpened its ability to see, to observe, to perceive what is going on both externally and internally, and to respond accordingly (see Chia, this volume). Organizational awareness is enhanced by the extent to which members of an organization collectively become skilful perceivers of the business environment (see Schwandt and Gorman, this volume). The ability to perceive is sharpened through increasing the individual and organizational capacity to see differences. This is easier in the case of individuals, such as for example the Canadian retailer Sam Steinberg, who was the first to launch his business into shopping centers in the early 1950s in Canada (Mintzberg and Waters, 1982). As Mintzberg (1994, p. 232) points out, incipient discontinuities in the business environment tend to be spotted by individuals who have a deep understanding of an industry and its context (see Fuller et al., this volume).

However, as research in artificial intelligence shows, such a sophisticated form of pattern recognition for discontinuities cannot be formalized and, insofar as this is the case, it cannot be turned into formal organizational systems and routines (Dreyfus, 1997; Penrose, 1994; Searle, 1997). Ansoff's (1984) "weak signals" – the signals that give an organization a clue for discontinuities to come – are potentially infinite. Which ones will turn out to be critical cannot be formally articulated but informally intuited (Mintzberg, 1994, p. 233; see Seidl, this volume), which is why foresight tends to be an important feature of successful entrepreneurs who do not have to articulate and justify their choices and actions to outside audiences.

For an organization to sharpen its collective capacity to perceive is more difficult than for individuals. The reason is that, as argued at the beginning of this chapter, organizing is the process of generating recurrent behaviors, namely a process for reducing differences among individuals through institutionalized cognitive representations (Tsoukas and Chia, 2002, p. 571). This is what gives organized systems predictability and efficiency; but this is also what gives them rigidity and crudeness. Organizing induces abstraction and generalization in social activities for coordinated purposeful action to become possible. Thus, in strictly organizational terms, a "broken photocopier" is an abstract entity, as malfunctioning as any other, and this is what enables a photocopier company to issue repair manuals to its service technicians (Orr, 1996). Organizations, however, are far more than abstract systems: they are activity systems (Blackler, 1995; Spender, 1996). A particular broken photocopier is not a an abstract entity that simply features in repair manuals, but a material machine that is used in specific contexts by specific individuals, which will be repaired by specific technicians.

An organization develops its ability to see differences by the extent to which its members do not merely draw on institutionalized cognitive representations and routines ("a broken machine," "if this happens then do that") but improvise and adapt them to local contexts, and undertake situated action that compels organization members to partially revise the cognitive representations they draw upon (see Cunha, this volume). The more sensitive organizational members are to differences between institutionalized representations and routines on the one hand and the local contexts of action on the other, the more perceptive they will be. Just as a good painter brings to our attention something we had seen but not noticed (Bergson,

1946), so an organization becomes perceptive by sharpening its members' attention through helping them spot differences between how things canonically and routinely should be on the one hand and how they actually are and/or might be, on the other. Notice that what is important here is not forecasting what exactly "might be" but using plausible versions of the latter in order to juxtapose them with current representations, routines, and assumptions, and draw out the implications. Maintaining the difference – the tension – between "what should be" and "what is" as well as between "what is" and "what might be" activates the organizational sensory system, just like the human sensory system is activated by difference (Bateson, 1979).

It is in that sense that SBOL creates "memories of the future" (Ingvar, 1985). Through preparing scenarios about different futures, an organization can see plausible changes in the environment and how they will probably impact the organization. Although none of those scenarios may come true, the jolt that is delivered to the organization through them is often strong enough to make the organization challenge its business-as-usual assumptions, its current cognitive models and routines (van der Heijden et al., 2002, p. 176; Wright and Goodwin, 1999).

Van der Heijden et al. (2002, p. 177) describe how a scenario project in an Asian multinational corporation made the company perceive more clearly the changes in its environment and their implications for the organization, as follows:

> The "jolt" in this case was that on considering the scenarios, there was a realization within the senior management team that their success formula – which had served them well for 20 years – was unlikely to generate the same success in the future. It did not matter much which scenario one looked at; there were a number of changes in the contextual environment which they had not previously heeded, and which made it unlikely that the organization could continue to succeed in the future without fundamental rethinking taking place in the organization.

In other words, the scenario project re-focused senior mangers' attention and made them notice changes that they had probably seen but not noticed – the price of being both an organization in general (reducing differences) and a successful organization (complacency) in particular (Miller, 1990). The process of constructing and reflecting on a scenario set enabled senior managers to "visit" the future ahead of time, thereby creating "memories of the future," and juxtapose those "memories" with current practices. It is the difference between "how things may turn out to be" and "how they currently are" that spurred managers to action. The organization now could not go on as before pretending it did not know: things would have to change.

Notice that, seen this way, foresightful action – action in conditions of limited knowledge concerning both the extent to which future events may be anticipated and how to deal with them – is possible through greater *self-knowledge*. Knowledge about the future and how to handle it may be difficult to obtain, but it is within our power to enhance what we know about ourselves. This should not be confused with the case of self-prediction – self-knowledge is valuable not because it leads to self-prediction but because it sharpens one's ability of perception and, thus, enhances one's capacity for action.

As MacIntyre (1985, pp. 95–6) persuasively argued, self-prediction is impossible because an actor's future actions cannot be predicted by him/her since they depend on the outcomes of decisions as yet unmade by him/her. Self-knowledge is clarity about one's behavioral tendencies. In organizations, it is particularly strengthened when senior managers envisage different ways in which the future may turn out and how the organization would accordingly respond. That kind of knowledge makes the organization more aware of its potentiality and, to the extent this happens, it contributes to organizational self-knowledge.

This is in line with Dewey's understanding of "potentiality." For him potentiality is not teleologically defined – namely defined as the unfolding on an inner essence in the pursuit of a fixed end – but interactively produced (Dewey, 1998, p. 223). Potentialities are known after interactions have occurred. There are, at a given time, unactualized potentialities in an organization because, and in as far as, there are in existence other things with which it has not as yet interacted. Scenarios of the future are such things with which an organization is asked to simulate "interacting" and, by doing so, it obtains a clearer picture of its potentiality.

Dewey (1988, p. 143) has observed that "the object of foresight of consequences is not to predict the future. It is to ascertain the meaning of present activities and to secure, so far as possible, a present activity with a unified meaning." And, later on (1988, pp. 143–4), he continues:

> Hence the problem of deliberation is not to calculate future happenings but to appraise present proposed actions. We judge present desires and habits by their tendency to produce certain consequences.... Deliberation is not calculation of indeterminate future results. The present, not the future is ours. No shrewdness, no store of information will make it ours. But by constant watchfulness concerning the tendency of acts, by noting disparities between former judgements and actual outcomes, and tracing that part of the disparity that was due to deficiency and excess in disposition, we come to know the meaning of present acts, and to guide them in the light of that meaning.

In the context of this book, Dewey's argument can be seen as a wonderful advocacy of organizational learning. While the distinguished philosopher points out the futility of trying to forecast the future, he is sensitive enough to realize that intelligent (or in his terms, "deliberative") action is one that: (a) springs from knowledge of past experience that reveals current tendencies; and (b) is quick enough to link outcomes to expectations in a continuous manner (see Lipshitz et al., this volume). Dewey seems to have in mind here both retro-knowledge and how important it is in helping actors understand current tendencies *and* fore-knowledge and how significant it is in inducing re-consideration of old aims and habits in light of expected outcomes. Like the executives of the Asian multinational mentioned above, organizations need to keep ascertaining the meaning of their current activities – their active tendencies – for by doing so they keep their activities alive, stop them from becoming routine habits. The meaning of current activities is ascertained by juxtaposing them with activities in the past and, more importantly, with likely activities in the future.

While organizational learning partly relies on retrospective sense making, whereby we obtain a clearer picture of our actions through making sense of them ex post facto

(Weick, 1995), it also partly relies on prospective sense making, whereby an organization ascertains its tendency to yield certain results through comparing its current modus operandi with the anticipated challenges of the future. In other words, in Dewey's terms, an organization is likely to act foresightfully when it obtains the necessary self-knowledge of its current tendencies. This happens when it systematically links both expectations to outcomes and current practices to anticipated futures. Foresightful action is thus inextricably linked to learning and sense making. Dealing effectively with the future is not so much about getting it right ex ante as about preparing for it. Whereas forecasting activities focus on outcomes, organizational learning (especially scenario-based and analogical organizational learning) focuses on process – preparing the organization to spot differences soon enough and act before or better than others.

## Foresightfulness as Coping

From the above it follows that an actor is foresightful when it has the propensity to act in a manner that coherently connects past, present and future (Tsoukas and Hatch, 2001; Weick and Roberts, 1993; see chapters by Cunha, and Lipshitz et al. this volume). At an elementary level, this happens when an organization forecasts, for example, demand for next year and adjusts accordingly its policies (e.g. production capability, prices, marketing campaign) in anticipation of the new demand. Forecasting techniques tackle this sort of problems rather well. For this simple form of foresightfulness to be effective, organizations need to have a memory in which past incidents are recorded, and to have deciphered certain relations between the items stored in memory, which enable the organization to anticipate future incidents.

A second, more complex way of relating past, present, and future is for an organization to hypothesize that certain events will take place in the future and work backwards to the present state to decide what it would need to do should these prognostications come true. This, as argued above, can take the form of contingency planning or scenario planning.

An organization also fully develops the pervasive *skill* of foresightfulness when its members systematically treat time as a stream, namely when they forge a coherent relationship between past, present, and future or, between memory, attention, and expectation respectively (Tsoukas and Hatch, 2001; Weick and Roberts, 1993). Through the use of stories, scenario-based organizational learning provides practitioners with flexible means to connect data dispersed in time. Plausible futures need to be narratively connected to current tendencies and past experiences.

The pitfalls for organizations here are threefold. Too heavy an influence by the *past* results in incapacity to see what has changed in the present and what is the likely shape of things to come. This is a problem inherent in formal organization. The latter tends to perceive the world predominantly in terms of its own cognitive categories, which are necessarily derived from past experiences. The world may be changing but the cognitive system underlying formal organization, a system that reflects and is based on past experiences, changes slowly (see chapters by Durand, and Henderson and Blackman in this volume).

Too much concentration on the *present* task makes the organization unappreciative of all the small changes that are taking place in the wider environment. Van der Heijden (1996, pp. 115–16) mentions a major company in the mainframe computer industry in the 1980s that found it nearly impossible to notice the huge changes that were taking place in its industry. They were very capable of forecasting demand for computing power (tellingly, expressed in "millions of instructions per second" – a key term in the mainframe business) but unable to work out the *form* the market was slowly taking before their own eyes (i.e. the emergence of distributed computing).

Finally, too tight a focus on the *future* per se risks making the organization a victim of fashions. As Mintzberg (1994) has pointed out, moving in and out of diverse markets, following the fashion of the day, without properly considering the organizational capabilities a firm has historically developed, may lead a company to reckless decisions. Diversifying into new businesses should not be a mere exercise in linguistic re-description ("reinvent your business") but a balanced consideration of a firm's capabilities. "Knowing thyself" is as important as "dare to be different."

Foresightfulness becomes an *organizational skill* when future-oriented thinking ceases to be a specialized activity undertaken by experts and/or senior managers, in which they engage from time to time in order to deal with something called "the future," but acquires the status of expertise that is widely distributed throughout the organization and is spontaneously put to action. Forecasting techniques, simulation methods, even scenario planning, all are designed to be used or engaged in by experts, or senior managers, who focus explicitly on the future and treat it as if it was a separate entity. While this is important, for all the reasons mentioned above, it is even more important that foresightfulness becomes an embedded organizational capability, a set of actions that do not spring so much from explicit reasoning about "the future" but from an "immediate coping" (Varela, 1999, p. 5) with what is confronting the organization. Just like "a wise (or virtuous) person is one who knows what is good and spontaneously does it" (Varela, 1999, p. 4), so a foresightful organization is one whose members spontaneously forge connections between past, present, and future. In other words, organizational foresightfulness is fully developed when it becomes an institutionalized capacity of unobtrusively responding to an organization's circumstances so that the organization may get around in the world.

The notion of *coping*, drawn from Heideggerian philosophy (see Dreyfus, 1991; Wrathall and Malpas, 2000), implies that dealing with the future is a pervasive, *background* organizational skill, not a focal act. In executing its primary task – be it treating patients, serving customers, teaching students, or whatever – an organization acts necessarily in the present. The future is not some entity to engage with in the same way, say, a bank engages with a customer. A bank sells its services in the present and organizes itself to be able to carry out this task in the future as effectively as it can. To be able, however, to *continue* selling services to customers, it needs to be concerned not just with the present but with the future as well. A foresightful bank is *subsidiarily* aware of the past and the future while focally engaging in the present (Tsoukas, 2003). It is aware of the fact that it ought to be able to continue being attractive to customers in the future, while serving them in the present on the basis of abilities it has acquired in the past. While engaging in its primary task, it is unobtrusively adjusting its service to carry on drawing in customers in the future (McSweeney, 2000).

An organization develops its subsidiary awareness of the future by developing its *distentive* capability – the ability to narratively link past, present, and future. *Distentio* is an Augustinian idea offered by Ricoeur (1984) to describe the stretching of consciousness through simultaneous attention to memory and expectation. When memory and expectation are engaged, they enlarge the consciousness of the present – know-how is brought forward from the past and extrapolations to the future are made. Narratives are a means for letting us experience time by bringing memory and expectation to bear on the present. Narratives enable us to appreciate the temporal dimension of human experience and think in "time-streams" (Neustadt and May, 1986).

An excellent example of such a highly developed distentive capability – the ability to be subsidiarily aware of the past and the future -is shown by George Marshall, the Chief of Staff of the US Army during World War II. In the spring of 1943, in the midst of the War, Marshall called John Hilldring to his office to discuss how Hilldring, a two-star general, should go about organizing military governments for countries that had been liberated or conquered by the Allies. Hilldring reported what Marshall said to him as follows (cited in Neustadt and May, 1986, pp. 247–8):

> I'm turning over to you a sacred trust and I want you to bear that in mind every day and every hour you preside over this military government and civil affairs venture. Our people sometimes say that soldiers are stupid. I must admit at times we are. Sometimes our people think we are extravagant with the public money, that we squander it, spend it recklessly. I don't agree that we do. We are in a business where it's difficult always to administer your affairs as a businessman can administer his affairs in a company, and good judgement sometimes requires us to build a tank that turns out not to be what we want, and we scrap that and build another one ... But even though people say we are extravagant, that in itself isn't too disastrous ...
>
> But we have a great asset and that is that our people, our countrymen, do not distrust us and do not fear us. Our countrymen, our fellow citizens, are not afraid of us. They don't harbor any ideas that we intend to alter the government of the country or the nature of this government in any way. This is a sacred trust that I turn over to you today ... I don't want you to do anything, and I don't want to permit the enormous corps of military governors that you are in the process of training and that you're going to dispatch all over the world, to damage this high regard in which the professional soldiers in the Army are held by our people, and it could happen, it could happen, Hilldring, if you don't understand what you are about.

This is a remarkable speech for it skillfully weaves together past, present, and future, and shows how a policy maker may indeed be foresightful. Marshall, remember, was busy fighting a terrible war and, yet, he was capable of seeing far ahead to ponder the post-war situation. He looked ahead with a clear awareness of the past. He showed a deep understanding of US military–civilian relations (the criticism of, but also the crucial trust of, the US armed forces by the people) and, implicitly, of how the same relations had had a different history in other counties. He urged Hilldring to make day-to-day decisions while thinking of their long-term consequences. Marshall coped with the future spontaneously: the situation – advising a subordinate – brought forth the action; the future did not become a separate object of analysis but was spontaneously brought to the present and was coherently linked to the past. Foresightfullness is shown here to be not a specialized activity, which is to be occasionally engaged in, but a pervasive mode of being. As Neustadt and May (1986, p. 248) aptly remark: "By looking back, Marshall looked ahead, identifying what was worthwhile to preserve from the past and carry into the future. By looking around, at the present, he identified what could stand in the way, what had potential to cause undesired changes of direction. Seeing something he had power to reduce, if not remove, he tried to do so."

## Overview of the Book

The chapters in this book are derived from the *First International Conference on Probing the Future: Developing Organizational Foresight in the Knowledge Economy*, which was organized by the Graduate School of Business, University of Strathclyde, in July 2002, in Glasgow, UK. The conference sought to provide a forum in which important questions, conceptual and empirical, concerning organizational foresight could be debated in a scholarly fashion.

Several authors explore ways in which organizations make sense of their environments and of themselves in order to cope with the uncertainty of the future. Two distinguished academics with significant corporate experience as well, Spyros Makridakis and Kees van der Heijden, long-time students of how organizations manage the future, have contributed, especially for this book, a foreword and an afterword respectively. The book is structured in three parts, each of which addresses a particular question. Part I ("Making Sense of Organizational Foresight") addresses the question: "How should 'organizational foresight' be conceptualized?" Part II ("Foresight and Organizational Learning") includes chapters that deal with the question: "How do organizations make sense of themselves and their environments, and, accordingly, how do they organize their learning in order to cope with the future?" The authors in Part III ("Developing Foresightful Organizations") address the question: "How can organizations become foresightful?"

In Part I Robert Chia ("Re-educating Attention: What is Foresight and How is it Cultivated?"), using Whitehead's definition of foresight as the philosophic power of understanding the complex flux of the varieties of human societies, compares how we might cultivate foresight with how we are inclined to cultivate foresight. He draws the reader's consideration towards a number of ways in which our attention needs to be re-educated. We forget, he says, that we have a partial perspective of a system made up of an infinite number of futures and so tend to see the future through a single, or at most, a small number of perspectives. Tacitly, we always pay attention to one aspect of knowledge to the detriment of another, yet we rarely use our ability to reflect on the gestalt bias of our knowing in our hurry to know. Given these tendencies, the author advocates re-educating attention towards micro level developments in the environment and the periphery of our own consciousness to avoid premature closure around a single future. Visionaries are seen as being particularly in tune with the (unconscious) processes in societies underlying how the future unfolds, rather than possessing an uncanny ability to forecast the future. Perspectivism is thus held in tension with pragmatism, in a way which addresses how our tendency to control the future makes us less open to as yet unseen combinations.

V. K. Narayanan and Liam Fahey ("Invention and Navigation as Contrasting Metaphors of the Pathways to the Future") argue that different firms tend to conceive of the future in different ways – as invention and as navigation – and claim that these views are incommensurable. A company that faces the multiple uncertainties of new science, technological overlap, and unknown customer adoption rates of radically new products, tends to operate with the "invention" metaphor of the future. The future emerges from a dynamic marketplace. In contrast, an organization working in an established field, operates with customers directing extensions of the product line, making "navigation" a more appropriate metaphor of the future. The authors state that the assumptions underpinning these realities are incommensurable and, consequently, there is no single, or correct, way of seeing the future. Organizations need to consider how different communities, time lines, and boundaries make invention or navigation a more suitable way of thinking about the future. Equally, whereas "navigation" has a known vocabulary, which can be built upon in a linear fashion, "invention" involves the creation of a new vocabulary and the emergence of new meanings.

T. K. Das ("Strategy and Time: Really Recognizing the Future") explores the notion that clock-time may be too simple a conceptualization of time for strategy making. The author advocates that a more sophisticated concept of time be adopted, since time is conceptualized differently by different individuals, but these differences are infrequently considered when making strategy. The author explores the implications of treating time as psychological and subjective. This stance implies the need to focus on how time affects individual and organizational behavior, as opposed to how individuals and organizations behave in time. The author highlights how different conceptualizations of time influence strategic planning in the form of the development of visions, plans, milestones, and the approach to strategic change.

In Part II, David R. Schwandt and Margaret Gorman ("Foresight or Foreseeing: A Social Action Explanation of Complex Collective Knowing") consider the generation of foresight as being particularly complex when operating within a collective in which knowledge is unevenly distributed. Social action is seen as taking place against a backdrop of knowledge flow moderated by organizational patterns, reflection, organizational goals serving as reference points, structures created by roles, and sensemaking through stories and language. As social action occurs through these forms of media, the outcome is reasonable or inquisitive, goal referencing either routine or experimental, the treatment of new information non-equivocal or equivocal and structuring is either closed or open. A case study serves to illustrate the explanatory power of the framework and considers four pathologies of foreseeing. First, new information is brought in to the collective by new team members, meaning there is too little shared past to make sense of this new information. Second, there is too little reflection, as reflection is considered to be a waste of time, so assumptions are not challenged. Third, the design of the team leads to a form of structuring, which inhibits experimentation. Finally, role confusion ensues when expectations about what it means to be foresightful are not explicit. This chapter conceives of foresight as collective knowledge production, and improvements in foresight as a function of understanding how the dynamics of knowledge production are altered by context.

Raanan Lipshitz, Neta Ron and Micha Popper ("Retrospective Sensemaking and Foresight: Studying the Past to Prepare for the Future") draw on Weick's theory of sensemaking to analyze a case of team learning, which is atypical from the standpoint of Weick's theory, in that accuracy rather than plausability is the focus of organizational operations. Foresight is shown to be a function of learning in a situation where the future is different from the past, even if not radically so. Each one of Weick's seven defining characteristics of sensemaking are considered in light of the case and are all found to be relevant. In particular, the usefulness of critical thinking within a group, directed at an individual's performance within a highly competitive organizational culture and setting, is analyzed. An important connection is made between the past, in the form of retrospective sensemaking, and the future, in the form of improvisation, despite the future being uncertain because it is different from the past. It is proposed that the ability to improvise under conditions of uncertainty is enhanced by the richness and complexity of what is already known, which, in turn, can be increased through retrospective sense making created during a learning exercise. Thus the authors create a relationship between memory and improvisation and, hence, between the past and future, suggesting foresightfulness is, at least in part, a function of this relationship.

Rodolphe Durand ("Can Illusion of Control Destroy a Firm's Competence? The Case of Forecasting Ability") shows that if forecasting accuracy is considered as a competence, then firms that overestimate have a better performance than firms that underestimate. This effect is moderated by how firms rate themselves against others, in terms of critical success factors for the industry. Having a high opinion of oneself abets performance whereas a neutral view enhances performance. The chapter suggests that the relationship between forecasting accuracy and performance is complex; foresight involves more than the ability to accurately forecast macro phenomena, such as industry growth. Equally, the chapter suggests that the notion of competence is far more complex than a single ability (in this case to forecast the future).

In Part III, Miguel Pina E. Cunha ("Time Traveling: Organizational Foresight as Temporal Reflexivity") proposes that the ability to be foresightful involves being able to simultaneously consider and link the past, present, and future and, thus, to travel through time. Rather than dwell on these views as epistemologically incommensurable, a more pragmatic approach is taken. All possible combinations of the past, present, and future are considered and discussed in terms of the actual form they take in organizations. The framework shows how action-based managers transcend the boundaries between prediction and invention. There are advantages as well as dangers to time traveling. The past provides valuable experience and learning in the present as much as it provides availability bias. The future can be dream-like, but is achieved from a base provided by the reality of the present. In summary, the chapter highlights the need for a complicated understanding of foresight through proactive temporal coordination, articulation, and reflexivity. It provides both a theoretical and practical route into such an understanding.

David Seidl ("The Concept of 'Weak Signals' Revisited: A Re-description From a Constructivist Perspective") considers organizational foresight in terms of the weak signals that need to be noticed if an organization is to become aware of, and act upon, strategic discontinuities. Rather than view weak signals in Ansoff's sense of being "out there" in the environment, this chapter treats them as social constructions. As such, organizations need to adapt to their own constructions and, therefore, adapt to themselves. Weak signals are seen as social constructions in the sense of context being an important factor in defining how a weak signal is interpreted, whether it is believed, and how it relates to other weak signals. This socially constructivist inter-pretation of weak signals is extended even further by the author to incorporate autopoiesis, whereby weak signals become part of a closed and self-referential system. Connecting this stance to foresight, the chapter argues that organizations need to pay attention to their communication structures as they affect the creation and inter-action of (socially constructed) weak signals. Equally, although the environment cannot be foreseen, it might be possible to foresee likely constructions of the environ-ment, given communication structures direct what communication processes come about and hence what constructions are created.

Ted Fuller, Paul Argyle, and Paul Moran ("Meta-rules for Entrepreneurial fore-sight") view foresight through the eyes of the owner of a new economy company operating in a dynamic environment. Using complexity theory, bifurcation points in the history of the firm are seen as thresholds, which occur when the owner's personal identity and motives combine with changes in the environment to trigger and energize organizational change. Anticipation is seen as trying to turn weak signals into oppor-tunities, the restructuring of personal identity and behavior into new organizing domains, and a high quality of personal reflexivity. That said, above all, foresight takes the form of the entrepreneur's overriding desire to be successful resulting in dramatic changes in direction in order to remain aligned to the environment.

Unlike Seidl, Deborah Blackman and Steven Henderson ("Autopoietic Limitations of Probing the Future") critique the metaphorical application of "autopoiesis" to social systems. They argue that the managerial adoption of an autopoietic perspective might be damaging to an organization's ability to probe the future, or rather the autopoietic tendencies within a firm are likely to create dysfunctional organizational dynamics. The problems of a retail firm, which after many years of success went through a period of difficulty, are seen in terms of systemic change demanding non-autopoietic and hence non-self referential change. The years of success have however turned the organization into an autopoietic system, meaning that interaction of the organization with the system is always in terms of the organization's reference system. As such foresight becomes difficult, if not impossible. The authors argue that organ-izations can be so tightly coupled to their past and present that they cannot alter their dynamics to cope with a future that requires them to think in a way that does not refer to themselves.

# REFERENCES

Ansoff, H. I. (1984) *Implanting Strategic Management*, Englewood Cliffs, NJ: Prentice-Hall.

Bateson, G. (1979) *Mind and Nature*. Toronto: Bantam.

Bergson, H. (1946) *The Creative Mind*. New York: Carol Publishing Group.

Blackler, F. (1995) Knowledge, knowledge work and organizations: An overview and interpretation, *Organization Studies*, 16, 1021–46.

Brown, S. L. and Eisenhardt, K. M. (1998) *Competing on the Edge*, Boston: Harvard Business School Press.

Dewey, J. (1988) *Human Nature and Conduct*, Carbondale: Southern Illinois University Press.

Dewey, J. (1998) Time and individuality. In L. A. Hickman and T. M. Alexander (eds.), *The Essential Dewey*, vol. 1, Bloomington: Indiana University Press, pp. 217–26.

Dreyfus, H. L. (1991) *Being-in-the-World: A Commentary on Heidegger's Being and Time, Division I*, Cambridge: MA: MIT Press.

Dreyfus, H. L. (1997) From micro-worlds to knowledge representation: AI at an impasse. In J. Haugeland (ed.), *Mind Design II*, Cambridge, MA: MIT Press, pp. 143–82.

Dreyfus, H. L. and Dreyfus, S. E. (1986) *Mind over Machine*, New York: Free Press.

Elster, J., Offe, C., and Preuss, U. K. (1998) *Institutional Design in Post-communist Societies*, Cambridge: Cambridge University Press.

Giddens, A. (1990) *The Consequences of Modernity*, Cambridge: Polity Press.

Giddens, A. (1991) *Modernity and Self-identity*. Cambridge: Polity Press.

Glasmeier, A. (1997) Technological discontinuities and flexible production networks: The case of Switzerland and the world watch industry. In M. L. Tushman and P. Anderson (eds.), *Managing Strategic Innovation and Change*, New York: Oxford University Press, pp. 23–42.

Hassard, J. (2002) Organizational time: Modern, symbolic and postmodern reflections, *Organization Studies*, 23, 885–92.

Hogarth, R. M. and Makridakis, S. (1981) Forecasting and planning: An evaluation, *Management Science*, XXVII, 115–38.

Ilinitch, A. Y., Lewin, A. Y., and D'Aveni, R. (1998) *Managing in Times of Disorder*, Thousand Oaks, CA: Sage.

Ingvar, D. (1985) Memories of the future: An essay on the temporal organization of conscious awareness. *Human Neurobiology*, 4, 127–36.

MacIntyre, A. (1985) *After Virtue*, 2nd edn., London, UK: Duckworth.

Makridakis, S. (1990) *Forecasting, Planning, and Strategy for the 21st Century*, New York: The Free Press.

Makridakis, S. and Hibon, M. (1979) Accuracy of forecasting: An empirical investigation, *Journal of the Royal Statistical Society*, CXLII, 97–145.

McSweeney, B. (2000) Looking forward to the past, *Accounting, Organizations and Society*, 25, 767–86.

Miller, D. (1990) *The Icarus Paradox*, New York: Harper Business.

Mintzberg, H. (1994) *The Rise and Fall of Strategic Planning*, New York: Prentice Hall.

Mintzberg, H. and Waters, J. A. (1982) Tracking strategy in an entrepreneurial firm, *Academy of Management Journal*, 25, 465–99.

Mintzberg, H., Ahlstrand, B., and Lampel, J. (1998) *Strategy Safari*. London: Prentice Hall.

Neustadt, R. E. and May, E. R. (1986) *Thinking in Time: The Uses of History for Decision Makers*, New York: Free Peess.

Orr, J. (1996) *Talking About Machines*, Ithaca, NY: ILR Press.

Penrose, R. (1994) *Shadows of the Mind*. Oxford: Oxford University Press.

Popper, K. (1988) *The Open Universe*, London: Hutchinson.

Ricoeur, P. (1984) *Time and Narrative*, vol. 1. Chicago: University of Chicago Press.

Rorty, R. (1989) *Contingency, Irony and Solidarity*, Cambridge: Cambridge University Press.

Searle, J. (1997) Minds, brains and programs. In J. Haugeland (ed.), *Mind Design II*, Cambridge, MA: MIT Press, pp. 183– 204.

Spender, J.-C. (1996) Making knowledge the basis of a dynamic theory of the firm, *Strategic Management Journal*, 17(Special Winter Issue), 45–62.

Tsoukas, H. (1999) Reading organizations: Uncertainty, complexity, narrativity, University of Essex, Department of Accounting, Finance and Management, Working Paper Series No.16.

Tsoukas, H. (2001) Re-viewing organization, *Human Relations*, 54, 7–12.

Tsoukas, H. (2003) Do we really understand tacit knowledge? In M. Easterby-Smith and M. A. Lyles (eds.), *Handbook of Organizational Learning and Knowledge*, Oxford: Blackwell.

Tsoukas, H. and Chia, R. (2002) On organizational becoming: Rethinking organizational change, *Organization Science*, 13, 567–82.

Tsoukas, H. and Hatch, M. J. (2001) Complex thinking, complex practice: A narrative approach to organizational complexity. *Human Relations*, 54, 979–1013.

Tushman, M. L., Anderson, P. C., and O'Reilly, C. (1997) Technology cycles, innovation streams, and ambidextrous organizations: Organizational renewal through innovation streams and strategic change. In M. L. Tushman and P. Anderson (eds.), *Managing Strategic Innovation and Change*, New York: Oxford University Press, pp. 3–23.

Van der Heijden, K. (1996) *Scenarios: The Art of Strategic Conversation*, Chichester: Wiley.

Van der Heijden, K., Bradfield, R., Burt, G., Cairns, G., and Wright, G. (2002) *The Sixth Sense*, Chichester: Wiley.

Varela, F. J. (1999) *Ethical Know-How*, Stanford, CA: Stanford University Press.

Weick, K. E. (1979) *The Social Psychology of Organizing*, 2nd edn., Reading, MA: Addison-Wesley.

Weick, K. E. (1995) *Sensemaking in Organizations*, Thousand Oaks, CA: Sage.

Weick, K. E. and Roberts, K. H. (1993) Collecive mind in organizations: Heedful interrelating on flight decks, *Administrative Science Quarterly*, 38, 357–81.

Whitehead, A. N. (1967) *Adventures of Ideas*, New York: Free Press.

Wrathall, M. and Malpas, J. (2000) *Heidegger, Coping, and Cognitive Science*, vol. 2, Cambridge, MA: MIT Press.

Wright, G. and Goodwin, P. (1999) Future-focussed thinking: Combining scenario planning with decision analysis, *Journal of Multi-Criteria Decision Analysis*, 8, 311–21.

# Part One

---

# Making Sense of Organizational Foresight

# Chapter Two

# Re-educating Attention: What is Foresight and How is it Cultivated?

## Robert Chia

## Introduction

Foresight is a unique and highly valued human capacity that is widely recognized as a major source of wisdom, competitive advantage and cultural renewal within nations and corporations. The sometimes seemingly uncanny ability of great leaders, visionaries, and captains of industry to "foresee," "read," and then act pre-emptively to forestall disastrous outcomes is a quality much envied by those of us far too often caught up in the immediacy of daily life. To be able to remain finely tuned in to the undercurrents of ideological and political debates; to detect subtle shifts in cultural moods and attitudes towards societal concerns such as the system of representative democracy, the problem of public accountability, the effects of technological developments on issues as diverse as ethics, ecology, and biogenetics; to be well tuned in to contemporary problems of plurality, diversity, and change that may have important implications for policy formulation and corporate decision-making; to accurately register subterranean drifts in the collective psyche of the developed economies and to understand their wider import for business, profit, growth, and capitalism; to detect the changing composition of international markets and the ongoing reconfiguring of global business sectors – these are all vital capabilities that no forward-looking nation or organization can afford to ignore. Foresight, is the "philosophic power of understanding the complex flux of the varieties of human societies," an "unspecialized aptitude for eliciting generalizations from particulars and for seeing the divergent illustrations of generalities in diverse circumstances" (Whitehead, 1933, pp. 119–20). It is a product of deep *insight* and understanding.

The ability to foresee, to be farsighted and see ahead, involves a regaining of what the art critic John Ruskin calls the "innocence of the eye," that almost child-like ability to see afresh "as a blind man would see them if suddenly gifted with sight" (Ruskin, 1927, vol. 15, p. 27). Such a penetrating vision derives from a rare state of conceptual *naiveté* in which all our prior intellectual fabrications have been momentarily set aside and we are then able to experience things as they are in themselves, devoid of all their functional implications. This is the ultimate ground of unmediated encounter from which insight and foresight emanates and it is this generative field of potentiality that underpins all forms of successful speculation including especially corporate visions, scenario-planning, and strategic decision-making. Great leaders, compelling visionaries, successful discoverers, accomplished futurists and scenario-planners are deeply perceptive *antennas of society* blessed with an instinctive ability to read the deeper conversations of mankind.

The word speculation often invites an imagery of wild and unjustifiable postulations and pronouncements. Proper disciplined speculation, however, is a truly rigorous scientific method which, like the flight of an aeroplane "starts from the ground of particular observation . . . makes a flight in the thin air of imaginative generalization; and . . . again lands for renewed observation rendered acute by rational interpretation" (Whitehead, 1929, p. 5). The essence of successful speculation is the attainment of a deeper existential encounter with the seemingly disparate material events surrounding us and the subsequent relating of these events into a coherent explanatory schema. Visions and scenarios are creative products of such intellectual efforts. They are thought experiments designed to aid us in ordering our perceptions and in helping us formulate strategic decisions that will be appropriate for all plausible futures (Schwartz, 2002). Farsighted and successful visionaries and scenario-creators are able to detect and disclose almost imperceptible shifts in societal tendencies, aspirations, and preferences and ordering them in such a way as to produce a compelling system of explanation (Spinosa et al., 1997).

Understood in this broadest sense, foresight is a refined sensitivity for detecting and disclosing invisible, inarticulate or unconscious societal motives, aspirations, and preferences and of articulating them in such a way as to create novel opportunities hitherto unthought and hence unavailable to a society or organization. Foresight is achieved through a re-education of attention. It requires a sustained and painstaking dismantling or deconstruction of the "unconscious metaphysics" (Whitehead, 1933) shaping our dominant habits of thought. Like the air we breathe, our culturally inspired beliefs, assumptions, and practises are so translucent, so pervasive and so seemingly necessary that they inevitably direct our focus of attention and guide the processes of scanning, perception, and information-pickup. In so doing they often prevent us from achieving deeper insight into the human condition. In a word, both blindness and insight are inextricably linked to the entire socio-cultural and cognitive processes.

The purpose of this chapter is to elaborate on the basic claim that foresight is essentially about the *re-education of attention* and that it can be systematically cultivated through visual strategies that privilege *peripheral* rather than *frontal* vision as the basis for human understanding. We learn more fundamentally from *glancing* rather than from *gazing*; from *scanning* and *browsing* than from *looking*; from immersion in *vagueness* than from attending to already-formed *gestalt* figures. In all attempts to probe into the future it is the quality of foresight which determines the success or failure of such speculative endeavors. In order to show why this is the case, we begin first by explaining how traditional forecasting with its emphasis on accuracy, precision, and prediction is increasingly giving way to the currently more fashionable notion of scenario-spinning with its open-ended speculative emphasis. This shift signals an important epistemological readjustment from the idea of a singular universal truth to the ideas of multiple perspectives, interpretation, and conceptual pluralism. *Perspectivism* provides the overarching principle for legitimizing the generation of multiple scenarios in place of the search for a singular accurate forecast. Modern perspectivism, however, while an important first step in encouraging conceptual agility, remains unnecessarily limited precisely because of its obsession with the generation and juxtaposing of alternative scenario futures. Attention is focused on the generation of alternatives rather than on the cognitive structure of the framing process itself. There is a reluctance to examine the *forming* aspect of in-form-ation. An overemphasis on attending to the gestalt figure of a scenario seriously underplays the fundamental role that *unconscious scanning* and *tacit knowledge* play in directing attention, structuring sense-making, and guiding comprehension. We argue here that the cultivation of a kind of *scattered attention* or *eye-wander* is fundamental to the process of developing insight and foresight. We then go on to explore how foresight and the *farsightedness* associated with it can be systematically developed through the internalizing of an open-ended nomadic, as opposed to a systemic, visual strategy.

## Applications of Foresight: Prediction, Forecasting, and Scenario Planning

> Too many forces work against the possibility of getting *the* right forecast. The future is no longer stable; it has become a moving target. No single "right" projection can be deduced from past behavior. (Wack, 1985, p. 73)

The desire to understand and predict future outcomes has been integral to our ongoing attempts at continued survival ever since mankind emerged from a life of bare subsistent existence. One consequence of this has been the gradual development of a systematic method for dealing with the future by analyzing present conditions, projecting continuity and possible changes in the future, and then speculating on what such changes in the future might hold for us. Some generic form of forecasting has always existed in human consciousness since some level of predictability and hence productivity are a prerequisite for the eventual emergence and development of civilized life. Without some form of predictability we could not develop norms and expectations and hence would only live for the present. Without some form of predictability there would be no incentive to discover, produce, store, build, and exchange. The ideas of design and planning – human activities that require imaginative projections into the future – would be non-existent. Society and the modern nation-state with all its complex institutions, laws, rules, procedures, norms, and expectations would not be at all possible. Some level of successful forecasting and prediction, therefore, has always been an essential factor in humankind's rise into dominance.

However, it has only been in the early part of the twentieth century that forecasting has emerged as a respectable scientific subdiscipline that relied substantially on mathematical formulations and the calculations of probabilities of occurrences to aid predictions regarding future outcomes. In relatively stable and hence more easily predictable environments forecasting remains a highly valued technique for prediction. Indeed, sometimes its very success in predicting the future has been its own downfall as Pierre Wack (1985, p. 73) the "founding father" of scenario planning at Shell observed:

> Forecasts are not always wrong; more often than not, they can be reasonably accurate. And that is what makes them so dangerous. They are usually constructed on the assumption that tomorrow's world will be much like today's. They often work because the world does not always change. But sooner or later forecasts will fail when they are most needed.

However, the increasing turbulence of the past three decades in particular has seen the gradual replacement of forecasting by a more open-ended and generative technique for projecting futures that has been called scenario-planning (Fahey and Randall, 1998; Schwartz, 2002; van der Heidjen, 1996; Wack, 1985). Unlike forecasting, scenario-planning is ostensibly less about predicting what is likely to happen than it is about the imaginative visualizing of plausible alternative futures and of subsequently designing flexible strategies of action that will enable an organization to respond effectively to any of these eventualities. To use a popular metaphor often employed by scenario-planners, scenarios are like "test conditions in a windtunnel" (van der Heidjen, 1996) that can enable us to observe the effects of a variety of possible external conditions on an organization. Scenario-spinning creates alternative and internally consistent descriptions of possible futures that challenges us to consider their likely consequences (van der Heidjen, 1996). Unlike forecasts, scenario-creators maintain that scenarios are ostensibly *not* predictions (Schwartz, 2002). Instead, it is claimed, they are useful conceptual vehicles for learning about the environment.

While traditional forecasting unashamedly seeks to arrive at a most probable future with the greatest degree of assurance, scenarios have a more ambiguous status. Unlike forecasting which is intentionally focused, systematic, linear, and fundamentally reductive and rational, scenarios are ostensibly emergent, creative, and often even playful re-formulations of current conditions. Scenario-spinning is more like a strategic conversation (van der Heidjen, 1996), or a form of story-telling that attempts to develop convergent thinking about divergent futures (Schwartz, 2002). It is argued that the creation of alternative plausible scenarios forces mental stretch and challenges the dominant mind-sets of decision-makers. They take decision-makers "into new substantive terrain; they require them to be willing to suspend their beliefs, assumptions and preconceptions; they compel them to grapple with questions that previously were not raised or were . . . quickly shunted aside. . . . Scenario learning therefore . . . challenges conventional wisdom, historic ways of thinking and operating, and long-held assumptions about important issues" (Fahey and Randall, 1998, p. 5). In a world that is increasingly perceived as rapidly changing and fraught with uncertainty, scenario-planning has overtaken forecasting as the more appropriate vehicle for basing strategic decisions (Fahey and Randall, 1998; Schwartz, 2002; van de Heidjen, 1996; Wack, 1985). In so doing scenario-planning has ostensibly abandoned any attempt to predict the future and instead scenarios are viewed as mechanisms for confronting decision-makers with the implications of their own deeply held assumptions about the way the world works.

The replacing of forecasting with scenario-planning is an important first step but one that does not go far enough analytically. By supposedly abandoning the quest for accuracy in prediction, scenario-creators are unable to address the deeper question of why ultimately some scenarios appear more compelling than others. What differentiates a "better" scenario from a less sound one? Even scenario-planners have to come to these implicit judgements. The answer is simply that compelling scenarios reflect the possession of a deeper insight into the current situation. And it is this insight that produces the ability to foresee likely future outcomes. Ultimately, the success of scenario-creation is not just about achieving mental agility, an important quality though it be, but about attaining a deeper level of insight and foresight regarding the prevailing conditions, ephemeral though they often are. This is what Whitehead (1933, p. 120) meant when he said that foresight is fundamentally an "unspecialized aptitude for eliciting generalizations from particulars."

In this regard, although it is patently true that in human social systems the relationship between cause and effect, between past, present, and future, and hence the problems of predictability, are at best "loosely coupled" (Weick, 1979) and at worst seemingly totally unrelated, this in no way suggests that there are *no* underlying regularities at all on which a relative degree of consistency of understanding can be established sufficient for norms and expectations and hence some degree of predictability to prevail in human societies. There may well be multiple perspectives and interpretations of a given situation, but this in no way suggests that there are no relatively enduring structures of comprehension shaping our perception and understanding. Relativity, *not* rampant relativism, underpins theoretical pluralism. This implies that at some point, sooner or later conceptual formulations, including especially visions and scenarios generated must touch base and resonate with ongoing material experiences. Some attempt to anchor plausible scenarios must be made and hence some level of forecasting and predictability is implied, even in the seemingly freewheeling process of scenario-spinning.

## Scenario-spinning in an Age of World Picture

> Perceiving is an achievement of the individual, not an appearance in the theater of his consciousness. It is a keeping-in-touch with the world, an experiencing of things rather than a having of experience. (Gibson, 1979, p. 239)

In a perceptive analysis of the visual character of human cognition, the ecological psychologist J. J. Gibson (1979) noted that the modern civilized individual, for the most part, adopts a perspectival view of the world almost as a matter of instinct. We moderns, says Gibson, spend most of our time indoors in enclosed spaces and are thus so accustomed to looking *at* things, whether it be on a page, on a television screen, on the Internet, through a picture frame, or through a window. Even when we are outdoors under the sky, we are more likely to be driving an automobile and looking through the windscreen or windows than being directly surrounded by the environment itself. We moderns are actively discouraged from using our eyes as prosthetic devices to probe our surroundings and to turn our heads to scan *around* us as well as to move *around* things. Moreover, unlike a horse or a rabbit that is equipped with lateral eyes, humans have frontal eyes that limit the scope of view so much so that the natural blind region is relatively large. We can only see very selectively by looking *at* that which comes naturally into our frontal vision. Our frontal focus prevents us from being alert to events developing at the fringes; at the periphery of our vision. We "spend most of our time *looking at* instead of *looking around*" us (Gibson, 1979, p. 203). We are culturally programmed to *gaze* and not to *glance* (Chia, 1998). It is as if we are spectators on the scene observing the situation as we do a framed picture.

As a result the world appears to us as somehow ready-made and pre-framed before our arrival hence our awareness of the possibility of alternative readings of the situation is radically diminished. We thus develop a perspectival approach to life and it is this idea that we can have nothing more than a perspective on the world that has inspired the shift away from a singular accurate forecast to the idea of multiple scenarios. Instead of the search for one accurate representation of what the future might be, we now settle for the creative proliferation of multiple possible futures each as plausible as the other. In all this, however, what remains unchanged is the idea of the world around us grasped in pictorial form. Heidegger (1977, p. 129) calls ours the age of the "world picture." The colloquial expression "I get the picture," exemplifies this pervasive way of thinking about the world that surrounds us. It implies the necessity and externality of frames and the objectivity and fixity of our gaze as well as the universality of this practice. In this regard the attempt to generate alternative scenarios, to force us to re-perceive what we apprehend, is a laudable project. But it does not go far enough.

Framing presupposes perspective and selectivity and it is this selective process of attending and dis-attending to which remains unexamined in the study of scenario-planning and in our attempts to understand foresight. What we do in the process of theorizing is to "*harness up* reality in our conceptual systems in order to drive it better" (James, 1909/96, p. 248). In so doing, in creating this order out of the chaos of raw experience, however, we necessarily create excesses: a "penumbra" of rejected experiences that are no less real but that are denied an ontological status in our scheme of things. Yet they are ever present as a background shadow that constantly threatens to overflow our logic and representation. All visions and scenarios are products of *di-vision*. They are underpinned by an empirical "remainder" that *reminds* us what has been left out. And, it is this empirical remainder that forms the basis for insight and foresight.

## Limits of the Perspectivist Paradigm

> *perspectivism* is the conception according to which the world is inhabited by different sorts of subjects or people…which apprehend reality from distinct points of view. (De Castro, 1998, p. 469)

To fully appreciate the limits of the perspectivist paradigm with its accompanying emphasis on the generation of multiple perspectives or scenarios, it is necessary to very briefly trace the epistemological roots of this worldview. Much of modern perspectivism and the accompanying pluralism it promotes has been justified by a selective appropriation of the insights of philosophical *pragmatism*. It is, therefore, necessary to articulate what pragmatism entails and what perpectivism understates by its emphasis on the generation of alternative readings of a particular given situation. To begin with, genuine pragmatists like William James and John Dewey deny the claim that reality, as it is in itself, is already-formed, stable, and "thing-like." Instead, the REAL, for these pragmatic thinkers is construed as fluxional, transient, formless, and ceaselessly changing. It is simply a "big blooming buzzing confusion, as free from contradiction in its 'much-at-onceness' as it is all alive and evidently there" (James, 1911/96, pp. 49–50). Before conscious thought and our linguistic interventions, lived experience is nothing more than "a shapeless and indistinct mass" (Saussure, 1966, p. 111). And it is out of this infinite potentiality that we call reality that human acts of *vision* and di-*vision* work to construct order, identities, objects, and the subsequent productive elaborations that we commonly call culture. Human life, therefore, is an endless series of self-constitutive acts in a world characterized by perpetual incompleteness, decay, and disappearance. This is the essence of the human project – to fix, order, and structure an otherwise wild, intractable, and amorphous lifeworld and to make it respond positively and productively to our needs, concerns, and aspirations.

Unlike traditional realists who believe that ultimate reality is somehow preordered and law-like in character, and hence already there awaiting our discovery, pragmatists maintain that the reason why we have this impression is because language, which is a cultural artifact, is itself so structured. And, since we can only consciously apprehend reality through language, including especially the language of mathematics, it follows that reality readily takes up the shape of the very conceptual templates we use to apprehend it. The essential difference, therefore, between traditional realism and pragmatism is that for the former *"reality is ready-made and complete from all eternity,"* while for pragmatists *"it is still in the making, and awaits part of its complexion from the future."* On one side "the universe is absolutely secure, on the other it is still pursuing its adventures" (James, in McDermott (ed.), 1977, p. 456, emphasis original).

More importantly, however, for pragmatists, and this is what modern perspectivism ignores, what haunts our culturally shaped consciousness is a vague but persistent *awareness* of the selective partiality of knowledge. We have a deep intuition of the existence of an invisible remainder that has been left out of our structures of comprehension. For William James (1911/96), all of life is underpinned by an essential ambiguity or vagueness and it is out of this that the visible and the identifiable are extracted. The social philosopher Michael Polanyi (1967) has also insisted that all explicit knowledge is abstracted from a vague, inarticulate but nevertheless primary source. Focusing on the formed visible figure of articulated knowledge incurs a hidden cost, which we deeply intuit. What is made present, therefore, is always haunted by a complementary absence. What is visible and present is a "present," a *gift* that is provisionally given to us by an invisible force that we can only vaguely divine. Presence intimates an immanent yet ungraspable absence that serves as the background to the visible figure we apprehend.

What perspectivists overlook and what pragmatists seek to remind us is the importance of attending to the structure of the framing process itself and how it acts to limit our vision and direct our focus and attention. By overly attending to the generation of a plurality of perspectives, what scenario-planners fail to address is the underlying residual consistency and resonance which enables us to still determine which of the scenarios generated is more likely than the others to come true. That is the true nature of foresight and the "sixth sense" that van der Heidjen et al. (2002) allude to in their most recent book. The fact that we can generate multiple alternative perspectives or scenarios does not necessarily mean an abandoning of any attempt to predict the future as is sometimes claimed (Schwartz, 2002). Rather the real purpose of exercising intellectual agility is to allow us to see past the various perspectives generated to the underlying hidden order and hence to productively foresee how events are likely to unfold. This intimating of an underlying hidden order occurs in the realm of the tacit, the inarticulate, and the unconscious.

## The Tacit Dimension

> Principles em-bodied...are placed beyond the grasp of consciousness, and hence cannot be touched by voluntary, deliberate transformation, cannot even be made explicit. (Bourdieu, 1977, p. 94)

In a series of powerfully argued seminal works, the scientist-turned-social philosopher Michael Polanyi (1962, 1967, 1969) drew attention to a crucial missing element in our understanding of the structure of knowledge and of human comprehension – the tacit dimension. Polanyi believed that throughout most of Western philosophy from Plato onwards, what constitutes proper knowledge has been defined far too narrowly in terms of the explicit and the visible so much so that the tacit elements underlying our epistemological endeavors have been surreptitiously ignored. Polanyi makes an important claim for the primacy of an elementary form of *tacit* knowing, which we will always find difficulty articulating. The ineffable nature of this kind of knowledge does not in any way detract from the fact that we do actually know many things that cannot be rendered explicit through language. This claim is easily verifiable through our common-sense experience of, for example, being able to recognize people we know without being able to specify exactly what it is that enables us to make these correct judgements. Alternatively, an airline pilot may develop a vague and uneasy sense that something is wrong even though his autopilot and his flight instruments appear to indicate perfectly normally. An important distinction, therefore, exists between explicit knowledge and a more basic form of vaguely intuited tacit knowing that somehow seems to defy linguistic articulation.

In developing his argument for the primacy of tacit knowledge Polanyi distinguished between *focal awareness* and *subsidiary awareness*. Focal awareness refers to the consciously directed attention one gives to an object of interest while subsidiary awareness is that which provides the background or context within which focal awareness operates. Thus, when we use a hammer to drive in a nail we attend to both the nail and the hammer but in significantly different ways:

> The difference may be stated by saying that the latter (i.e., the hammer) are not, like the nail, objects of our attention, but instruments of it. They are not watched in themselves; we watch something else whilst keeping intensely aware of them. I have a *subsidiary awareness* of the feeling in the palm of my hands which is merged into my *focal awareness* of my driving in the nail. (Polanyi, 1962, p. 55)

This distinction between focal awareness and subsidiary awareness is formulated in recognition of the essentially *vectorial* character of human comprehension. In other words, conscious awareness is, of necessity, *directional*. Explicit knowledge is always knowledge *of* something. Thus, as you the reader, focus on the meaning of the words written here, you will be only subsidiarily aware of the fact that they are written in English and that they observe certain rules of grammar and so on. If you begin to focus on the grammatical structure of this sentence, its meaning and content moves to a subsidiary level. The relationship is one of figure and ground. Thus, it is possible to fully understand what a piece of text is saying but be completely unaware of its linguistic status. Polanyi who is Hungarian by birth, tells the story of a regular breakfast routine in which he reads his mail and then occasionally passes it on to his son often unaware that the letter had not been written in English.

> My correspondence arrives at my breakfast table in various languages, but my son understands only English. Having just finished reading a letter I may wish to pass it on to him, but must check myself and look again to see in what language it was written. I am vividly aware of the meaning conveyed by the letter, yet know nothing whatever of its words. (Polanyi, 1962, p. 57)

According to Polanyi, *focal* and *subsidiary* awarenesses are mutually exclusive in the sense that one cannot focus on what is presently functioning subsidiarily since awareness is, by definition, always vectorial. This figure/ground relationship is one that is familiar to those who have seen pictures used to evoke the imagination in creativity exercises.

The important thing to note in such pictures is that only one aspect of the picture can be focused on at a time and to the untrained eye, it is virtually impossible to see both images together at the same time. Yet, each aspect requires the other as background for us to register its profile. Accentuating certain preferred figurations, articulating favored scenarios and projecting potential outcomes incur a hidden cost that we deeply intuit. Like the background lining of a kimono that enables it to keep its form, this subsidiary awareness of the other shapes the epistemological contours upon which much of human comprehension and decisional action rests. It is a tacit "foreknowledge of yet undiscovered things" (Polanyi, 1967, p. 23). To possess foresight, therefore, is to intuit an as-yet unformulated problem or to perceive an opportunity that is still hidden, inarticulate, or not yet revealed. It is an "intimation of the coherence of hitherto not [yet] comprehended particulars" (Polanyi, 1967, p. 21). Polanyi argues that it is precisely this kind of foreknowledge that is crucial to scientific discoveries. This is what the Copernicans must intuitively have had when they insisted that the heliocentric theory was not merely a convenient way of computing the paths of the planets but that it was actually how things were. Such foreknowledge is registered in the realms of the unconscious.

## Tacit Foreknowledge and Foresight in "Unconscious Scanning"

> There are other forms in a painting unseen.... I refer to the minute, almost microscopic, scribbles which make up the technique of a great draughtsman or the brush work of a great painter. (Ehrenzweig, 1965, p. 30)

We are culturally biased to notice simple, discrete, compact, and precise forms and to generally ignore vague, incoherent, and inarticulate forms in our perception. Because of our deep cultural programming, our eyes are always eager to perceive a good gestalt: a clear picture, form, or shape, the familiar features of someone we know, the distinct outlines of a building etc. We are guilty of a haste-of-wanting-to-know. Because of this overpowering urge, we invariably overlook those inarticulate micro-forms or tentative formations that collectively make up a crucial aspect of our cognition and comprehension. Conscious perception or focal awareness, because of its gestalt bias, excludes what has been called "eye-wander" (read, *Art and Industry*, in Ehrenzweig, 1965, p. 22). We are impatient for outcomes, for achieving a coherent, complete, and recognizable form and hence tend to gloss over the hesitancies, detours, false starts, and digressions that have taken place in the course of its emergence. We become only concerned with ends and outcomes not with means and process. Instrumentality governs much of our conscious attention.

Unconscious scanning and registering at a subsidiary level, however, does also take place side-by-side with this dominant instrumentality. But we are often unaware that that is occurring. Glancing and "eye-wander" are two aspects of this kind of peripheral vision that take place at the level of subsidiary awareness. Eye-wander is best exemplified by our occasional experience of absent-minded browsing in the retail shops and bookstores while waiting for someone or for something to happen. It is undirected, scattered attention that glosses over outlines and details and it is during these moment of non-purposeful attention that we, in fact, become much more observant and "in-tune" with our surroundings. There is a certain uncontaminated "purity" in our seeing which we loose the moment we begin to become conscious of it. This is what Ruskin called the "innocence of the eye" and what Matsushita (1978/ 1986) meant by a *sunao* (meek, open-hearted, innocent) mind. This is also what artists are specially trained for in order to detect those inarticulate forms that conscious attention overlooks.

The art theorist Anton Ehrenzweig (1965, 1967) calls this subsidiary awareness diffused or "scattered attention." However, while Polanyi insists on the mutual exclusivity of focal and subsidiary awareness what Ehrenzweig maintains is that it is actually possible through disciplined application and training to equip ourselves with the capacity to hold both figure and ground together in a unitary act of comprehension. This is what marks out the accomplished artists. For instance, in the case of music, the surface gestalt figure is typically represented by the melody. The melody draws our conscious awareness and keeps it as the focus of attention. The accompanying voices serve only as a background and are not as pregnant and "ear-catching" as the main melody itself. The serious music student, however, gradually realizes that what is called the accompaniment really consists of several voices which "form more or less continuous melodies in their own right" (Ehrenzweig, 1965, p. 41). The pupil's attention is thus directed away from an exclusive concentration on the main melody and made to simultaneously follow the several competing melodies unfolding at the same time in order to truly begin to appreciate the rich polyphonic character of music. Instead of focusing singularly on the melody the student is now able to scatter his/her attention and concurrently follow several lines of development.

The same thing applies in art. Here, like the student of music, the student of art learns to deliberately work *against* the gestalt principle. "When the art-school student takes up drawing he is made to watch not only the outline of the object he draws (the figure of Gestalt psychology), but also the negative forms which the figure cuts out from the background" (Ehrenzweig, 1965, p. 28). In other words, art students are taught to observe, simultaneously, the unfolding of the negative form as its outline emerges at the tip of the pencil. They are taught to attend to the varied minute combination of these invisible negative strokes that will make for a great improvement in the general impression of the formed figure. Unconscious scanning involves a subliminal sensitivity to the hesitant details of emergence that are generally overlooked by the untrained eye. In both instances of music and art training what is developed is the capacity for a kind of "scattered" or dispersed attention that is able to follow multiple lines of possibilities of development without the compulsion to prematurely achieve closure. The poet John Keats called this ability to resist premature closure a "negative capability." Such a capability can be cultivated in a number of ways, not least of all in the kinds of mental exercise ranging from doing crosswords, to the playing of combination games like chess and bridge, and to more polyphonic structures like crime novels and the artistic craft. To cultivate this sensitivity we must first recognize a different logic in operation.

## From State Logic to Nomadology

> the difference is that Chess codes and decodes space, whereas Go proceeds altogether differently, territorializing or deterritorializing it. (Deleuze and Guattari, 1988, p. 353)

In their influential text, *A Thousand Plateaus*, the French philosopher Giles Deleuze and his psychoanalyst friend Felix Guattari make the important observation that much of modern thinking remains dominated by a binary logic of state: a logic best exemplified by the root–tree metaphor. According to this *genea-logical* approach it is possible to trace the lineage of a decisional event from an individual occurrence through the branches, to the trunk and eventually to the roots. Such a logic presupposes linearity, traceability, progression, multiplication, and an overarching unity. Thus even a book or a chapter such as this one embodies this familiar kind of root–tree logic. We have an established procedure involving a title, an introduction, various sub-sections and a conclusion. As the ideas we are trying to deal with get more complicated we invent ever-more sub-categories to account for detailed differences. Thus it acquires a tree-like structure beginning with a singular trunk or the main theme of the book, branches and sub-branches and so on. One begets two, two begets four, four begets sixteen and so on . . . Most importantly, all the elements down to each individual leaf can be traced back to the trunk and ultimately to the root that nourishes it. The equivalent concept of such traceability in modern thinking is the notion of causal chain and our ability to trace every effect to a specific cause. Similarly we talk of "decision-trees" in our analysis of the decision-making process and of the "tree of knowledge" in our attempts to understand nature. Deleuze and Guattari call this logic the logic of "State." This is true in two senses. For one thing, it is a logic that emphasizes fixed "end-states" and for a second, it is a logic employed by the State as a control apparatus. The purpose of the State apparatus is to locate and represent each of its members so that it can achieve precision, mastery and overall control over its subjects. Each of its subjects can then be maneuvered into place to serve a specific societal role. Chess is a good example of how Statehood is played out. "Chess is a game of State, or of the court . . . Chess pieces are coded; they have an internal nature and intrinsic properties from which their movements, situations and confrontations derive. They have qualities . . . Each is like a subject . . . endowed with a relative power" (Deleuze and Guattari, 1988, p. 352).

Chess is about the arrangement, coding and decoding of a restrictive space in order to achieve overall mastery and control. It is like a State war machine that can go to war with clearly specified tasks and clear battle-lines. There are clear rules of engagement and the status of each piece is well defined hierarchically. The object is conquest and subjugation of the opponent. Chess is the ultimate example of the conscious focused planning of field maneuvers.

In contrast the Chinese game Go (or Wei Chi as it is more traditionally called) is also played on a board much like chess except that its units are simple pellets or discs, anonymous arithmetic units without any privileged status and that only have a collective function. While chess pieces entertain bi-univocal relations with one another, and with their adversary's pieces, A Go piece has only extrinsic relationships that only exist within a nebula or constellation where it fulfils its function of "insertion or situation, such as bordering, encircling, shattering" (Deleuze and Guattari, 1988, p. 353). Go is a kind of war without battle lines, with neither direct confrontation nor decisive retreats. Go is more like terrorism and guerrilla warfare, the enemy is often unknown or invisible and the attacks are sporadic and can come from any direction. In Go small seemingly insignificant moves can have massive repercussions.

Playing Go is a matter of "arraying oneself in an open space, of holding space, of maintaining the possibility of springing up at any point: the movement is not from one point to another, but becomes perpetual without aim or destination, without departure or arrival" (Deleuze and Guattari, 1988, p. 353). In chess you win by defeating the opponent and when you win you know it. The victory is decisive. It is all or nothing. In Go you win by occupying more territory and hence have a greater leverage than your opposition. Your adversary may be weakened but not destroyed. Go is the logic of nomads and rhizomes, not a root–tree logic, the logic of State.

Chess and Go represents two diametrically opposed ways of thinking about strategies, futures, and possibilities. One is linear, focused, and mission-led. The other is open, dispersive, and opportunity seeking. One is rational the other a creative search. State logic orders the relentless flow of crude and inarticulate experiences into readily identifiable finite units in order to control and manipulate them to its advantage. It is preoccupied with positions, fixities, and stable relations. It relies upon a precise logic of focused attention, clear judgement, structured reasoning, and controlled action. Nomadic logic, on the other hand, is that which dwells in the undifferentiated and pre-linguistic stream of experience and resists all premature attempts to translate such experience into secondary structured forms. It scatters attention, encourages eye-wander, and is thus able to handle open-ended situations without the compulsive desire to "round them off" prematurely. It celebrates the possibilities that come with the vagueness, ambiguity, and fluidity of experience. To achieve deeper insight and hence foresight it is necessary to cultivate this quality of nomadology.

## Cultivating Foresight

A journey of a thousand miles begins with the first step. (Old Chinese proverb)

The classical rational mind with its focus on immediate, visible material outcomes, and end-states finds it difficult to understand how it is possible that major outcomes can be attained by sometimes seemingly insignificant events occurring remotely or peripherally both in space and time. Chaos and complexity theories now, however, reveal the possibilities of what is popularly called the "butterfly effect" where small seemingly inconsequential events occurring often unnoticed at a periphery can trigger off major catastrophes. Small remote peripheral causes can create dramatic effects and consequences. The possibilities of *non-local causality* are forcing us to re-evaluate our understanding of the traditional relationship between cause and effect. It forces us to expand our vision and to look further afield for causal connections. Yet the wider our scan the more uncertain and ambivalent the causal possibilities appear. What we have called a nomadic logic urges us to dwell in the open-ended, incomplete, and ambiguous without prematurely seeking closure and allows us to see how it is possible for seemingly peripheral events to substantially influence central outcomes in the fullness of time. In art, as we have seen, the student is taught to attend to the microscopic scribbles or the individual strokes of brushwork instead of the dominant form figure and to attend diligently to these peripheral activities. The good artist knows from wide experience how important it is to be aware of these "invisible" chaotic scribbles because of the overall impact they will have on the general impression of the picture. In music, the pupil's attention is similarly turned away from an exclusive concentration on the surface gestalt (which in this case is the melody) and made to observe the polyphonic character of the accompanying voices. In both instances it is the seemingly inconsequential details and peripheral micromovements that are observed at the "corner-of-the-eye" so to speak. In both instances it is the nomadic logic that is cultivated and a scattered attention or eyewander encouraged. It is this seemingly marginal activity that allows us to develop the necessary sensitivity for foresight.

However, the learning of this form of *subsidiary awareness* or *unconscious scanning* is not just restricted to music and the arts. It can also be cultivated in a number of ways including the playing of a variety of combination games (albeit in a much more limited manner) and in the reading of crime novels. According to Ehrenzweig (1967, p. 38):

> An exaggerated need for clear visualization will even be harmful in playing a comparatively simple combination game like chess or bridge. The playing of combination games is not unlike creative work. It too requires the scanning of serial structures in order to decide strategy.

In all such instances the creative thinker has to make a decision based on inadequate information. That is the essence of creativity. However, there are significant differences in degrees of creative search beginning from crossword puzzles, combination games like chess and bridge, and much more open-ended ones like Go as we have tried to argue. Go is much more like a crime novel as we shall see in a moment.

In crossword puzzles the search is limited to a relatively narrow range of combinational possibilities. It is a puzzle with a fixed final outcome. You either get it right or not at all. In some ways a crossword puzzle represents an appropriate metaphor for the kind of traditional forecasting now increasingly discredited. There is an inbuilt assumption that situations do not materially change. The playing of Chess however, is far more complex in that it can have a large number of final outcomes depending on the interaction of both players and on how the game progresses. Yet, as we now well know it is possible to programme a computer to learn sufficiently about these combinations to actually pose a real threat to the Chess masters and even to beat them convincingly. Deep Blue is one example of this triumph of the power of information processing. Given a large enough processing capability a computer can become better than a human being in the game of Chess. The playing of Go, on the other hand, is much more open-ended and does not, as of the present, lend itself to the kind of programming attainable in Chess. It is closer to that of a crime novel.

In the case of a good crime novel, the reader is often left in suspense right until the end of the novel, or sometimes even then the culprit is not identified. The crime novel appeals more through the skill of its construction than by its content or outcome. Suspense and intrigue are built into the plot. Its technique can be called one of deliberate ambiguity. A good author never ever allows the clues he/she surreptitiously inserts ever so discretely to narrow down prematurely so that the culprit can be identified early on. Instead he/she keeps these clues as discrete, disconnected, and as ambiguous as possible. As this chaotic complex of information mounts in the reader's mind the reader has to bear the tension and suspense only because he/she assumes that, in the end, all will fall into an orderly and logical pattern. The final twist comes when the reader is somewhat surprised or taken aback by whom the culprit turns out to be. A few odd bits, which had been smuggled in unnoticed under a dazzling camouflage of insignificant details, are then triumphantly dragged out and delivered as the logical outcome of the unfolding story.

Writing a really good crime novel is no mean achievement since it requires several sub-themes and hence several series of accompanying clues to be kept running simultaneously much like the polyphonic character of music. The reader is not allowed to concentrate on the development of a singular plot. Instead there are multiple possible lines of development and the reader's attention is constantly diverted from one possibility to another. He/she follows the "unfolding of the whole intentionally incoherent and ambiguous story in a state of diffused attention with one or the other possibility dimly flickering and extinguishing again, but never attracting attention exclusively" (Ehrenzweig, 1965, p. 44). The crime novel technique is a supreme example of a nomadic logic and a guide as to how we should be re-educating our attention so as to achieve a deeper insight and foresight into the situations in which we find ourselves.

Foresight is the ability to hold in abeyance our need for premature closure and to see multiple possibilities developing in an open-ended situation. It relies on a heightened sensitivity to the micro-development of material events taking place at the periphery of human consciousness. In this regard the cultivation of foresight and the far-sightedness that it instils entails a shift in attention away from focal awareness to the concerns of *subsidiary awareness.* Learning to develop foresight is learning to resist the seductions of premature closure. The experience of art, music, drama, and the playing of increasingly more open-ended combination games helps develop the kind of scattered attention and the cultivating of the "negative capability" required for achieving a deeper resonance with the material events taking place around us. This is a vital quality for successful visioning and scenario-creation.

## Conclusion

What we have argued in this chapter is that foresight is essentially about the *re-education of attention*. We are culturally programed to attend to the visible, the articulate, the compact, the precise; to gaze and not to glance. The frontal *gaze* is abstracting, objectifying, and passive. The sideways *glance*, on the other hand, is furtive, movement-sensitive, and interactive. The latter is much more sensitive to event-happenings at the periphery of vision and hence more able to grasp the unfolding minutiae of event-situations. To shift our attention away from focal aware-ness we must first appreciate that such an emphasis derives from a dominant binary logic of "state" which privileges clarity, stability, linearity, and outcomes. This pre-occupation with form and figure prevents us from engaging in the much more messy and ambiguous character of event-happenings in the real world.

What is needed in the place of state logic is a *nomadic logic* that encourages us to scatter our attention and to resist any attempts at premature definition or closure. It encourages eye-wander and is better able to handle open-ended situations and resisting the compulsion to "round them off" prematurely. It celebrates the potenti-alities and possibilities that accompany vagueness, ambiguity and the fluidity of experience. It enables us to intuit the fore-structure of event-happenings by causing us to attend not so much to the content of information but to the hidden structural order that underlies seemingly disparate activities and events. When visionaries and leaders, when futurists and scenario-planners appear prophetic and farsighted it is because they are deeply tuned in to the unconscious structures of comprehension that are inaccessible to the conscious mind.

Sensitivity to such deep structures can be systematically cultivated through a variety of ways. Crosswords and the playing of combination games such as chess go some way to helping us to be more sensitized to the alternative possibilities confronting any given situation. Go and crime novels represent a much more radical extension of this kind of dispersive activity that is inspired by the *nomadic logic* we refer to here. They blur lines of confrontation, level out hierarchical differences and confuse simple cause and effect thinking. The extreme case is in great works of art, poetry and music, which plumb the depths of human consciousness and are able to achieve magnificent glimpses of the inherently open-ended and creative nature of the human condition. This is why Ruskin was able to inspire Mahatma Gandhi with his prophetic words:

> Hundreds of people can talk for one who can think, but thousands can think for one who can see. . . . To see clearly is poetry, prophecy and religion. John Ruskin (1985, *Unto this Last*, p.21)

# REFERENCES

Bourdieu, P. (1977) *Outline of a Theory of Practice*, Cambridge: Cambridge University Press.

Chia, R. (1996) *Organizational Analysis as Deconstructive Practice*, Berlin: De Gruyter.

Chia, R. (1998) From complexity science to complex thinking: Organization as simple location, *Organization*, 5(3), 341–69.

De Castro, V. (1998) Cosmological deixis and Amerindian perspectivism, *Journal of the Royal Anthropological Institute*, 4, 469–88.

Deleuze, G. and Guattari, F. (1988) *A Thousand Plateaus*, London: Athlone Press.

Ehrenzweig, A. (1965) *The Psychoanalysis of Artistic Vision and Hearing*, New York: George Braziller.

Ehrenzweig, A. (1967) *The Hidden Order of Art*, Berkeley: University of California Press.

Fahey, L. and Randall, R. M. (1998) *Learning from the Future*, Chichester: John Wiley & Sons.

Gibson, J. J. (1979) *The Ecological Approach to Visual Perception*, Boston, MA: Houghton, Mifflin Co.

Heidegger, M. (1977) *The Question Concerning Technology*, New York: Harper and Row.

James, W. (1909/96) *A Pluralistic Universe*, Lincoln and London: University of Nebraska Press.

James, W. (1911/96) *Some Problems of Philosophy*, Lincoln and London: University of Nebraska Press.

Matsushita, K. (1978/1986) *My Management Philosophy*, Singapore National Productivity Board Publication.

McDermott, J. J. (1977) *The Writings of William James*, Chicago: University of Chicago Press.

Polanyi, M. (1962) *Personal Knowledge*, New York: Harper and Row.

Polanyi, M. (1967) *The Tacit Dimension*, London: Routledge and Kegan Paul.

Polanyi, M. (1969) *Knowing and Being*, (ed. M. Grene), Chicago: University of Chicago Press.

Ruskin, J. (1927) *The Complete Works*, London: Nicholson and Weidenfeld.

Ruskin, J. (1985) *Unto This Last and Other Writings*, London: Penguin Books.

Saussure, F. D. (1966) *Course in General Linguistics*, New York: McGraw Hill.

Schwartz, P. (2002) *The Art of the Long View*, Chichester, New York: John Wiley & Sons.

Spinosa, C., Flores, F., and Dreyfus, H. L. (1997) *Disclosing New Worlds*, Cambridge, MA: MIT Press.

van der Heijden, K. (1996) *Scenarios: The Art of Strategic Conversation*, Chichester, New York: John Wiley & Sons.

van der Heijden, K., Bradfield, R., Burt, G., Cairns, G., and Wright, G. (2002) *The Sixth Sense*, Chichester: John Wiley & Sons.

Wack, P. (1985) Scenarios: Uncharted waters ahead, *Harvard Business Review*, 85(5), 72–89.

Weick, K. E. (1979) *The Social Psychology of Organizing*, Reading, MA: Addison-Wesley.

Wilson Allen, G. (1973) *A William James Reader*, Boston: Houghton Mifflin.

Whitehead, A. N. (1929), *Process and Reality*, Cambridge: Cambridge University Press.

Whitehead, A. N. (1933), *Adventures of Ideas*, Harmondsworth, Middlesex: Penguin Books.

# Chapter Three

# Invention and Navigation as Contrasting Metaphors of the Pathways to the Future

*V. K. Narayanan and Liam Fahey*

## Introduction

Strategy is meaningful only with reference to the future. Yet attention to how and why the future might unfold often remains less than explicit across the sub-strands of both theoretical and applied approaches to strategy determination. Strategy analysis methodologies stemming from diverse disciplinary underpinnings (e.g. economic, psychological, sociological, and political) all too often focus on efficient and effective pathways to some (often not well-articulated) future. Methodologies range from predominantly descriptions of the current and immediate term as in industry analyses (Porter, 1980) to broad-brush projections of alternative futures exemplified in scenarios crafted by *World Future Society* and many corporations. Rarely, however, does the discourse across these strategy sub-literatures transcend to the meta-theoretic level, questioning the epistemological bases of these analyses of the future.

We start with the premise that "the future" is a *cognitive construction*. Because the future has not yet happened, it must be conceived, imagined, or otherwise created as an explicit cognitive act by one or more individuals. For our purpose, we assume that the relevant individuals or group have some *action* purpose for doing so. Hence, we argue that the concepts and methodologies that underlie such constructions of the future can and should be erected upon sound epistemological foundations.

Building upon the work on Nicholas Rescher, we offer an epistemological analysis of two different approaches to the future *invention* and *navigation*, which in various guises are evident in the strategic management literature. We organize our analysis into five sections. First, we briefly make the case that any effort to construct the future unavoidably confronts epistemological challenges. Second, we outline how Rescher's view of epistemology, embedded in his systematic articulation of conceptual idealism, offers the necessary analytical *framework* to address the challenge of how individuals construct the future. Third, in order to demonstrate the power and relevance of Rescher's epistemological framework, we briefly articulate two differing, but popular pathways to the future evident in a variety of literatures – invention and navigation. Fourth, we then show how invention and navigation are propelled by their own distinctive epistemology, one critical result of which is that movement from one to the other is fraught with the challenge of incommensurability. In the final section, we address the organizational implications that stem from subjecting the two modes of future analysis to serious epistemological scrutiny.

## The Future as an Epistemological Problem

Any effort designed to project and interpret the future confronts two fundamental analytical/intellectual questions:

1 What allows us to have *confidence* in our ability to peer into the future? Stated differently, how do we deal with the basic and unavoidable epistemological issues involved in grappling with the future?
2 Assuming we can come to grips with the epistemological issues, how *can* we look into the future? What methodologies enable us to do so?

The first question directs attention to the epistemological anchors of our assertions about the future whereas the second focuses attention on the methodologies that are invoked to depict how the future might unfold. The two questions are indeed linked: the underlying epistemological premises invest the methodological outputs with varying degrees of credibility, and thus elevate them to something approaching "truth hood."

Epistemological concerns flow axiomatically from our overarching premise that the future is always a cognitive construction. Some of these concerns emanate from the nature of things in the world we inhabit. Ontologically, the future is non-existent, thus, empirical verification of any assertions about the future will have to wait for the future to unfold. Second, only in a totally deterministic world, can we say that the future is causally encompassed in the present. Stated differently, the future is causally underdetermined by the realities of the present and is open to the development of wholly unprecedented patterns due to the interactions and contingencies of actors and trends. Third, the future as such, cannot exert any *causal* influence on the present – though of course our *ideas* about it will have a major formative impact in what we think and do.

Confounding these ontological considerations is the fact that the future may *also* be *cognitively* inaccessible due to the incompleteness of information. First, we may not be able to secure the needed data. Indeed, it is often surprisingly difficult to obtain the requisite data to develop deep understanding of the past and present as one input to developing future possibilities. Second, we are not able to ascertain the patterns embedded in or lurking behind the available data necessary to posit the underlying operative laws with respect to how and why alternative futures might unfold. Third, interpreting data and underlying regularities (patterns, operative laws) involve dynamics and complexities that simply exceed our innate cognitive capabilities.

One outcome of these two sets of interacting considerations is that all our claims about the future necessarily involve varying degrees of facts (data) as *observed* and "facts" (data) as *conjectures*. We simply cannot rely solely on our observation or understanding of the present and past as *the* platform to develop futures projections. In short, therefore, the future cannot be depicted without the intervention of the human mind: we cannot project what we cannot conceive. How well we conceive of the future in light of the ontological and cognitive considerations just noted thus depends upon our conceptual abilities, both as individuals and collectivities. Because whatever methods we employ to construct the future will, therefore, be at the mercy of the human mind with all its frailties, limitations, and predispositions, we need to retreat to disciplines and rigors of epistemology to depict and assess the elements of the operative methodology, if its outputs are to be invested with any claims remotely approaching "truth hood," or "correctness." Rescher's emphatic focus upon the role and importance of the *conceptual* in shaping our understanding of how we construct knowledge in any organizational context renders his epistemological position and propositions ideally suited for any effort to construct and assess methodologies to grapple with the future.

## Rescher's Epistemological Framework

Rescher's epistemological framework is systematically depicted and clearly articulated in his prolific writings under the rubric of conceptual idealism (Rescher, 1992). It builds upon the nineteenth and early twentieth century European philosophers and is thus classical in nature. A preeminent philosopher of science, Rescher has devoted significant attention to the future (see, for example, Rescher, 1998), having been involved in the invention of the Delphi technique while at Rand Corporation. His focus is primarily cognitive, but he admits pragmatism in his discussion, especially in his treatment of technological constraints on science. While a detailed account of the Rescherian position is beyond the scope of this chapter (the interested reader may examine several books referred to in the bibliography), we will delineate the key elements of his framework relevant to exploration of the future.

## *A Complex of Two Cycles*

Rescher traces the claims of any school of thought to "knowledgehood" to the underlying cognitive enterprise on which the claims are founded. Rescher's position is best summarized in his own words:

> Acceptance-as-true is in general not the starting point of inquiry but its terminus. To begin with, all that we generally have is a body of prima facie truths, that is, propositions that qualify as potential, perhaps even as promising, *candidates* for acceptance. The epistemic realities being as they are, these candidate truths will, in general, form a mutually inconsistent set, and so exclude one another so as to destroy the prospects of their being accorded in toto recognition as truths pure and simple. The best that can be

done in such circumstances is to endorse those truths that best cohere with the others so as to make the most of the data as a whole in the epistemic circumstances at issue. Systemic coherence thus affords the criterial validation of the qualifications of truth candidates for being classed as genuine truths. Systematicity becomes not just the organizer but the test of truth. (Rescher, 1992, p. 157)

Rescher uses systematic in a unique sense, referring to a complex of two cycles, each reinforcing and restraining the other, the *theoretical cycle* of cognitive coherence and the *pragmatic cycle* of empirical validation. Although coherence is a primary criterion for judgment, the two cycles emphasize different modes of coherence. The former cycle uses coherence with available or emerging theoretical scheme whereas the latter cycle looks to empirical evidence to judge the validity of truth claims. Thus, the first focuses on the *intellectual* aspect of description, explanation, and understanding, the second the *pragmatic* aspect of prediction and control over nature. Both cycles are present in any epistemology, although the substance and emphases may vary from one epistemological platform to the other. In emerging fields theoretical coherence may be weak, and there may be greater sensitivity to "facts," real or imagined; in ideology theoretical coherence is a primary criterion even in the presence of contradictory "facts" that are automatically screened out.

Rescherian epistemology thus highlights a web of beliefs, but Rescher distinguishes between "facts" and "concepts" that may constitute the web. Prediction may involve new facts, thus it serves not only to verify available truth candidates, but also to discover new facts, as in the case of Leverrier and Adams, who by using Newton's laws of motion deciphered the position of Neptune. Concepts, however, represent types of facts and hence are more general. What may be a new fact may not be a new concept; the concept must already have subsumed the fact. Thus the epistemic status of a belief depends upon its location in the web: facts are lower than concepts in status.

## Coherence Process

Given the process orientation inherent in the two cycles, Rescher expects epistemological platforms to cohere. He thus insists on harmony between explanation and prediction. Of course, change is ever present: Whereas harmony is ideal, Rescher expects knowledge regimes to be superseded, much like the paradigm shifts observed by Kuhn. The process is timeless, although constrained by available technology (a point we will elaborate later); and the goal of the enterprise is primarily cognitive.

Rescher insists on the *process of knowledge generation* as the key to his epistemological framework. Rational inquiry, in turn, lies at the heart of the two cycles, the interaction of which powers the (continual) generation and testing of knowledge. Thus, Rescher does not insist on the truth of facts in the beginning: since the starting conditions of inquiry may be far from the truth and the truth-as-accepted itself is susceptible to be proven otherwise, Rescher locates rationality in the process of knowledge generation. Rescher follows Kant in asserting that cognitive reflexivity dogs every postulation of a "fact." Similarly, he acknowledges the gap between the real and ideal, a gap that gets closed only in ideal circumstances. This incompleteness of science is countered by the arbitrament of praxis, which affords an inquiry-independent standard for assessing the adequacy of the cognitive endeavor.

Rescher views the end of science as a myth: there are no limits to inquiry in the cognitive sense. But he argues that the technological and economic constraints may slow the cognitive enterprise, as the marginal increment in knowledge requires ever increasing cost in technological and methodological developments. Technology is thus servant of inquiry, but extracts an economic price.

## The Role of Conceptual Innovation

The import of a Rescherian framework for problems of the future hinges on perhaps its key constituent element – *conceptual innovation*. It emphatically alerts us to the central and critical *need* to engage in (re)conceptualization: to continually reframe the world as we understand it. It reminds us that knowledge advancement, whether discontinuous or incremental, always traces its impetus to change in (our understanding of) concepts: developing new concepts, adapting old concepts, looking for connection among concepts. Such innovation in how we conceive of the world, in short what we see in the world, how we see it, and indeed, why we see it, thus must become a preoccupation of those who consciously tackle the problem of the future. Conceptual innovation further admonishes us to accept that the acquisition or creation of new data and information always compels us to assess whether our long-held concepts are adequate to describing and explaining the world around us, not to mention the world as it might be at some future point in time. To cite a common example, new data about customers' buying preferences could cause us to redefine our concept of customer need or our conception of speed with which customers might move to rivals' products. Further up the ladder of conceptualization, a set of managers by identifying and reconceiving connections among a number of unfolding data points such as customer, competitor, and technology change might reason through a process of causal linkages that a radical new market opportunity would soon present itself.

## Real and Possible

Conceptual innovation extends the knowledge domain beyond the realm of what is (description) and current know-how (control). It takes us beyond "facts" as descriptive truths about the "real" world. Because we as "knowers" conceptually innovate, using causal principles and laws, we think not just in terms of "what does happen?" but "what would happen if?" Such principles and laws "encompass not only the actual but the hypothetically possible as well" (Rescher, 1992, p. 312). Conceiving (that is, detecting and projecting) "this realm of mere possibility" (ibid.) of what is not actually present as part of the physical, or social, or political reality but accessible only because we make and commit to assumptions, suppositions, hypotheses, is something that only those endowed with minds can do – and something that becomes necessary in any endeavor to understand possibilities about the future.

## Mind Involving and Invoking

Rescher distinguishes between mind involving and mind invoking. Of course, use of existing data and theories to make sense of the future – mind involving is always present. Yet this does not capture the full import of explicit "mind-invokingness" (Rescher, 1992, p. 311), i.e. the mind's ability to resort to assumptions, suppositions, and hypotheses. The capacity to invoke visions about an organization's alternative futures or aspirations about the customer value-generating possibilities of the firm's next generation of products depend singularly upon the mind's ability to invoke (conceptually) views of the future, views that could not exist except through the thought processes of mind-endowed creatures. "Mind-invokingness" allows managers and others to articulate complex scenarios projecting, for example, alternative industry futures, or simulations depicting potential evolutions of complex sets of interacting variables (such as intricate supply–demand interactions across multiple time periods). Without resort to "mind-invokingness," the future to the extent it is dramatically different from today will remain outside our conceptual reach.

"Mind-invokingness," in turn, exemplifies the almost limitless sources and range of data and information inputs to the cognitive enterprise. Data are not merely gathered and orchestrated; often they are created. Sense-data, the stuff of day-to-day experience, can be sifted, reconfigured, and interpreted to generate meaning that is far afield from initial observations. Thus data, even where they meet some test of "facts," always reflect the circumstances of their being a human creation. Data are always formed through the use of mind-made conceptions. Truth, or more generally, the insight value of data, stems not from its local and isolated aspects (e.g. the extent to which the data have been validated), but from the broader context of which the data are but one part. Facts in isolation possess limited power to convey meaning.

Yet the mind-involved and mind-invoked conception of the world does not give rise to an egocentric, self-referential stance. Rescher rejects all claims to a privileged status for *our own* conception of things (Rescher, 1992, p. 189, emphasis in original). This is so for many reasons, but perhaps the most critical is that we "knowers" or inquirers can never be in a position to realize *how* our current conception of a thing is inadequate – we can only realize *that* it may well be so on the basis of retrospect (ibid., p. 184, emphasis in original). Thus, the cognitive enterprise at the heart of knowledge generation and assessment requires extensive and intensive communication and interaction – in short, real dialogue with others. Inquiry therefore becomes, and must be, a communal project of investigation. Studying the future must involve others outside our "circle."

## Language and Community of Inquiry

But what is the nature of this communal form of inquiry? How do the conceptually and experientially generated inputs get transformed into outputs? Language becomes the purposive instrument by which individuals' communicate the data and information (with all the inherent limitations and infirmities) required for the interpersonal exchange needed for the coherent pursuit of individual goals and for the coordination of effort in the pursuit of common goals. But the raw content of such interpersonal exchange, by definition, entails the distinct, indeed idiosyncratic, viewpoints of each participant: the conceptions and their interconnections formed by each individual constitute the grist for the exchange among and between individuals. The mind-centric buttress of conceptual idealism inevitably leads to only one way out of the morass of myriad viewpoints, reasoning that manifests the hallmarks of "rational" discourse. The knowledge process thus must articulate arguments involving clear connections among elements in the reasoning – often reflecting causal linkages, assumptions underpinning viewpoints, and most critically, persistent and pointed challenges to key elements in the reasoning process resulting not just from conceptual grounds but from learning due to monitoring and reflecting on the results of action.

Persistent and intense interpersonal exchange, driven by different viewpoints, results in cognitive change; but such cognitive change, among other things, requires that each "knower" begins from a premise that his/her viewpoint may embody conceptions (data, information, assumptions, presuppositions, etc.) that are not only (potentially) at variance with those of others but may need to be changed in the face of superior evidence and/or argumentation. Thus, even apparently self-evident descriptions such as customers' buying patterns, or straightforward explanations such as customers' own judgments about why they purchase one product rather than others, must be subjected both to the assessments of others as well as practical experience of what customers actually do and say. Exposure to data and information *outside* one or more individuals' conceptual frame of reference may alter dramatically otherwise previously strongly subscribed to, descriptions and explanations. In short, knowledge is an artifact not only of our minds but also of how our minds work. Thus, different views of the future rest upon methodologies *fashioned* to reflect and enable our minds to work in quite distinct ways.

In summary, the Rescherian epistemological framework allows us to portray the essence of any approach to the future along several key features:

1  the relative emphasis on the two cycles of conceptual coherence and empirical validation:
2  the process of internal coherence;
3  the role of conceptual innovation;
4  the sources and mix of the real and possible;
5  the relative degree of mind-invoking and mind-involving in the cognitive component of the approach to the future; and
6  the requirements of language and the nature of the inquiring community.

CHESTER COLLEGE WARRINGTON LIBRARY

To test the applicability of these features, we now turn to two common approaches to grappling with the future – invention and navigation.

## Two Alternative Metaphors for the Future

The received wisdom in strategic management exhorts organizations to peer into the macro environmental (that is, the political, social, economic, technological, and ecological milieus) and competitive contexts. Projections about these contexts fuel the search for new business opportunities and threats to current or potential strategies, as well as the appropriate organizational actions to take advantage of these insights.

This need for projection is translated into practise in different ways in contemporary approaches to strategy formulation. We can characterize the approaches along a two dimensional plane: accuracy and time horizon, as shown in Figure 3.1. Inevitably, beyond a certain horizon, projections become *cognitively* infeasible. Even when we confine ourselves to the feasible boundary there is a trade-off between time horizon and accuracy of forecasts, as shown in the figure.

At the risk of simplification, we can identify two major approaches to projection. Labeled *invention* and *navigation*, the two approaches occupy different regions of the accuracy/time horizon plane. Below we discuss each approach with the help of two disguised cases (see Box 3.1). In Table 3.1 we highlight key differences between the two approaches.

### *Invention*

The inventive mode, as a form of depicting the future (sometimes simply referred to as prediction), has featured prominently in the intellectual tradition of many fields of

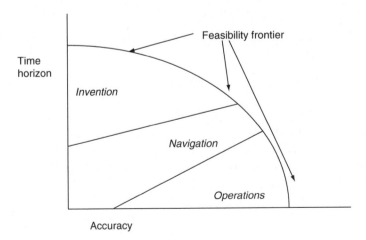

**Figure 3.1**   Modes of projection

# Box 3.1   Invention and Navigation Illustrated

## FullCon

FullCon, a division of a large technology firm, faces a future festooned with uncertainties in an emerging market space. Without exception, all the current and potential players proclaim that this market space five years hence will bear little if any resemblance to any product-market segment today. Sharp discontinuities currently characterize a variety of "applications" technologies. New technologies, at varying stages of development, are anticipated to reach the market over the next five years. Reports emanating from key technology houses suggest that the functionality and performance capabilities of some of these technologies are likely to be grossly overstated but that if they meet or exceed the expectations of some "insiders" (individuals involved in firms developing these technologies), the potential to create radical new customer functionalities will be reminiscent of the emergence of the mainframe computer or the personal computer. Some of these technologies, and perhaps some technologies yet to be conceived, will also be heavily influenced by work taking place in basic and applied research across a number of science domains – some of which at first glance may seem to outsiders totally disconnected from the solution space at issue. Moreover, the range of potential interactions among these technologies is such that even the "experts" place little credibility in any single "forecast" as to what the technology future might look like four or five years out. Adoption and use of the potential solution, in any of its forms, will also require dramatic shifts in the technology infrastructures, work practices, and organizational cultures in all potential customer organizations. Yet the alleged value and benefits of the potential solution may be sufficient to propel corporate organizations to adapt to its demands.

## SemiCon

SemiCon is a leading provider of a long established line of manufactured products. These products serve as components in the process technologies employed by a wide variety of manufacturing firms. Although new rivals have entered the business over the past 10 years or so, it was only in the past few years that the core product had begun to reflect advances in its constituent technologies. SemiCon executives felt that the firm was now, perhaps for the first time, facing an opportunity to extend the product line. A small subset of the firm's customers has brought a particular operations problem to the firm's attention.

The details of the problem remain murky: different customers have specified the problem in different ways. Given one articulation of the operations problem, alternative technical specifications of a product solution were quickly generated by the firm's engineers. Yet, in customer focus groups, the firm's product development team discovered that the real operations problem being experienced by some customers involved a far more critical technical challenge. If that challenge could be solved, it would fill the firm's declared need to extend its existing product line by greatly broadening the applications uses of its core product line. Customers have also informed SemiCon that one or two of its principal rivals have been talking about new R&D commitments exploring new product solutions to address these operations problems.

**Table 3.1** Invention and navigation as alternate modes of prediction

| Key dimensions | Navigation | Invention |
|---|---|---|
| 1 Conception of the future | 1 Patterned evolution that can be deterministic or probabilistic<br>2 Only partially understood by human actors | 1 Future as fundamentally open, manipulable by human action<br>2 Gnomic uncertainty |
| 2 The role of the mind | Mind-involving through induction and extrapolation of data | Mind-involving through induction and mind-invoking through imagination |
| 3 Method | Low cost experiments, Swift feedback, and Rapid adaptation | Pattern assimilation, Imagination, and Design of knowledge domains |
| 4 Central actors | Interacting and competing organizations | "Elites" as orchestrators, and idea generators within a system |
| 5 Applicability | Dynamic environments of medium time frame | Uncertain environments of long time frames |
| 6 Requirements of organization | Technical and operational flexibility | Emphasis on strategic flexibility |

inquiry or disciplines, although the vigor of its promulgation and attractiveness has waxed and waned according to the predilections of the times. It springs from one overarching premise: the future can and should be designed. This premise is not accidental: it simultaneously stems from the deep-seated desire of human beings to control their destiny and exalts their ability to do.

The inventive mode is approximated in FullCon's[1] attempt to project what the future might be in one emerging market space (see Box 3.1). The uncertainties and ambiguities associated with the potential technologies, how they might interact, what the configuration of products, markets, and customers might be, and what roles and functions different market players might assume combine to generate a myriad of possible futures. Not the least of the difficulties facing FullCon's managers is that little in their present or past experience prepares them for thinking about what this market space might look like in terms of products, customer functionalities, and market dynamics.

The inventive mode as a means to confront this type of intellectual/analytical challenge has been center stage in the work of authors as diverse as Emery and Trist (1973), Jantsch (1980), and Ackoff (1970). Emery and Trist (1973), for example, drawing upon Vickers (1968), Sommerhoff (1969) and Lewin (1951) explored diverse futures in the realm of social ecology; their primary focus was the institutions of society. Jantsch (1980), in his assessment of forecasting tools as means to grapple with the future's uncertainties was arguably the first one to use the term "inventive" explicitly. Ackoff's (1970) "idealized design" applied in contexts ranging from the technological to the design of complex systems, captures the thrust of the ideas underpinning and spurring invention. In short, invention aims either to create possible futures or craft possibilities for a desired future, somewhat distant in time. In either case, it combines extrapolation from the known (understood broadly) with "disciplined imagination" (Weick, 1989).

Invention's objective is to *alter the shared mind-set of organizational members* by exploring possibilities that are neither currently in existence nor even previously conceived. Hence, its outputs are directional, not prescriptive. FullCon is trying to depict what this market space might look like. Given alternative depictions of what the market space might look like, it can then assess what, if any, business opportunities and threats might lurk in each, and what it would take to exploit them. Thus, invention differs fundamentally from a "plan" (Mintzberg, 1987) or a "strategy" (Porter, 1980) – both of which give rise to immediate decision, resource allocation, and action consequences.

Invention emanates from and is made possible by a specific conception of the future. The future is fundamentally open and manipulable by social and human action. It is thus neither inevitable nor controlled by immutable laws, even if they are not well understood. It accepts the value of scientifically generated knowledge[2] for grounding extrapolations of current trends, but underscores the need for knowledge creation as a parallel and requisite activity in the invention of future. Put another way, inventors may have to invent new branches of knowledge, or create new connections across established knowledge domains or disciplines, in their endeavors to posit descriptions of possibilities. In the case of FullCon, many potential technological possibilities lie utterly outside its current technology base. It is trying to imagine customers' uses of these technology connections in ways that require a fundamentally new way of thinking about how a corporation would define and integrate core operating functions. The role of the mind is thus three-fold: assimilate data to extrapolate, imagine possibilities, and design processes of inquiry into what the mind does not yet know.

The critical actors in the invention mode fall into two overlapping clusters: *orchestrators* and *idea developers*. Orchestrators are typically the elites within a system, be they in society or in an organization. Invention-focused scholars typically prefer democratic processes in the design of values, but expertise in the design of processes. Orchestration is however confined to the "cognoscenti," who fully endorse the idea that the ability to generate ideas is widely distributed across populations. Of course, the emphasis on altering the mind-set predisposes them to democratic processes. In this sense, invention can be seen as an antidote to the folly of ignorance usually ascribed to centralized planning approaches by the Austrian school (Hayek, 1988).

Invention, when successful, creates discontinuities (Drucker, 1969): the future evolves through a series of disruptions that reflect distinctive breaks in apparent patterns. Such waves of "creative destruction" (Foster and Kaplan, 2001) provoke contingencies reflecting surprising and often unanticipated interactions among social, political, economic, technological, and cultural factors. FullCon is forced to imagine what would have to happen to enable specific technology disruptions and how they could create the next round of disruptions through product creation and changes in customers' infrastructure to adopt and leverage the new solutions. Invention celebrates deviations or errors as opportunities to build coherent, but different possibilities, thereby creating dynamic and turbulent environments.

FullCon's experiences suggests that invention demands organizational commitment to crafting foresight that is unrecognizable when viewed from the vantage point of prevailing views of the future. Such foresight in turn both foments and requires a willingness to radically reshape strategy and reconfigure the current organizational form. Invention is thus ideally suited for long-term efforts to fundamentally reconceive strategy and transform the organization. The fundamental strategy and organizational shifts undertaken by DuPont and Monsanto, as they move from traditional chemistry and pharmaceuticals respectively to exploit the opportunities presented by research and technological discontinuities in the life sciences, capture significant facets of the inventive mode.

## Navigation

Navigation as a metaphor for designing the future has enjoyed a schizophrenic existence. Although selective features of navigation have been widely practiced in organizations, only recently has it been recognized as a distinct means of understanding and dealing with the future. Its early genesis can be traced to the depiction of most organizations as "muddling through" and later as engaging in logical instrumentalism (Quinn, 1980). In the past few years, navigation has emerged under the banners of strategic experimentation (McGrath and MacMillan, 2000), competing on the edge (Pascale et al., 2000), and surfing the edge of chaos (Brown and Eisenhardt, 1998).

Navigation ascribes the emergence of the future to a patterned evolution from laws, or at least, some forms of "regularities." It admits both deterministic and probabilistic laws. It acknowledges the limitations of human and social knowledge, i.e., the laws are only partly understood by human and social actors. However, its underlying philosophy or esprit remains optimistic about the human capability to extract the requisite knowledge for managing strategy and organizational form.

SemiCon's managers evidence these tendencies. By committing themselves to identifying and unraveling change in rivals' actions, product developments, customers' responses, and other market developments, they believe that they can determine the "true nature" of the emerging customer opportunity and the best way to respond to it. The uncertainties can be identified; developments along them can be tracked; and inferences can be drawn to suggest preferred action plans.

SeminCon illustrates how navigation endorses the present as the source of the most appropriate indicators of the future. Since the world is evolving according to partially understood laws or more broadly, patterns with known form, navigation requires human and social actors to engage intensely with the world around them. The role of the mind is to discover patterns of evolution so that the journey to the future can be charted on firm cognitive foundations. Thought and action are conjoined as a tight system with limited temporal distance between the two. Although navigation recognizes the role of strategy (Porter, 1980), it underscores the limitation to our knowledge, by augmenting the notion of strategy with a perspective and praxis on evolution.

Navigation views the future as much more destined than invention: the present and the emergent processes interact to largely determine future states. To circumvent ignorance of the underlying laws, navigation proposes a three-pronged method for detecting emerging and potential change and responding accordingly. First, unlike the grand conceptual schemes hatched under the rubric of invention, navigation proposes a series of *low-cost experiments* as the means to generate a significant portion of the requisite data. SemiCon's managers institute focus groups, customer visits, and trials of tentative customer solutions as a means to collect specific data sets. Second, navigation designs *swift feedback*: the data provide the basis for inferences and judgments about the laws. SemiCon managers lose little time in inferring some of the key attributes of a desired customer solution. Finally, the learning is rapidly *translated into action*. Witness how SemiCon reacts quickly to the data provided in focus groups by designing possible customer solutions – thereby instigating another round of data gathering, inference derivation, and action stipulation. The challenge addressed by navigation is not redesigning the future, but deploying a method of knowledge gathering.

The central actors in navigation are a set of often interacting and competing organizations. Given the characterization of organizations as a unitary actor for discursive purposes, proponents of navigation have no particular affinity to democratic processes. Rather they are truly "managerialist" in orientation: they prescribe what managers within an organization should do.

Unlike invention, navigation as illustrated in the case of SemiCon, naturally leads to a series of incremental customer (solution) innovations and amendments in organization form. It focuses on adaptation by emphasizing learning: detecting change and reducing errors in underlying knowledge structures. Stated differently, it does not purport to envision or create new notions of the environment (the future), but rather to anticipate and respond to short-run environmental change. Navigation's apparent popularity in organizations may well be due to the implied time horizons: most managerial careers depend upon accomplishments in the medium time frame.

Not surprisingly, given navigation's inherent orientation toward incremental innovation, it is silent on strategic flexibility. Rather, it demands both technical and operational flexibility. Rapid feedback from experiments, and indeed, from actions of all types, renders mandatory the ability to translate such learning into technical (product), operational, and organizational responses. Intel's decision to focus on microprocessors and the IBM turn around under Gerstner are evidence of major features of navigation.

In summary, invention and navigation thus represent two distinctly different modes of projection. We will, in passing, note three methodological differences between the modes:

1 The inventive mode tends to be highly tolerant of conceptual fuzziness (e.g. not being aware of what the critical uncertainties might be), especially in the early stages of the process. Navigation bows to the organizational reality; *the lack of tolerance of fuzziness in coordinated action*, and therefore views fuzziness as an error in the process.
2 The inventive mode accepts the probability of conceptual innovations, which, by and large, are not addressed in navigation.
3 Tactically, inventive mode considers the design of new knowledge domains (and their associated concepts and language) as necessary for projections about the future; navigation accepts the existing knowledge as the basis for projecting the future.

These epistemological differences set the stage for our discussion of incommensurability.

## The Challenge of Incommensurability

Our analysis above suggests that invention and navigation represent two distinct modes of future projection. Each requires and indeed is propelled by its own distinctive epistemology. Each epistemology constitutes an internally coherent system pivoting around fundamentally distinct future-specific questions and ways of grappling with them. In short, the future-directed content and epistemological differences characterizing invention and navigation are not merely ones of degree, but ones of kind.

One overriding consequence of these fundamentally distinct epistemological systems is that movement from one future-projecting mode to the other is fraught with the challenge of *incommensurability*, as highlighted by Kuhn (Conant and Haugeland, 2000). Incommensurability becomes relevant once the need surfaces to translate one's system's concepts, terms, and language into the other. Such is the case when managers endeavor to combine both modes or to transition from one to the other. Although Kuhn (1962, in Conant and Haugeland, 2000) elaborated and demonstrated the power and importance of incommensurability in the context of successive scientific theories, the concept is especially relevant to isolating and assessing the implications for organizational decision making of the differences between invention and navigation as two modes of future-projection. As described by Kuhn (Conant and Haugeland, 2000, p. 34):

> Each of us [Kuhn was referring to Paul Feyerabend and himself] was centrally concerned to show that the meanings of scientific terms and concepts – "force" and "mass" for example, or "element" or "compound" – often changed with the theory in which they were deployed. And each of us claimed that when such changes occurred, it was impossible to define all the terms of one theory in the vocabulary of the other. The latter claim we independently embodied in talk about the incommensurability of scientific theories.

As in the case of scientific theories, the two modes of future projection may use identical or similar terms. However, the terms may have distinctly different meanings. Moreover, as noted previously, invention may require the development of a new vocabulary – terms that possess meaning within the context of inventing a future. Take for example the concept of scenarios. The participants involved in projecting an invented future have little choice but to construct a language that captures and describes the invented future, in part because by its very nature its content will be strikingly dissimilar to the present or indeed, anything likely to evolve from a navigated future. Stated differently, although some commonality of vocabulary associated with scenarios across the two modes will ensue, the fundamental differences in the underlying epistemologies result in futures so radically distinct from each other that the very meaning of the word "future" is not likely to travel easily from one mode to the other. Moreover, the differences inherent in constructing the scenarios, judgments made in the choice of relevant data and evaluative criteria, the practice or procedures in shaping the "end-state" and the "plot" to get there – render each mode irreducible to the other.

Five different strands of incommensurability can be identified:

1  *Availability of antecedent vocabulary.* Our understanding of any future must be language formulated before it can be communicated and analyzed. Otherwise, it remains our private domain. In this respect, the navigational mode benefits from an existing language and vocabulary associated with the present that facilitates description, communication, and assessment, in short, inquiry among inquirers. Hence, these inquirers can be reasonably confident they understand their colleagues in the inquiring journey. New vocabulary evolves over time, thus providing enough time to understand the trajectory of development even for those not involved in the process. The inventive mode, on the other hand, requires the

creation of new language. As it lays out a new understanding of the future, the language will be understood initially only by the participant in the process. To the extent they do not have direct empirical referents in the current world, it will hinder communication across groups of inquirers, especially to those not involved in the inventive process.

2 *Challenge of definition.* Terms and concepts acquire meaning through their use. Yet developing definitions of new terms and concepts is both necessary and difficult. Defining new terms and imbuing them with distinctive meaning is easier in navigation, in part because they can easily be linked to older terms from which they originated. In the inventive mode, terms both new and old need to be defined, and this is not a trivial exercise. As Kuhn illustrated in the case of scientific theories, the inventive mode most likely alters organizational paradigms (the embedded assumptions about the world and how it works), and this requires learning a new language. Terms cannot be taken for granted since they have different meanings, especially since they are linked to other terms.

3 *Holistic nature of language.* The availability of well understood terms and antecedent vocabulary enables navigation mode to represent alternative futures in linear terms, while the participants and non-participants can fully grasp the holistic nature of the projection. Invention requires holistic descriptions, and may have to employ metaphors and evocative language to communicate to the non-participants the holistic character of the projections.

4 *Dispersion of tacit knowledge.* Underpinning the above discussion is the idea that navigation can take for granted a vastly dispersed fund of tacit knowledge that has accumulated over the years within the organization. This renders communication speedy, efficient, and relatively free: meaning is established quickly through the use of largely familiar terms, concepts, and phrases. Invention, on the other hand, does not enjoy the benefits of such an inheritance. The dominant tacit knowledge may not be amenable to formulation of an entirely new worldview. Moreover, the relevant tacit knowledge, to the extent it exists, will not be widely dispersed; rather it will be confined to small groups involved in the invention journey thus rendering it mandatory to involve others in the process so that a shared understanding of the new future is allowed to crystallize in an ever broadening group.

5 *Methodology.* The way the forecasting tools are deployed in invention and navigation, in other words, the methodology, is vastly different. How the two modes cope with epistemological questions and errors of prediction differ significantly, as narrated in an earlier section. Thus, forecasting tools such as scenarios, often used in either mode, will have drastically different characteristics. The similarity in appearance should not mask the fundamental epistemological differences between the navigation and invention modes. Table 3.2 summarizes our discussion of incommensurability in the context of scenarios.

A focus on the epistemology of navigation and invention and the incommensurability between the two modes has significant organizational implications, a point to which we now turn.

**Table 3.2** The challenge of incommensurability

| Manifestations of incommensurability | Tension between invention and navigation | Illustration in the case of scenarios |
|---|---|---|
| 1 Antecedent vocabulary | The imperative of description is fundamental in invention. | Invention scenarios require construction of vocabularies. |
| | Navigation can rely on a relatively extensive antecedent vocabulary. | Navigation scenarios can invoke familiar evocative terms. |
| 2 The role of definition | During invention, terms are developed from practice, definitions are not useful. | Invention scenarios are understood by the participants; they are communicated primarily through illustration. |
| | Navigation is facilitated by definition of new terms of the older terms. | Navigation scenarios can invoke established vocabulary. |
| 3 Systemic nature of language | Communicative basis of invention should be holistic. | Scenarios need to retain holistic character in invention. |
| | Navigation can be linear. | Navigation can rely on reductionism. |
| 4 Dispersion of tacit knowledge | Invention creates tacit knowledge. | Tacit knowledge is confined to elites (under invention). |
| | Navigation can rely on a widely distributed tacit knowledge. | Is more easily dispersed in navigation. |
| 5 Methodology | Incompatible methodologies. | Criteria for feasibility for scenarios are different. |

## Organizational Implications

In this chapter, we have argued that "the future" is a cognitive construction, and that the process and output of this construction rest on central epistemological premises. If we take seriously the proponents of organizational learning (e.g., Argyris and Schön), who have reminded us that reflective learning is crucial to effective strategizing, then we have to accept the inevitability that an appreciation, if not careful selection, of the epistemological premises is a primary key to successful practice in future projects. Based on our discussion of the two modes of future-projections, we can offer two major implications for organizations that wish to engage in "managing the future."

## *Appropriateness of the Two Modes*

As we noted earlier, the two modes, invention and navigation, represent incommensurable epistemological approaches for an organization to simultaneously identify, test, and refine both its conceptual view of the future and its strategic and operational application. The inventive mode facilitates developing and adopting a radical set of future-specific premises compared to the status quo. Embedded in these premises is likely to be an understanding of how the future could unfold that most likely was never previously contemplated by any organizational members. The navigational mode, on the other had, allows the organization to modify its extant conceptual depiction of how the present will evolve in the immediate future. Its dominant incremental tone enables managers to refine continuously its world-view by testing ideas and assessing the results of experiments. Navigational mode operates within a reasonably coherent worldview, whereas inventive mode creates one. The incommensurability between the two is often masked by the use of similar sounding tools such as scenario planning; but the application of the tools differs fundamentally in their epistemological premises. We suggest that the appreciation of the premises is a prerequisite to the conscious choice of the mode for the future project.

As the feasibility frontier (Figure 3.1) suggests, invention and navigation are appropriate for different contexts. It is fairly clear that within a 10 year horizon, population demographics in advanced industrial societies can reasonably well be extrapolated, and neither invention nor navigation is necessary. However, if our focus is sources of energy, not population demographics, then linear extrapolations are ineffective. As this book goes into press, the major preoccupation in the US with respect to the sources of energy is the dependence on Middle Eastern oil. Under navigation mode, the scenarios being drawn up would focus mostly on *known* sources of energy, taking into account the turbulence due to the global *real politic*. An inventive mode, on the other hand, would focus not merely on the known but on the *possible* sources of energy, although no commercial or government enterprises may actually be involved in producing them. The scenarios constructed under the inventive epistemology will include probable paths to the possible sources, although currently there are few self-interested advocates of these possible futures. Scenarios can be constructed under *either* mode with very *different* cognitive processes and outcomes.

Given the incommensurability between the two modes, we are less persuaded by the sanguine prescriptions currently popular in literature. Consider, for example, the frequent advocacy of navigation-like stratagems in turbulent competitive contexts. Such advocacy may well be misplaced. Capturing signals (inferences of potential change) from a diverse set of indicators, but operating within an accepted worldview, could easily lead to superficiality in understanding of drivers of change, connections among them, and thus implications for action. Such fragmentation of understanding may even inhibit the organization from developing an integrated conceptual picture of the turbulence: various units or even individuals within the organization may possess and be testing distinctly different cause – effect models of what is transpiring in the external world. Indeed, it may well lead to further efforts (experiments, etc.) to capture the next stages of the unfolding change, thus further disaggregating the organization's understanding of the world around it. While we believe that the choice between the two modes, invention or navigation, is ultimately an organizational *decision* (conscious or otherwise), and may indeed rest on pragmatic considerations, we are less convinced by the claims to "truth hood" made by some advocates of navigation. As Rescher has forcefully reminded us, the future is an epistemological construction, and cannot be judged as true or false.

## Design of Community of Inquiry

The challenges to the organization's prevailing epistemology raise profound issues about the design and management of the necessary community of inquiries. If knowledge is an artifact not only of our minds but also of how our minds work, then how we structure and orchestrate the inquiring community assumes the highest importance. Because of the fundamental differences in their underlying epistemology, invention and navigation call for different communities. The differing requirements of concept and language development, and the interpersonal exchanges, need to be managed by an appropriate *composition of the groups, timelines, and organizational boundaries*. Invention requires longer time spans (deadlines) for accomplishment, individual inquirers who are both idiosyncratic in their viewpoints and open to the opinions and perspectives of others, and lesser intrusion from existing organizational practices to maintain cognitive tension among unfamiliar ideas. In navigation, where the cognitive endeavors are translated into action much quicker, shorter timelines, greater similarity among participants, and greater adherence to existing organizational processes should be the norm.

Perhaps, even more fundamentally, the mind-invoking conception of the world that lies at the heart of invention should remind both individuals and organizational units that they must reject all claims to a privileged status for their own conception of how the world works or will work. This acquires especial importance in efforts to project how the world may turn out at some point in the future: we simply can't allow our current understanding of things to overshadow how we imagine they could be in the future. Thus, a central organizational implication of the notions of invention and navigation is that members' minds must be conceptually unleashed to imagine alternative views of the future through the power of invoking assumptions, presuppositions, and hypotheses. The ability to literally create data about the future may be the mind's most distinguishing feature in the context of inventing futures. In short, organizations may have to commit to an epistemology that grants individuals and communities the license to engage in thought processes and forms of dialog in full public view of their peers and colleagues. For most companies, this will involve nothing short of a radical overhaul of their traditional cultures.

### NOTES

1  FullCon and SemiCon, which follows it, are disguised versions of scenario-learning cases in two companies with whom we have had a long-term association.

2  There is no presumption in the use of the term "scientific," to limit the types of sciences admitted. Indeed our reference to Trist is intended to underscore the role of sciences in this process, in addition to the so-called "hard sciences."

# REFERENCES

Ackoff, R. (1970) *A Concept of Corporate Planning*, New York: Wiley Interscience.

Brown, S. and Eisenhardt, K. M. (1998) *Competing on the Edge*, Cambridge, MA: Harvard Business Press.

Conant, J. and Haugeland, J. (2000) *The Road Since Structure*, Chicago, IL: The University of Chicago Press.

Drucker, P. (1969) *The Age of Discontinuity*, New Brunswick: Transaction Publishers, (1992).

Emery, F. E. and Trist, E. L. (1973) *Towards a Social Ecology*, New York: Plenum Publishing Corporation.

Foster, R. and Kaplan, S. (2001) *Creative Destruction*, New York: Doubleday.

Hayek, F. A. (1988), *The Fatal Conceit: The Errors of Socialism*. In W. W. Bartley III (ed.), vol. 1 of *The Collected Works of F. A. Hayek*, London: Routledge, and Chicago: University of Chicago Press, (1989).

Jantsch, E. (1980) *Self-organizing Universe*, Oxford: Pergamon.

Lewin, K. (1951) *A Field Theory in Social Science*, (D. Cartwright (ed.)), New York: Harper.

McGrath, R. and MacMillan, I. (2000) *Entrepreneurial Mindset*, Boston: Harvard Business School Press.

Mintzberg, H. (1987) Crafting strategy, *Harvard Business Review*, 65, 66–75.

Pascale, R. T., Millemann, M., and Gioja, L. (2000) *Surfing on the Edge of Chaos*, New York: Crown Business.

Porter, M. (1980) *Competitive Strategy*, New York: Academic Press.

Quinn, J. B. (1980) *Strategies for Change*, Homewood, IL: Richard D. Irwin.

Rescher, N. (1992) *A System of Pragmatic Idealism*, Princeton, NJ: Princeton University Press.

Rescher, N. (1998) *Predicting the Future: An Introduction to the Theory of Forecasting*, Albany, NY: The State University of New York Press.

Sommerhoff, G. (1969) The abstract characteristics of living systems. In E. E. Emery (ed.), *Systems Thinking*, Harmondsworth, Middlesex: Penguin Books.

Vickers, Sir Geoffrey (1968) *Value Systems and Social Process*, London: Tavistock Publications.

Weick, K. E.(1989) Theory construction as disciplined imagination, *Academy of Management Review*, 14(4), 516– 31.

# Chapter Four

# Strategy and Time:
# Really Recognizing the Future

*T. K. Das*

## Introduction

The literature on strategy has thus far largely failed to recognize the significance of the temporal dimension beyond acknowledging that there is a conflict and potential trade-off between the short term and the long term. This situation needs to be corrected through continued efforts at bringing forth reasoned arguments to establish the premise that the temporal dimension deserves comprehensive study because it constitutes a fundamental dimension of strategy making. This chapter is an attempt in that direction.

The chapter is divided into four parts. First, it makes the case for integrating the future time dimension in the strategy making enterprise. Second, it proposes that time should be treated as a problematic matter – as a variable rather than a constant – and discusses the significant consequences of "problematizing the future" for both research and practice of strategic management. Third, it delineates several implications of adopting the proposed future-salient view of strategy making, including changing from the problem-solving approach to the opportunity-adoption approach in strategic management, making strategy analysis and competitor analysis explicitly oriented to the future, and reconsidering strategy implementation decisions in terms of the future orientations of individual executives. Finally, the chapter briefly discusses the future directions of temporal research in strategy.

## The Neglected Future Time Dimension in Strategy

It would seem self-evident to most people that strategy making is necessarily concerned with the future. This, however, may not always be the case in actual practice. Too often, the seemingly obvious purpose of an activity is lost sight of in the course of time. In strategy making, the acknowledged essence of the activity is the effective navigation of an organization in the future time. This plainly calls for an understanding of that future time. In practise, though, strategy making seems to have become the compilation and analysis of increasingly voluminous data about the organization and its environments. The strategic essence of keeping the organization continuously relevant to the unfolding future time is unthinkingly ignored. Thus, it is neither obvious nor redundant to state that strategy making has to be future-salient. This also provides the rationale for understanding the role of the future orientations of the individual executives in the strategy-making enterprise (Das, 1986).

Strategy necessarily involves the dimension of time. In particular, the existence of strategy is intrinsically related to the future segment of the temporal dimension, although the past and the present circumstances provide the history and the foundation. However, the literature on strategy has thus far largely failed to recognize the significance of the temporal dimension beyond acknowledging the different implications of short-term and long-term decisions. A major part of this neglect can no doubt be ascribed to the fact that "many authors have found it difficult to get articles that deal with time orientation published. The front door has been locked to researchers who wish to explore and discuss this area" (Thoms and Greenberger, 1995, p. 272).

One important reason for the lack of attention to the future dimension of strategy is that the meaning of the term "the future" has been left unexamined while considering strategy. It is as if the role of the future dimension in the strategy-making process is unambiguous and unchanging, and hence unremarkable and unworthy of scholarly examination. The implication is that all strategy makers conceive the future in the same manner. In other words, the future is a constant and not a variable in the strategy-making process.

This non-problematic conception of the future time dimension is evident in the recent publications where time has been discussed in the strategic management literature. Almost all these writings stress the efficient use of time in the corporate and business domain. They relate to the strategic importance of speed in bringing products to the marketplace (Meyer, 1993; Stalk and Hout, 1990). The point about the desirability of reducing the product development time and other such activities is unexceptionable. This point is the business equivalent of the topic of personal and professional time management for individuals.

A straightforward clock-time view of the temporal dimension – that is, as a constant for all purposes – is a very limited one. It could also be a misleading conception of time when it relates to strategy making (Das, 1991). The essence of strategic decision making is the attempt to navigate the organization over time – which we call "the future". These decisions are made by individual strategy makers, whose psychological views of time cannot be ignored. Hence, a linear, clock-and-calendar conception of time may be much too reductionistic for the strategy-making process.

The only way to begin having a sense of the true nature of the onrushing future is to free ourselves from the comfortable embrace of familiar knowledge about the world of business. The means–end logic by which we construct our business world would make progressively less sense in the coming years of the knowledge-based economy. The tendency all too often is to extrapolate the past and the present into the future, instead of exploring the potential future options based on a temporary suspension of the insidious stranglehold of present circumstances. People indeed differ in the extent of their future orientation, as well as in the nature of their assumptions about the future.

## Problematizing Time in Strategy

Briefly, the question of treating the time dimension in strategy making as a problematic one is critical in two significant ways. First, it recognizes that individual strategy makers differ in their conception of future time, so that the temporal factor is itself a variable and not a constant. And second, it argues for the explicit consideration of future time as an essential factor in strategy making simultaneously with other traditional factors such as internal capabilities and external environmental forces. To establish these points, it would be helpful to briefly review the role of the time dimension in management and organizational research. This role can be delineated in terms of psychological time and individual future orientations.

## *From Clock-Time to Psychological Time*

It is becoming increasingly evident that, despite its relative neglect in business and organizational research, the time dimension has generally been attracting increasing interdisciplinary notice in recent years (Bluedorn, 2002; Das, 1990, 1993; Das and Teng, 2001; Jaques, 1982; Lee and Liebenau, 1999; Whipp et al., 2002). In specifically assessing the strategy area, while the output continues to be meager, contributions are growing steadily in both practitioner and academic arenas (Ackoff, 1981; Das, 1986, 1987, 1991; Hamel and Prahalad, 1994; Hay and Usunier, 1993; Judge and Spitzfaden, 1995; Mosakowski and Earley, 2000; Ramaprasad and Stone 1992).

Early last century, Taylorism recognized time as a scarce resource, the allocation of which determined organizational efficiency. The clock-time conception of the time dimension is evident in most of the strategy literature. For example, the prescriptions for fast cycle capability are based on the assumption that speedier production and delivery of products is a matter of better management, assessed in terms of time as clock-and-calendar. The same calendar time applies to the notion of planning horizons.

The extant conception of the time dimension in the management and organizational literature generally considers it only in its mundane, clock-time form. Very little attention, unfortunately, is given by researchers to the phenomenon of "the psychology of the future." The significance of this phenomenon is evident when we consider that the most critical aspect of organizational functioning and viability, namely, the process of strategic management, is centrally concerned with the future time dimension and, hence, with how the strategic decision makers perceive it. It is a disquieting feature of temporal research that it has yet to be integrated with other research areas even when its relevance seems obvious.

While the role of long-range thinking is readily acknowledged, the flow of time in the future as visualized by the strategy makers is routinely treated as non-problematic.

However, temporal studies that treat time as a subjective notion have been under-taken only recently and sporadically (Das, 1993). Individual temporal orientations are usually viewed in two basic ways. First, time orientations to past, present, and future as they relate to achievement motivation and information processing. And second, differing time horizons as they relate to the planning function. It may be helpful, at this stage, to briefly note that time has traditionally been seen in two basic ways:

> Students of time are aware of McTaggart's (1927) famous A and B series. The former relates to physical time and is reflected in the notions of earlier than, simultaneous with, and later than a chosen physical event. The latter relates to mental time and is anchored to a changing reference point called *now* or *present*, so that there are varying degrees of mind-dependent pastness and futurity. Thus, time in physics is an objective feature of the world, and events are mutually related in a permanent manner. This is not so with mental time, in which everything revolves around the now, so that all statements are inevitably tensed. Because physics is essentially presentless, one can reasonably say that the flow of time has to be mind-dependent. (Das, 1992, p. 479)

We need to note also the critical point that most of the thinking in the temporal research area, with very few exceptions, is based on the unexamined assumption of the linear flow of time or clock-time conception of the time dimension. The research carried out by Das (1986) with senior business executives suggests that a clock-and-calendar conception of time is not appropriate for studying strategy making, which is intrinsically founded on a human or psychological conception of time and the future. He found that, rather than a linear conception of time, business executives held divergent individual psychological views of the future within the same organizational milieu.

It is somewhat perplexing that the so-called time research, even when published, continues to ignore the need for understanding the nature of time as it relates to management and organization and concentrates, instead, on research about what individuals and organizations do *in* something known as time. Because of this limited and ultimately self-defeating conception of time research, it is not surprising that attention is mostly confined to questions that have measurable statistics in terms of the clock and the calendar. This is analogous to trying to understand human behavior *in* organizations while ignoring the question of what constitutes the organizational milieu. In other words, the germane issue for us should be how such individual behavior is affected by the organization or by virtue of a person being in an organization. To do justice to that issue, one needs to first understand an organization. In the same way, time studies in the business and management field should consider how time affects individual and organizational behavior, not how individuals and organizations behave *in* time. Thus, we need to make some minimum effort to be clear about how we apprehend the nature of time as we engage in temporal research.

Admittedly, publishing research that encompasses a distinctive conceptual under-standing of time, as contrasted with basically assuming its linear and objective character, can be a relatively formidable proposition. The easier course is to describe how things are in areas that proffer empirical data. Especially because temporal research is a new and unexplored (albeit significant) subject, the publication task becomes doubly onerous, because journal reviewers are more comfortable in approving papers on the basis of their traditional clock-time orientation. That orientation also facilitates the assessment of technical competence with methodological and statistical procedures that apply to other accepted concepts. A cursory survey of the published literature would tend to support this observation. The temporal research that has been published is very largely based upon temporal assumptions that are either completely unarticulated or clearly of the clock-time variety. The most notorious misconstrual of time is, of course, reflected in the widespread belief that all longitudinal issues fall under the rubric of time research. This is like believing that all research that includes measurements of the three spatial dimensions somehow constitutes research on space. If one were to go by these lights, then just about all research on activities in the management and organizational area could properly be designated as time research!

## *Individual Future Orientations*

The literature in various disciplines shows that people have inherent differences in their orientation toward the flow of time (Cohen, 1981; Cottle, 1976; Doob, 1971; Fraisse, 1963). In particular, individual orientations toward the future may differ in the relative degree of cognitive dominance of the near versus the distant future. This basic individual perspective on time would influence a person's general view of an undulating future in which certain salient life events occur (Cottle, 1968; Doob, 1971; Kastenbaum, 1961; Kelly, 1958).

In an early article, Das (1991) approaches time from the viewpoint of the strategic decision maker and makes two initial assumptions that take issue with the traditional approach to time. The first assumption is that the differences in the future time orientations of individuals have differential impacts on the nature of their decisions; the second assumption, and in our view the more provocative one, is that these orientations are not consciously acknowledged by the individual. While some managers will base future decisions merely on historic events, others have an enhanced capability to comprehend the future in its own right, and are therefore better positioned to make quality assessments or perform valuable sensitivity analyses regarding future probabilities. At the same time, the differences in future orientations between individual decision makers are neither recognized nor utilized to the organization's advantage.

The first point to note is that people who make strategy differ in the ways they visualize the future. This individual difference has two aspects. One aspect has to do with the fact that people differ in their conception of what constitutes the short-term and the long-term. Hence, obviously, the meanings of those terms are not shared by different strategy makers. The other aspect relates to the differences in the capacities of individuals to visualize or grasp future time. This capacity has a direct bearing on the quality of strategy making, because an individual with a comparatively restricted capacity to grasp the distant future would be unable to bring to the strategic decision making process any insight about that distant future. In contrast, an individual with a greater capacity to see into the distant future would have a more relevant input for the strategic decision making processes (Das, 1987; Das and Teng, 1997). Thus, the significance of the role of psychological time in strategy making needs to be recognized and examined.

The second point is the relevance and goodness of a strategy are directly tied to the projected temporal life of that strategy. Thus, it is important to examine the temporal dimension of strategy – that is, the nature and length of future time need to be explicitly considered as essential factors in constructing a strategy. These two related factors have to be assessed simultaneously with the other traditional factors such as the external environment and organizational capabilities. Clearly, one would be unable to assess the effectiveness of a strategy if the intended time period were left unstated. But furthermore, it does not make sense to even begin choosing among potential alternative strategies without full regard for the time periods over which the strategies are proposed to bear fruit (Das, 1991). A simulation of the outcomes of different alternative strategies, however roughly carried out in the minds of the strategy makers, has to incorporate the crucial factor of the time period. Unfortunately, both research and practise of strategy making continue to treat the future time dimension as a non-problematic factor, largely as something that is constant, objective, undifferentiated, and commonly understood.

These two problematic aspects of time in strategy are interrelated. In the next section, we discuss several topics that, taken together, should help us begin to appreciate the complex nature of the temporal aspects of strategy making, and underscore the significance of recognizing the role of the future time segment as perceived by strategic decision makers.

## Toward Future-salient Strategy Making

We discuss below some of the implications of including the future as a foundational component of strategic management. Specifically, we will mention some of the topics that illustrate the kinds of fresh approaches and insights that could be generated by an explicit recognition of the temporal aspects of strategic management. These illustrative topics are relevant to key aspects of activities generally associated with strategic management, namely, environmental scanning, strategy analysis (external and internal) for strategy formulation, and strategy implementation. The topics are:

1 future-salient vision;
2 opportunity adoption as the proper future-oriented approach (instead of the extant problem-solving approach, which is basically present-centered) during the creative or entrepreneurial stage of strategy formulation;
3 future-salient strategy analyses, which would focus on assessing the potential for developing alternative strategies for different time periods, such as "Future SWOT" to supplement the current present-centered SWOT analyses, as the proper way to analyze future conditions;

4  the relationship between individual future orientations and the choice of strategic planning horizons; and

5  future-salient modes of implementing strategic change, which would basically involve a choice between a one-shot and an incremental approach to carrying out strategic changes, contingent upon the individual future orientations of the top executives.

## *Future-salient Vision*

Most people in organizations unthinkingly consider strategy makers as relatively competent in terms of having a handle on the future. The perception, indeed, is that these top echelon personnel are where they are precisely because they are decidedly more future oriented than the general run of organizational members.

However, a vision has to be broadly shared by the organization's stakeholders. This shared view is one that is evolutionary in character, and needs to be consensually forged on an ongoing basis in the life of an organization. Plainly, such key goals cannot be left unstated. This underscores the need to arrive at a wide understanding of what it is that an organization intends to attain in the long run. At a minimum, this should facilitate concerted actions and effective allocation of organizational resources. For otherwise, different people will be faithfully pulling the organization "forward" in different directions, especially because individual cognitive biases of people tend to affect strategic decision processes (Das and Teng, 1999). Much, if not all, of these sincere energies could (indeed, must) be harnessed to commonly agreed ends in a coordinated fashion. The danger of an organization being misled by energetic, well-meaning, and competent people in the absence of a preexisting, accepted, future scenario is clear. Such a scenario, or vision, or direction, or strategic intent, should serve as both a beacon and a self-imposed instrument of organizational discipline. However, the construction and meaning of such a vision is problematic if we acknowledge that different organizational members have different views of what constitutes the future in which the vision resides.

## *Strategy Making as Opportunity Adoption*

Considering that the rationale for strategic management lies in having to address conditions in the future, it would seem appropriate to recast the essence of strategic decision making as one of preparing an organization for exploiting future opportunities. The relevant thinking perspective is one of "adopting" the opportunities as a prior and certainly more critical activity than thinking about the solvability of potential problems (or of overcoming constraints). In the terminology of problem-solving, this may be re-stated as follows: the "problem" to be solved is the identification of opportunity to be adopted in the future time period, and the "objective" to be attained thereby is the determination of what decisions need to be made at the present time.

Strategic decision-making has traditionally been predominantly conditioned by an approach that is clearly one of solving problems. Alternative strategies are developed to address recognized problems or opportunities. According to Simon (1976): "the activity called human problem solving is basically a form of means–end analysis that aims at discovering a process description of the path that leads to a desired goal". Simply put, problem solving connotes going from an initial state to a desired goal. It typically involves recognizing the symptoms of a problem, making a diagnosis, and finding or developing a prescription or solution.

In practical terms, the guiding mindset in problem solving produces solutions (strategies) that are usually out-of-date by the time they are arrived at for implementation. This is because problem solving is essentially based on present- and past-oriented conceptions of organizational activities. Fundamentally, problem solving tends to concentrate on known or existing conditions (including the condition of future opportunities as perceived in the present), not those that reside in potential futures. By the time an organization is ready to act, conditions inevitably change in non-extrapolatory ways, so that the analytical methodology of rationally making sense of extant problems and perceived opportunities fails to really tackle the emerging future conditions.

We propose that a more effective approach to ensure the requisite future orientation is to explicitly alter the thrust of strategic management from one of finding, defining, and solving problems to that of searching for and "adopting" opportunities (external as well as internal), which lie, by their very nature, in the future time period. The difference in the strategic decision mode is essentially that, instead of addressing problems in an effort to reach a goal (future opportunity), which is the problem-solving approach, the exact reverse should be done, namely, one should adopt the opportunity and then find out the manner in which the initial state (the present conditions) can be "reached." Such an inverted procedure would eliminate all inhibitions and hang-ups that unconsciously and devastatingly restrain creative strategy making. This methodology could in some sense be considered as "opportunity solving" or "problem solving in reverse." The distinction between the conventional problem-to-opportunity and the proposed opportunity-to-problem approaches to strategy making, while seemingly subtle, is central to appreciating the "future perfect" mode of thinking (Davis, 1987; Schutz, 1967) that characterizes genuine strategy making.

The process can be explained with the help of Figure 4.1. In problem solving, one attends to Problem P (same as Opportunity P) at present Time T. In due course when the solution is arrived at, the future would already be at hand. The contours of the earlier Problem P would by then have changed and the solution would no longer be valid. In the opportunity-adoption approach, however, the Opportunities Xn residing in Time Period T+1 in the "near future" are the ones that are identified and attended to in present Time T. There is thus a greater likelihood that the organization would be adequately prepared with a strategic posture suited to exploiting Xn when T+1 rolls around. We have termed this process of getting ready in the present for exploiting conditions in the future as *opportunity adoption*. In a similar fashion, as Figure 4.1 illustrates, Opportunities Yn and Zn in Time Periods T+2 and T+3 (in the "middle

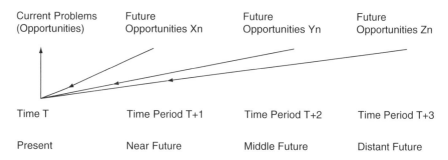

**Figure 4.1**   Solving problems versus adopting opportunities

future" and "distant future" time segments) need also to be "adopted" in the present.

An important point that is not ordinarily recognized in the literature on strategy making is that by simultaneously dealing with the three categories of future time periods, the organization is better able to appreciate the potential constraints and trade-offs in strategy making in relation to the different future time zones. In this approach, strategic management would mean managing the organization in such a manner that it is always ready in the present time period, and would always be ready in every future time period, to exploit the selected, "pre-adopted" opportunities foreseen in different future time periods. In the problem-solving strategic decision mode the goal is given and is like the weathervane, in contrast to the opportunity-adoption mode, in which the goal is to be selected and is akin to the compass.

The adoption of opportunities is predicated upon a markedly different kind of orientation, an orientation that relies on a strategy maker's ability to better "grasp" the flow of future time and the events that populate that future time period (Das, 1991). As we discussed in the previous section, research in psychology has shown that not all individuals are equally competent in grasping the flow of distant time. In other words, some individuals have a superior conception of the future time period than others, and are thus better able to avoid having to merely extrapolate past and present trends and analyses as a proxy for appreciating future conditions. In Figure 4.2, we set out the appropriate strategic decision orientations for individuals with near-future and distant-future orientations. The proposition that needs to be tested empirically is whether persons with near-future orientation tend to resort to a problem-solving strategic decision mode, while those with a distant-future orientation tend to adhere to an opportunity adoption strategic decision mode.

The opportunity adoption approach obviously calls for and depends upon future-competent decision makers. The traditional view of thinking about the future is largely non-problematic, quantitatively conceived, and extrapolatory in nature. In this chapter we suggest that future-competence is based upon the idea that "time" and "future" are problematic concepts for decision makers and that not all individuals are future-competent in equal measure.

In sum, it would seem appropriate to recast the thinking perspective of strategic management to one of "adopting" the opportunities lying in the future as a prior

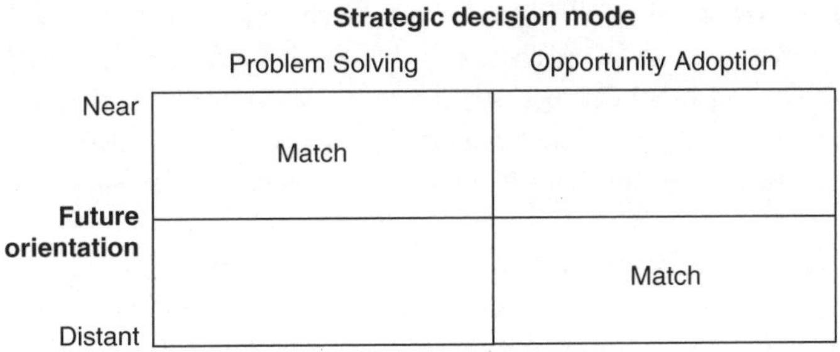

**Strategic decision mode**

| | Problem Solving | Opportunity Adoption |
|---|---|---|

Figure 4.2   Future orientation and strategic decision mode

and certainly more critical activity. An opportunity adoption approach is more appropriate for strategic management than the extant problem-centered approach. This is so because the rationale for strategic management lies in the future time period, the conditions in which can be molded into opportunities (rather than left unattended) through conscious advance action in the present via future perfect thinking. This would be in contrast to the extant problem-centered approach that emphasizes the solvability of potential problems (or of overcoming constraints). Problem solving tends to be past-oriented in contrast to the opportunity-adoption approach, which is intrinsically future-oriented (in consonance with the essence of strategic management). By the time one is ready to act, conditions inevitably change in non-extrapolatory ways and the solutions (strategies) arrived at through the traditional approach become out-of-date by implementation time. This suggests the need to find ways to develop future-competent executives, who would be capable of employing the proposed opportunity-adoption approach.

## Future-salient Strategy Analysis

Most data analysis is past-oriented. This analysis is obviously needed. However, since we know that the future unfolds in non-extrapolatory, discontinuous ways, we need to stress thinking about the conditions in the future without a frozen and concrete anchoring in the past and present. Hence, while the usual SWOT analysis is relevant as a starting point – and only as an initial assessment – the really useful strategic analysis is "Future SWOT." A similar logic applies to other traditional analyses like "Future BCG/GE Matrix" and "Future 5-Forces Framework" (cf. Porter, 1980). The currently accepted formats are satisfactory as far as they go, but the exercise has to be supplemented with similar assessments relating to the near, middle, and distant future.

In organizational matters, it is much too risky to treat the future as a mere extension of the present. An organization's immediate problems and opportunities have their obvious urgency and importance. We submit, though, that such extant problems and their solutions ought to be left in the able custody of the existing operational structure. Sure the top managers can look into these current problems and offer suggestions. But that would be a misapplication of their labors. Their proper domain is the future. This translates to examining the constellations of potential opportunities and constraints in the relatively distant future. Today's problems may wither away or become intractable; today-based solutions may well create tomorrow's problems. The same uncertainty surrounds the future value of today's organizational resources, and, indeed, of the nature of the organization's future "business."

We have already mentioned that by the time an organization is ready with a solution for a current problem, tomorrow rolls around and the current definition of the problem no longer holds, rendering the ostensible solution obsolete and even misleading. The fact is that all organizations necessarily have to expend some time to develop solutions and gear up for implementation. Hence, especially in strategic matters, the only solutions that are relevant are those that are thought through in advance and are ready on the shelf for being applied to various *anticipated* or future problems (or opportunities). If the top managers are busy addressing today's problems, then they are merely engaging in "fire-fighting" activities, not building the organization to be effective in the competitive times ahead. Organizations should explicitly deliberate in the context of potential *future* opportunities and *future* capabilities, *without treating the "futures" as extrapolations of the past and the present.*

In sum, to be effective in the future, we must be prepared for that future. Preparation inevitably takes time, but it is usually more than that. It means starting with a conception of the future, having a vision about what we wish to be in that future, selecting organizational strategies for attaining that vision, and a strategic plan to be set in motion in the current period so that the organization is poised to function effectively when that future arrives. All strategic decisions are in the "present" time-zone, although they relate to the "future" world. A strategic implementation plan is ensconced in the activity-filled present-to-the-future time-zone. Strategic decisions are not decisions to be made in the future – they are decisions about the future made in the present. As has been observed often, the tight logic of the temporal sequence of the different elements is sometimes lost sight of in the press of daily organizational activities. It is a futile exercise to try to attend to today's strategic problems by developing solutions (decisions) today.

The essence of these remarks is that strategy makers should locate their task of strategy analysis in a time-frame at several years from now, that they should deliberate on developing a few worthwhile future scenarios, and concentrate on developing effective strategies to start reconstructing the organization toward those selected future scenarios. They also need to be aware of the very problematic nature of providing for alternative scenarios while building their organizations in optimum ways.

It would be unfortunate if the organization should end up with future scenarios conditioned by a self-set straitjacket of present circumstances, without at least exploring some of the reasonable alternative futures. What is important to put in place is a process that attends to strictly "future" matters, with full cognizance of where an organization is at the present time. In that exercise, an organization should not be paralyzed by the present, nor should it be too quick to conclude that its extant conditions militate against any far-reaching changes.

The sole task of the top strategy makers, to put it in a nutshell, is developing a few worthwhile alternative scenarios for the organization's future to meaningfully weigh the options (aided by comprehensive information, thoroughgoing analyses, implementation strategies, and a clear evaluation of relative merits).

An organization needs to explore whether it can aspire to a different institutional persona, one that would continue to cherish its traditional endowments, strengths, and distinctive competencies, but one that would additionally have a much more substantive standing than the present in terms of its part in the business world of the future. Obviously, one should not settle for an expectation of a bigger and better version of the currently defined organization. The strategy makers should explore potential alternative futures for the organization that would do justice to its potentials and obligations. At a minimum, a thoughtful and well-constructed vision is needed, buttressed by a strategic plan, so that it is prepared to continue making substantive contributions in the face of inevitable external as well as internal pressures.

## Future Orientations and Strategic Planning

It seems clear that the dimension of time has not received adequate attention in the literature, and that researchers have been remiss in analyzing time as a separate and variable planning factor. What is particularly disconcerting is that, when time is considered, it is relegated to its classical function as an objective linear scale against which productivity or planning is assessed, rather than a subjective valuation that determines whether individual planners excel or fail.

The fact that not all organizational members are "predisposed toward, say, a 1-year or a 5-year planning horizon" (Das, 1991, p. 53) has important implications for firms, especially in light of the fact that the members are not consciously aware of their individual future orientations. The implicit conclusion here is that longer planning horizons have value only to the extent that they reflect a more insightful vision of future events, and Das (1991, p. 56) makes this point when he states, "A longer planning time horizon would be a hollow development if it were not based firmly upon an improved subjective 'grasp' of the future." Throughout the planning cycle, then, decisions are being made at all levels of the organization that will be contingent upon each decision maker's grasp of future eventualities. Indeed, as Das (1986, 1987) found in an empirical study with senior business executives, there is a significant linkage between the future orientations of individual decision makers and their preferences for different strategic planning horizons. In fact, those executives who had more distant-future orientations seemed to prefer longer planning horizons, whereas the near-future oriented ones preferred relatively shorter horizons. Clearly, in the case of conflicting choices of planning horizons, the decisions made at the higher levels of organizations are the ones that would prevail. However, these decisions are superior only if we assume that the upper hierarchical levels imply increasing degrees of future awareness. This, of course, is not necessarily so. Also, since time and organizations are dynamic, not only should planning horizons preferred by corporate executives be reassessed, but they should be reevaluated periodically against objectives.

Another aspect of time that is relevant to strategic planning is the treatment of it as a scarce resource that can be used as an exchangeable coin in the economic marketplace. We can employ this analogy to identify how time, as an economic resource, may be incorporated optimally into the planning process. As Das (1991, p. 54) observes, "when, for instance, a longer planning horizon is selected for a particular objective, it is equivalent to employing 'cheaper' temporal means." This implies that given less time pressure for the generation of results, one can use more time ("economize with more abundant time"), and thereby achieve cost savings that may not be forthcoming with a shorter time horizon. Sometimes decision makers unknowingly debate the achievability of business targets within a given planning period that has a different meaning and weight for each individual involved. They engage in what has been called by Das (1986, 1987) as the "silent politics of time." This is an interesting point, because it tells firms that there is a cost–benefit analysis appropriate to the planning function that is solely dependent on time. There is little doubt that few firms if any undertake this kind of temporal analysis when formulating strategy.

## Future Orientations and Strategic Change

We propose a framework that links the individual future orientations of top executives with both the scope and pace of strategic change in organizations. The framework proposed here basically consists of individual future orientations (near versus distant) of the top executives, scope of strategic change (limited versus comprehensive), and pace of strategic change implementation (one-shot versus gradual).

There are basically two distinctive ways of approaching the strategic change process. First, a comprehensively designed, fully operationalized, fully staffed implementation process which would be initiated reasonably energetically right from the beginning. And second, a flexibly designed, gradually developing change process, whose long-term and medium-term configurations have been only very broadly delineated.

To contrast with the first approach, the incrementalism of the second approach would have the following benefits:

1  a fairly early starting date, which would help engender a sense of achievement of change and provide some momentum for various related activities;
2  permit the organization to get started with the existing production or service activities along with whatever initial new activities that can be introduced;
3  adjust the organization gradually according to the availability of executive energies, etc.;
4  minimize the risk of too many resistance centers that are likely to develop if a one-shot, full-blown strategic change were to be attempted; and
5  there would be sufficient time to permit the management systems and other bureaucratic decision-making processes to be completed for each of the components of the organization being strategically changed.

We propose that strategic change configurations adopted in organizations are contingently related to the existing individual future orientations of their top executives. It is worthwhile exploring whether the more distant-future oriented executives are likely to adopt strategic change configurations that are more comprehensive in scope and to implement them at a relatively more gradual pace than the more near-future oriented executives. We should also consider the practical implications of the association between the individual characteristics of top executives – in terms of both "future competence" and "change competence" – and the effectiveness of specific kinds of strategic change approaches.

Two principal propositions may be developed here. The first states that the more distant-future oriented executives would be likely to adopt strategic changes that are more comprehensive in scope and to implement them at a relatively gradual pace. The second proposition states the diametrically opposite position, namely, that the relatively near-future oriented executives would be more likely to adopt strategic changes that are more limited in scope and to implement them in a one-shot fashion. These propositions seem to reflect the two archetypes of "strategic" and "operational" leaders found in the literature.

In sum, we have proposed that strategic change configurations adopted in organizations are related to the existing individual future orientations of the top executives. The more distant-future oriented executives would be likely to adopt strategic changes that are more comprehensive in scope and to implement them at a relatively more gradual pace than the more near-future oriented executives. We need to work out the practical implications of the association between the individual characteristics of top executives and the effectiveness of specific kinds of strategic change configurations. In particular, it would be useful to elaborate on the proposed notions of "future competence" and "change competence" of top executives, and to discuss their contingent relationships with different strategic change configurations.

## Temporal Research in Strategy

We have noted that temporal research in strategic management is lacking in conceptual scope and intensity. Whereas strategy scholars are increasingly acknowledging the need for such research, there is no clear agenda for this endeavor. There is evidently a need to examine in depth the principal reasons for the existing lack of research interest in studying the role of the psychology of the future in various strategic decision processes and also to devise fruitful directions of research to address these inadequacies.

The task, first, is to analyze the fundamental assumptions about the future among strategic managers as reflected in the published literature. After all, the future is in many ways a portmanteau idea (Das, 1984), in which contradictory meanings inhere, such that it is both closed and open, both mandated and yet verboten. Thus, any serious analysis would lead to a discussion of the inadequacies of the current conception of the future time dimension in relation to the essence of strategic management processes. Indeed, the point should be clear that the implicit acceptance of a basically clock-time orientation about the future is misleading and detrimental to the proper exercise of the strategic management function. Some of the empirical findings in this regard have been discussed by this author elsewhere (e.g., Das, 1986, 1987, 1991). Fortunately, there already exists a core of conceptual thinking in the interdisciplinary literature (see Das, 1990) that enables us to glean insights relevant to a better understanding of the critical role of the psychology of the future in strategic decision-making processes. One has, however, to borrow from the different social science disciplines outside of the traditional organizational and economic literatures that continue to dominate the strategic management field.

A review of the temporal research in management and organizational studies indicates that it is lacking both in number and conceptual scope (Das, 1993). Business researchers need to selectively review some of the interdisciplinary contributions regarding the concept of the psychology of the future, with a view to incorporating them in the conceptual framework of strategic management processes. From this effort, it should be possible to articulate the specific insights arising from this future-integrated conception of strategic management processes.

Our discussion has focused on the implications of treating time as a fundamental component of strategy making. Some key areas of research on strategy suggest themselves when time and future are considered as problematic constructs. Based on a review of the relevant interdisciplinary literatures on time, we can identify the following areas for strategy research that seem to hold promise for helping us understand the role of the future time dimension in strategy. They are:

1 the role and effects of psychological time on the process and content of strategy making;
2 the impact of executive characteristics on the content of strategy and its implementation, and the contingent relationships between the future orientations of executives and strategy process and content;
3 the issue of proper "timing" in strategy making; and
4 developing measures and measurement instruments for research rigor that is currently lacking.

In researching the above topics, we would need to be mindful of the endemic conflict between short-term and long-term strategies and the trade-offs that are involved.


## Conclusion

The concept of strategy has not so far incorporated the temporal aspect in any clear or substantive manner. The mind-set that should predominantly inform the strategy-making enterprise has to recognize the "future." Not the past, certainly. Not even the present. But the incessant, inexorable, soon-to-be-here future. The organizational reality is that effectiveness depends on having a fairly well-conceived vision (what should be our organization's "business"?; what are we to be all about?) consistent with the organization's distinctive competence and the resources that could be reasonably garnered, based on a "grasp" of the future.

Business executives and organizations have been faulted for being overly concerned with short-term performance results. Traditional suggestions such as instituting long-range planning and executive stock options have not had much success in curing this malaise. This chapter suggests that we should supplement corporate policies about encouraging long-term planning with attention to suitably placing individual business executives themselves for different kinds of strategic tasks, with diligent attention to their individual future orientations.

We need also to develop the practical implications of the association between the individual characteristics of top executives (in terms of both "future competence" and "change competence") and the effectiveness of specific kinds of strategic change configurations. Education and training should be attuned to developing future-competent executives, who would employ, for example, the opportunity adoption approach suggested here.

The conclusion of this chapter is straightforward. More research that specifically investigates the link between the future orientations of decision makers and strategic management processes is required in order to provide guidance to practitioners to enable them to manage organizations effectively. Our understanding of strategy making would need to be enhanced to include the specific dimension of the future, in addition to whatever ones the various scholars have proposed, such as direction, competitive stance, environmental adaptation, etc. In this endeavor, it is essential to acknowledge that the problematic character of "the future" would entail redefining the concept of strategy making, such that the future is recognized explicitly as a foundational factor.

## REFERENCES

Ackoff, R. L. (1981) *Creating the Corporate Future*, New York: Wiley.

Bluedorn, A. C. (2002) *Human Organization of Time: Temporal Realities and Experience*, Stanford, CA: Stanford University Press.

Cohen, J. (1981) Subjective time. In J. T. Fraser (ed.), *The Voices of Time*, 2nd edn., New York: George Braziller, pp. 257–75.

Cottle, T. J. (1968) The location of experience: A manifest time orientation, *Acta Psychologica*, 28, 129–49.

Cottle, T. J. (1976) *Perceiving Time: A Psychological Investigation With Men and Women*, New York: Wiley.

Das, T. K. (1984) Portmanteau ideas for organizational theorizing, *Organization Studies*, 5, 261–7.

Das, T. K. (1986) *The Subjective Side of Strategy Making: Future Orientations and Perceptions of Executives*, New York: Praeger.

Das, T. K. (1987) Strategic planning and individual temporal orientation, *Strategic Management Journal*, 8, 203–9.

Das, T. K. (1990) *The Time Dimension: An Interdisciplinary Guide*, New York: Praeger.

Das, T. K. (1991) Time: The hidden dimension in strategic planning, *Long Range Planning*, 24(3), 49–57.

Das, T. K. (1992) Mental colonization of the temporal. Review of the book *Time and Mind: Interdisciplinary Issues (The Study of Time VI)* by J. T. Fraser (ed.) [Madison, CT: International Universities Press, 1989], *Contemporary Psychology*, 37, 478–80.

Das, T. K. (1993) Time in management and organizational studies, *Time & Society*, 2, 267–74.

Das, T. K. and Teng, B. (1997) Time and entrepreneurial risk behavior, *Entrepreneurship Theory and Practice*, 22(2), 69–88.

Das, T. K. and Teng, B. (1999) Cognitive biases and strategic decision processes: An integrative perspective, *Journal of Management Studies*, 36, 757–78.

Das, T. K. and Teng, B. (2001) Strategic risk behavior and its temporalities: Between risk propensity and decision context, *Journal of Management Studies*, 38, 515–34.

Davis, S. M. (1987) *Future Perfect*, Reading, MA: Addison-Wesley.

Doob, L. W. (1971) *Patterning of Time*, New Haven, CT: Yale University Press.

Fraisse, P. (1963) *The Psychology of Time*, New York: Harper.

Hamel, G. and Prahalad, C. K. (1994) *Competing for the Future*, Boston, MA: Harvard Business School Press.

Hay, M. and Usunier, J. C. (1993) Time and strategic action: A cross-cultural view, *Time & Society*, 2, 313–33.

Jaques, E. (1982) *The Form of Time*, New York: Crane, Russak.

Judge, W. Q. and Spitzfaden, M. (1995) The management of strategic time horizons within biotechnology firms, *Journal of Management Inquiry*, 4, 179–96.

Kastenbaum, R. (1961) The dimensions of future time perspective: An experimental analysis, *Journal of General Psychology*, 65, 203–18.

Kelly, G. A. (1958) Man's construction of his alternatives. In G. Lindzey (ed.), *Assessment of Human Motives*, New York: Rinehart, pp. 33–64.

Lee, H. and Liebenau, J. (1999) Time in organizational studies: Towards a new research direction, *Organization Studies*, 20, 1035–58.

McTaggart, J. M. E. (1927) *The Nature of Existence*, Cambridge: Cambridge University Press.

Meyer, C. (1993) *Fast Cycle Time: How to Align Purpose, Strategy, and Structure for Speed*, New York: Free Press.

Mosakowski, E. and Earley, P. C. (2000) A selective review of time assumptions in strategy research, *Academy of Management Review*, 25, 796–812.

Porter, M. E. (1980) *Competitive Strategy: Techniques for Analyzing Industries and Competitors*, New York: Free Press.

Ramaprasad, A. and Stone, W. G. (1992) The temporal dimension of strategy, *Time & Society*, 1, 359–77.

Schutz, A. (1967) *The Phenomenology of the Social World*, Evanston, IL North Western University Press

Simon, H. A. (1976) *Administrative Behavior: A Study of Decision-making Processes in Administrative Organization*, 3rd edn., New York: Free Press.

Stalk, G. Jr. and Hout, T. M. (1990) *Competing Against Time: How Time-based Competition is Reshaping Global Markets*, New York: Free Press.

Thoms, P. and Greenberger, D. B. (1995) The relationship between leadership and time orientation, *Journal of Management Inquiry*, 4, 272–92.

Whipp, R., Adam, B. and Sabelis, I. (eds.) (2002) *Making Time: Time and Management in Modern Organizations*, Oxford: Oxford University Press.

# Part Two

# Foresight and Organizational Learning

# Chapter Five

# Foresight or Foreseeing?
# A Social Action Explanation of Complex
# Collective Knowing

*David R. Schwandt and Margaret Gorman*

## Introduction

The *Oxford English Dictionary* (1991) defines *foresight* as the action or faculty of foreseeing what must happen. Society has come to expect that our leaders must provide foresight. However, the complexity of the world and the information revolution have placed ever-increasing limits on their ability to foresee what is to come (Axelrod and Cohen, 2000). In response to this complexity, organizations have turned to teams of executives to develop strategy, coordinate functions, and make decisions (Gupta and Govindarajan, 2000; Hansen and von Oetinger, 2001). The assumption is that these individuals, occupying positions of authority and responsibility, will integrate their actions and communications to provide knowledgeable foresight concerning complex organizational and environmental issues. These assumptions are not always valid.

Although some voices have heralded the merits of executive teams (Bantel, 1994; Makin et al., 1996; Nadler, 1997; Nadler and Ancona, 1992), others now question the social circumstances and abilities of executives to actually function as a "team," let alone provide organizational foresight (Edmonson, 2002; Katzenbach, 1997; Lumsdon, 1995). The complexity of collective foreseeing arises not only from the multiple aspects of an equivocal and often confusing environment (Weick and Sutcliffe, 2001) but also from the realization that information and knowledge may be distributed both within and outside of the organization (Tsoukas, 1996). This chapter explores these social circumstances and associated pathologies of collective foresight through a sociological framework. It includes the application of the framework to a case of an executive team's foreseeing. It begins by constructing a theoretical link between collective foresight and social action, sensemaking, and collective cognition. The chapter ends with four pathologies associated with executive team foresight.

## Collective Foresight and Social Actions

Adding the modifier "collective" to the basic definition of foresight increases the complexity of the phenomenon by the inclusion of multiple actors in the process of "foreseeing what must happen." Collective foresight is operationalized as an "emerging" knowledge that is dependent on the actions of individuals, is guided by values, and occurs in the context of a social structure. This definition allows for potential variance in a collective's capacity for foresight based on actors' interaction, integration of collective values, and relative involvement in knowledge creation.

The emergent aspect of collectivity does not stand alone in the realm of social theory. It has been supported by theoretical works concerning the social construction of reality (Berger and Luckman, 1966), managerial sensemaking (Weick, 1995) and the creation of strategic meaning (Eden and Ackermann, 1998). Of particular note is the work of Taylor and Van Every (2000) and their argument concerning the importance of communications in the emergence of organization. They emphasize the temporal nature of emergent organization as a function of conversation and language. The continuous emergence of collective foresight, from conversations or negotiations (Eden and Ackermann, 1998), highlights the need to understand the actions and interactions within the social structure.

Understanding collective foresight, or the acts of foreseeing, in the context of an executive team requires us to draw on multiple theories of action and interpretation. Although some theorists advocate strict adherence to ontological heterogeneity (Burrell and Morgan, 1979), understanding the confounded world of the executive team requires the bridging of the functional and interpretive worlds of human interaction (Gioia and Pitre, 1990). After establishing collective foresight as an executive function, this section develops the relationship between collective cognition, sensemaking, and foresight.

## *Foresight as an Executive Function*

Nadler and Spencer (1997) describe the executive team as a new leadership model that has the potential for an "assembly bonus": the synergetic gain in output when people are brought together. This added value is not only a function of the number of members but also a function of performing the right work – including the right people – creating the right context (culture), and developing the right processes. "The core defining characteristic is the existence of a set of people who collectively take on the role of providing strategic, operational, and institutional leadership for the organization" (Nadler and Spencer, 1997, p. 9).

Executive team functions are characterized by: the team leader's being the "chief executive officer;" salience of the external environment; complexity of the task; competition and needs for power of the members; and intensified political behavior. As the interactions occur within the collective, interest and motivations change. This may lead to issues of "undiscussables," such as power between the CEO and others, succession issues, member relationships, level of risk taking, and conflict (Edmonson, 2002; Katzenbach, 1997; Lumsdon, 1995; Nadler, 1997). The recursive nature of this meaning construction process by the collective is mediated by variables such as power structures, interpersonal conflict, and reconciliation of multiple realities (Giddens, 1996). Thus, as organizations form executive teams, the assumption of interaction at the team level resulting in higher quality foresight may or may not occur because of these internal dynamics.

Internal dynamics of management teams drew interest from scholars during the 1980s such as Hambrick and Mason's (1984) work on upper echelons, Pfeffer's (1981) work on turnover in top management teams, Hackman's (1990) work on designing effective work teams, and Smith and Berg's (1987) relational and sociomotive life of teams, which refocused on internal dynamics associated with bringing together a collection of actors for decision making. All of these developments highlight to varying degrees the social dynamics related to effectiveness, as well as to how managers' cognitive frame (Gioia and Chittipeddi, 1991; Huff, 1990; Wiersema and Bantel, 1993) and conflict influence collective perceptual processes (Kinght et al., 1999). Heuristics models of group effectiveness (Cohen and Bailey, 1997) present frameworks that incorporate variables such as conflict, communication, and group psychological traits (e.g., norms, shared mental models), along with task design, group composition, organizational context, and environmental factors.

While the psychological literature support the general conclusion that team diversity is beneficial (Bantel, 1994; West and Anderson, 1996; Wiersema and Bantel, 1993), the organizational theorists have discussed the costs associated with socialization, communication, interpersonal conflict, and impact on information exchange (Jehn, 1997). The role of power in new groups (Hackman, 1990; Schein, 1996) and in teams (Barker, 1993) and interest conflict among top management groups (Ocasio, 1994; Pfeffer, 1981) have been highlighted in the literature. According to Guzzo et al. (1993), healthy teams accomplish, and power exchange impacts both task accomplishment and relationships. A hierarchic system of authority can be more constraining and rigid than that of the original manager-driven system that the system replaced (Barker, 1993).

The limitation of top management team literature lies with the research design, which often does not directly observe the power dynamics (Shen and Cannella, 2002) or dynamic sensemaking process among the team members. These designs limit the ability of researchers to capture the complexity of the top management teams' dynamics as they seek to make sense of their changing environment and/or negotiate plausible alternatives for strategic direction. These dilemmas lead us to consider the dynamics of sensemaking in an executive team.

## Foresight and Sensemaking

Knowing what must happen, or foresight, requires executive team members to collectively make sense of their environment. Sensemaking is about such things as placement of items into frameworks, comprehending, redressing surprise, constructing meaning, interacting in pursuit of mutual understanding, and patterning (Weick, 1995). Some researchers have defined the actions associated with the construct as being private and have only tangentially tied sensemaking to the assumptions and values of the collective (Gioia and Chittipeddi, 1991). Others, such as Weick (1993, p. 6), have conceptualized the construct as "grounded in both individual and social activity... and possibly not even separable."

Weick (1995) identified seven properties that distinguished sensemaking from other explanatory processes such as understanding, interpretation, and attribution: (1) grounded in identity construction, (2) retrospective, (3) enactive of sensible environment (i.e., action is a precondition for sensemaking), (4) social, (5) ongoing, (6) focused on and by extracted cues, and (7) driven by plausibility rather than accuracy. He made a strong case for extending his observations concerning sensemaking in highly critical situations, such as forest firefighting, to more routine organizational settings. These so-called normal settings can be characterized by "high noise levels" (e.g., poor communications), no clear reasons to change, lack of trust, high reliance on cause–effect relationships, lack of skills, fear of admitting failure, social dynamics such as pluralistic ignorance, and individual commitments to strong professional cultures (Weick, 1993). High noise situations characterize the environment in which the executives are expected to have foresight or knowledge about what must happen.

**Foresight and collective cognition**   An executive team's foresight must not only satisfy the need for enhanced firm performance but must also reflect aspirations to enhance the firm's knowledge through continuous collective critical inquiry (Scwandt, 1997; Schwandt and Marquardt, 2000). To help understanding of the influence of the team's social dynamics on its ability to foresee, this section of the chapter briefly describes a collective cognition framework based on social action theory (Parsons and Shils, 1952). The theoretical basis of action theory is grounded in the consideration of human interactions that perform critical functions for the social system's survival and are dependent on the mutual exchange of resources via interchange media (Parsons, 1975).

The collective cognition framework contains two major components. The first is comprised of four subsystems of collective action. The second is a set of four configurations of interchange media. The four subsystems of action, as illustrated in Figure 5.1, fulfill the social cognition function. These are as follows: the *Environmental Interface* subsystem, which contains those actions associated with filtering of information into and out of the firm; the *Action/Reflection* subsystem, which represents actions directed at reflection on information in the process of creating valued knowledge; the *Dissemination and Diffusion* subsystem, which represents actions directed at coordinating and controlling the flow of information and knowledge within the organization; and the *Meaning and Memory* subsystem, which represents actions directed towards maintaining the cultural patterns, values, meaning, and sensemaking processes for the learning system. These four subsystems represent the functions required by a collective to convert information into valued knowledge.

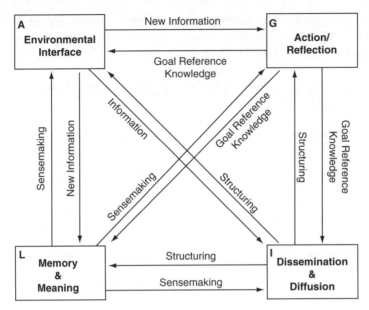

**Figure 5.1**   Collective cognition framework

Each action subsystem depends on the others for a critical "input" that enables it to carry out its function with respect to the purpose of collective knowledge creation. In a like manner, each action subsystem provides an "output" that is critical for each of the other subsystems. These inputs and outputs are called *interchange media variables*. They provide the means for interaction, for example the influence of norms and values in determining the filtering action associated with bringing new information into the collective (as depicted in Figure 5.1).

## Interchange Media Configuration and Foresight

Four interchange media configurations, clusters of interchange variables (Meyer et al., 1993), were created and given names that parallel those found in social action theory but that are representative of human cognition (see Figure 5.1):

1 *New Information*, which is the output of actions associated with scanning, collecting, and interpreting data;
2 *Goal Reference Knowledge*, which is a product of transforming information into valued knowledge through actions of reflection;
3 *Structuring*, which is the product of actions associated with the integration of organizational structures, roles, norms, and communications that provide a dynamic flow of information and knowledge; and
4 *Sensemaking*, which is the latent enactment of values, basic assumptions, language, and symbols to establish meaning.

Table 5.1 delineates the interchange media configurations and associated organizational variables that can be used to describe the outputs of the collective cognition framework's subsystems of action.

**Table 5.1**   Interchange media configuration and associated organizational variables

| *Interchange media configuration* | *Organization variables[a]* |
|---|---|
| New information | • Internal and external data |
| | • Customer feedback |
| | • Employee survey |
| | • Trend and scanning data |
| | • Competition data |
| | • Intuitive information |
| | • Results of an experiment |
| | • Program evaluation results |
| Goal reference knowledge | • Decision-making procedures |
| | • Knowledge structures/maps |
| | • Technical knowledge |
| | • Policies |
| | • Documentation |
| | • Routines |
| Structuring | • Roles |
| | • Leadership |
| | • Norms |
| | • Communication structure |
| Sensemaking | • Stories/memories |
| | • Meaning schemata |
| | • Language and symbols |
| | • Values and assumptions |

[a]This list of variables is not meant to be complete, only representative.

As the variables are described, the configurations begin to take on a characteristic orientation to performance or cognition, or some combination of both. For example, if a team member is describing his or her executive role (structuring) as coordinating and controlling, then structuring would be oriented more towards performance and characterized as "closed." However, if the member described his or her role as facilitating, then the structuring configuration would perhaps be more oriented towards collective cognition and be characterized as "open." The continuums of orientations of the interchange media configurations and their respective anchoring characteristics are listed in Table 5.2.

**Patterns of interchange media configurations**   The relative alignment on the continuum allows for the analysis of sets of patterns of interchange media configurations for any specific collective. For example, an executive team charged with the specific task of foreseeing might ideally reflect an orientation to the cognitive side of the configuration continuum. A team working toward short-term economic drivers, in contrast, might be more oriented towards the performing characteristics.

**Table 5.2** Interchange media configuration continuum

| Interchange media | Configurational characteristics | |
|---|---|---|
| | *Performance* | *Cognition* |
| Sensemaking | *REASONABLE* ⟵⟶ | *INQUIRY* |
| | Accurate | Plausible |
| | Present orientation | Future orientation |
| | Pragmatic | Theory |
| | Cynical | Receptive |
| Goal reference knowledge | *ROUTINE* ⟵⟶ | *EXPERIMENTAL* |
| | Action | Reflectivity |
| | Reduced | Available |
| | Useful | Risk |
| | Applicable | Untested |
| New information | *NON EQUIVOCAL* ⟵⟶ | *EQUIVOCAL* |
| | Rational | Nonrational |
| | Discernable | Ambiguous |
| | Predictable | Random appearance |
| | Justifiable | Chaos/complexity |
| Structuring | *CLOSED* ⟵⟶ | *OPEN* |
| | Tightly coupled | Loosely coupled |
| | Directive | Developmental |
| | Controling | Facilitating |
| | Rules | Guidance |
| | Rigid | Flexible |

The team's relative orientation will change depending on the tasks confronting them. The relative orientation of configuration does not, in and of itself, lead to pathological actions. However, misalignment of any one of the configurations with the others in an inappropriate context could lead to pathological behavior on the part of the team: e.g., "closed" structuring with "inquiry" sensemaking in collective foreseeing interactions might manifest itself in team members' discounting leader-manipulated inquiry. The framework provides six patterns of potential pathologies associated with the team's ability to engage in collective foresight (see Table 5.3). We will now turn to an analysis of these patterns and their associated pathologies in a case study of an executive team in their pursuit of foresight.

## Case Design and Methods

A case study design was employed to study one executive team and their foreseeing actions. Our methodology included both qualitative and quantitative strategies. Multiple open-ended interviews of the nine members were conducted to gather

**Table 5.3**  Interchange media configurational patterns

| *Performance* | | *Learning* |
|---|---|---|
| Reasonable | Sensemaking | Inquiry |
| Routine | Goal reference knowledge | Experimental |
| | | |
| Reasonable | Sensemaking | Inquiry |
| Non equivocal | New information | Equivocal |
| | | |
| Reasonable | Sensemaking | Inquiry |
| Closed | Structuring | Open |
| | | |
| Closed | Structuring | Open |
| Routine | Goal reference knowledge | Experimental |
| | | |
| Closed | Structuring | Open |
| Non Equivocal | New information | Equivocal |
| | | |
| Non Equivocal | New information | Equivocal |
| Routine | Goal reference knowledge | Experimental |

evidence concerning the nature of their perceptions of the team interactions. Observations of team interactions (coordinating meetings and offsite planning sessions) were made over a period of six months, and organizational documents were analyzed for triangulation concerning team output and organizational culture context. All interview transcripts were checked for reliability via member checks. Multiple independent researchers validated assignment of meaning to qualitative data.

Executive team members were given a survey to ascertain their values orientations with respect to the focus of the team (internal or external) and its structure (control or flexible) of management practices (Quinn, 1988). Participants were asked both to rate these values in the present and to predict future value orientations. The competing values survey provided an overall profile of each of the participants' perceptions of the organization's dominant characteristics, leadership, culture, climate, criteria for success, and management style (Berthon, Pitt and Ewing, 2001).

## Evolution of the Executive Leadership Team

Service Corp. is a well established, publicly held business services firm employing approximately 3,000 employees. It is positioned in the industry as a "boutique," with specialized expertise in particular services. Until the mid-1990s, it was the leader in its service niche; however, the market for its service has dwindled. Over the past 10 years, Service Corp. moved to a broader spectrum of business products. This broadening was accomplished mainly through acquisitions.

After five years of leadership turmoil and dwindling market share, the CEO was in search of the next product or service that would turn the company around. His orientation was characterized by an innovative approach to opportunities that he saw in the environment. He stated the problem as "No one internally sees the same opportunities that I do."

To spark recovery and innovation, the CEO and COO felt they needed to broaden the leadership base within the firm. They wanted to form a management team consisting of the managers of service units and other critical "special units." However, their estimates of the capabilities of these individuals were not high, especially with regard to executive insight and breadth of foresight. The purpose of this group was to help identify and implement the new future of the organization. This "new firm" was to include greater customer focus, new businesses services, increased use of technology, visionary leadership, expanded human resources, and, finally, a new set of cultural values for the organization. One of the underlying goals was the development of the members of the team. This "team" would be implemented differently from past management changes that had been characterized as destructive internal competition and as "individual deal making under the watchful eye of the CEO." The executive team was to be collaborative so as to provide the best thinking and foresight to highly complex and critical issues.

The CEO initially requested team members to engage in a range of efforts, to include collecting customer data, scanning the environment for new business prospects, developing a new image or brand recognition, establishing cross-unit sharing of knowledge and resources, and redesign in an effort to become the employer of choice within the industry. The CEO espoused a very proactive team that could anticipate client/market needs and would be linked by "one" organizational vision.

The new executive leadership team (ELT) was announced, and a one-day, offsite meeting was conducted. The team agreed on a list of organizational objectives that would form its agenda for the upcoming year's operations. Members began with high expectations; however, some of the members had reservations regarding the CEO and COO's commitment to the "team" based on past failed attempts to break the paternalistic culture that had existed for more than 100 years.

After one month, the ELT started experiencing paralysis. Little progress was being made in the generation of new foresight. At this point all members of the team began to question the legitimacy of the ELT structure. A second offsite meeting was conducted. Less enthusiasm was observed on the part of the CEO and COO. At the same time, the individuals selected for the ELT were pressing for greater role clarification (of both their roles and the CEO/COO's roles). Although the members felt capable of accomplishing the original objectives, there was a feeling that the sharing of information and decision-making would be easier if the structure of the organization were realigned to include new criteria for personal rewards other than unit productivity. The team executives saw a conflict between what they were being asked to do as a member of the ELT and what they were being rewarded for as unit managers.

By November, momentum was waning, and the team had become disgruntled. Many conversations reflected on past attempts (promises) that had been made by the CEO/COO. After members gave specific feedback to the CEO/COO concerning their relative roles' allocations, their value orientations, and the implication for cultural values, the team was disbanded. Thus, in a matter of three months, the formation and destruction of the ELT resulted in no significant gain in collective foresight. However, the CEO's and COO's sensemaking of this failure confirmed their doubts about the capability of their managers; in turn, this failure confirmed the managers' doubts about the commitment of the CEO and COO to an executive leadership team and its mission to look to the future.

## Results – Interchange Media Configuration

The results are delineated at two levels of analysis. The first level provides insights in terms of the four interchange media configuration. The second level provides insight in terms of four pathologies that emerged due to misalignment in the patterns of the interchange media configurations.

## *New Information Configuration*

The executive team did not suffer from the lack of new information concerning its new ventures and customers. In fact, the team may have had too much information. The CEO and COO were continuously asking the research department to generate analysis of market data. Much of the information concerned the competition and potential customers in the realm of the new business services the company was entering. In addressing the executive team, the CEO said, "We will aggressively accelerate the process of transforming from a single product specialist to a customer driven company. My decision was based upon input from our customers, our leadership and analysis of external and internal data that led quite convincingly to the conclusion."

During the period of the study, the team launched several initiatives to bring in new information. One executive saw these efforts in support of new products "in terms of what we needed to do externally, what we needed to bring in as expertise into the firm, to manage different types of products, to convince our client that we have the capability to do this, and that essentially they would be comfortable with our company stepping out of our traditional area." The nature of the industry had instilled in each of the members a value for information. As related by the CEO, "information in the business markets changes minute by minute, and not having the information precedes the death of the firm." This sentiment was common among all the members. In fact, each meeting, no matter the nature of the agenda, started with a discussion of the "current market action" and then moved to the current "price of our stock."

With the new acquisitions came the need to scan the environment for different cues that generated new information. New members, especially those dealing with large accounts and information management, did not regularly attend the team meetings. One executive team member remarked that "[the new product manager] seems to spend most of his time in the field and not taking care of the business." The new members did see themselves as having to "live in the environment" to be "on top of the information" so that they could make the quick decisions that were required. They had little interest in managing or leading an organization in the traditional sense. The result was that the other team members wondered what information they were not getting due to these absences; also, these behaviors generated questions concerning the absent members' commitment to the team.

The firm began a branding effort to enact in the public arena what the CEO and COO believed to be the organizational identity and mission. A brand consultant was hired to align the firm's identity with its image. The consultant worked only with the CEO and COO; other ELT members were not included in these branding sessions. This enactment effort resulted in the expenditure of millions of dollars on a failed national advertising campaign – Service Corp. had never advertised to the general public in its history.

The team was also exposed to non-technical information. An example of this was the review of an internal employee survey that was conducted by an external consultant. This information was quite negative concerning management systems and leadership behaviors. One executive team member reflected on this negative evaluation as "lack of management capacity." However, the team members dismissed the feedback because they felt "it reflects the way we used to be, and we are no longer that company." The survey was less than three months old.

The one message that was taken away from the survey by the CEO was that "the executive team should be more decisive." This information reinforced the CEO's opinion of the members of the team and became justification to provide more oversight to the team's actions. This one piece of information had become valued knowledge without any active reflection.

## Goal Reference Knowledge Configuration

Service Corp. had a long history of focusing on a niche strategy and therefore was noted for its specialist knowledge in that market. Even as the company explored new product lines, its reflection was dominated by "niche market strategies" as described by one member: "We probably will once again be relegated to niche status, but just a slightly different niche than we were before. So the window is – it's open now but probably closing very fast. It goes to the realization that growth opportunities in the business don't overlap our existing product set and expertise." Much of the company's present knowledge was directed toward government accounts that tended to allow for slow deliberate interactions across the firm. The CEO reflected on this issue as being present even before his tenure began: "For 30 years we talked about the risk of being a narrow product specialist." Although overspecialization was seen as vulnerability, it became accepted as the niche expertise.

With the expansion into more volatile venues, the process for reflecting on new information had to be changed. The firm knew how the government responded to their sales procedures, but the products had changed and so had their customers. This meant much of their knowledge concerning customer contacts and distribution would have to be changed. They would have to become more responsive. The legal counsel found this discomforting: "We seem to take actions without fully exploring the ramifications and exposure we will encounter." Meanwhile, other members of the team felt that too much deliberation resulted in missing opportunities. Thus, a continuous tension existed within the team concerning the decision-making processes it was using and the time it expended.

The executive team spent relatively little time together other than two offsite meetings and periodic coordination sessions. The topics of the coordination meetings ranged from deciding on the appropriateness of a "dress-down Friday" policy to solving integration problems with a newly acquired software firm. Even the offsite retreats eroded into dealing with the "immediacy" of operational issues, which then supplanted reflection on questions of "why."

The meetings were characterized by one of the team member as "a great opportunity to make my case for the additional people I need." These meetings were the only time the members were in the same room with the CEO and COO simultaneously; therefore, they were seen as opportunities "to present our issues." The director of human resources saw the meetings as "a three-ring circus. Too many agendas going on that prevent us from focusing on any real thinking. The CEO has his loyalists and so does the COO." One executive characterized their communications as "just very anecdotal. It's all just one-on-one conversations."

## *Structuring Configuration*

The data representing the structuring of the executive team can be seen from two perspectives: the relationship between the CEO and COO and its impact on the team, and the norms governing the actions and language of the team members.

The CEO had been a part of the Service Corp. "family" for more than 19 years, while the COO had been with the firm only 2 years. This differential placed a perceived burden on the CEO: " I have to develop [the COO] as a senior executive. It is a slow process." The COO responded to these perceptions by saying, "I have to manage my boss. His longevity with the firm has him in a box. I have to put business systems in place to increase our effectiveness." Review of their responses to a relative role analysis revealed disagreement on the perceived distribution of executive's roles concerning building commitment to the organization's strategy, both internal and external; primary responsibility for image, identity, and brand of the organization; management of resources across units and conflict resolution; the creation of structure for decision making; and leadership of the senior team and development of leaders. These differences in role perception resulted in contradictions in their interactions with the team members. The differences were also manifested in their respective understanding of the purpose of the executive team. The CEO saw "senior management working together in a leadership team that represents all aspects of operations and brings to the discussion a wealth of internal and external analysis to set the general direction of the firm." However, the COO saw "an opportunity to bring a more effective structure to our operations."

The team members acknowledged the CEO's words encouraging participation in "leadership" as a signal to be more proactive in their executive role. Yet when interviewed, team members said they felt that they did not have enough guidance from the CEO – or enough flexibility – to move on their own. Thus, the team members wanted to assert themselves through assuming more structural autonomy; yet any restructuring of the organization was seen by the CEO and COO as being very risky and providing too much flexibility to individuals whose actions could not be predicted. Team members missed the CEO's statement that "not all the skills that we need are present on our team at this time." Paradoxically, the CEO and COO were waiting for the team members to take actions in developing collective foresight, not necessarily the control of their independent operations. However, one of the members characterized this as follows: "a structure has largely broken down, and it doesn't seem to have accomplished the objectives enough so that I think the CEO has lost confidence in that structure's ability to get things done. So in some ways, we've reverted back to a paternalistic centralized decision-making structure, which is too bad."

## Sensemaking Configuration

Three interdependent aspects of sensemaking emerged that represent the team's collective memory and its attempts to make meaning of their situation: (1) the history and culture of a 100-year-old firm; (2) the emerging culture of the executive team; and (3) the values and assumptions associated with the industry. According to one member, "one of the biggest barriers was that internally we had been a company who had been there for a long, long time. Everyone was pretty comfortable. We had to bring new people in at really senior levels of the organization. And as we started to do that, there was a lot of resistance and a lot of questioning of whether this was going to unravel the cozy culture."

The firm's history and culture, as reflected in a book published during the company's centennial (displayed prominently on the CEO's desk), reinforced the values of hard work, independence, integrity, and importance of market research and specialized expertise. Although the message was uplifting, an underlying theme in the book was "reliance on research may help, but it does not eliminate the uncertainty of change in the industry." The CEO saw history's lesson as being that "expertise, investment diversity, and customer's security are our cornerstones. However, we have to be ready to capitalize on opportunities." He saw the culture of the firm in transition from a conservative culture – "minimize risk through excellent research and long-term customer dependence on niche products" – to an aggressive, customer-driven culture – "higher risk, multiple products, and quick response."

The executive team members encountered many competing values as a team. Value survey data from all members reflected a very high controlling structure, with a focus on internal as opposed to external issues. As for the future, all members, with the exception of the COO and general counsel, saw a need for more flexibility in team and organization structure, with a higher focus on the external environment. The team appeared to see one set of values as being good for the future (flexibility and external focus) but was employing the opposite values in its interactions in the present (controlling, internal focus).

Finally, the industry during this period of time was reflecting a high positive reaction to a growing business market. As reflected by one of the team members, "with the right 'deal,' we could launch this firm into a new era." The market was rewarding higher risk taking, customers were demanding quick response with multiple and broad product support, and money was there to be made. These market conditions propagated a fast-paced, quick-decision type of environment for the industry and a radical change for Service Corp.

## Results – Configurational Pathologies

Researchers classified each configuration as characterizing either collective performance or cognition. The preponderance of evidence and agreement by the researchers allowed for the relative placement on the continuum for pattern comparison as depicted in Table 5.4. The orientation of each of the interchange media configurations, in and of themselves, was not necessarily inappropriate. However, in the context of collective foreseeing, the patterns were expected to represent more of a cognitive orientation than performance orientation. Table 5.4 also shows how the team's actions continued to produce performance dominant configurations. An analysis of the patterns of interchange media reveals four pathologies that contributed to the breakdowns in the team's foreseeing actions.

### *Pathological Relationship between Collective Foreseeing and Sensemaking*

Table 5.4 makes it apparent that the only interchange media configuration characterized as cognitive was the equivocal nature of "New Information." Two types of new information were entering the team: (1) information concerning new markets and competitors and (2) internal information about the team and its operation as a team.

**Table 5.4** Service Corp.'s interchange media configurational patterns

| Performance | | | | Learning |
|---|---|---|---|---|
| Reasonable | X | Sensemaking | | Inquiry |
| Routine | X | Goal reference knowledge | | Experimental |
| | | | | |
| Reasonable | X | Sensemaking | | Inquiry |
| Non equivocal | | New information | X | Equivocal |
| | | | | |
| Reasonable | X | Sensemaking | | Inquiry |
| Closed | X | Structuring | | Open |
| | | | | |
| Closed | X | Structuring | | Open |
| Routine | X | Goal reference knowledge | | Experimental |
| | | | | |
| Closed | X | Structuring | | Open |
| Non equivocal | | New information | X | Equivocal |
| | | | | |
| Non equivocal | | New information | X | Equivocal |
| Routine | X | Goal reference knowledge | | Experimental |

However, the actions of the team resulted in no change with respect to sensemaking and structuring, which in turn reinforced only "existing" goal reference knowledge. Even with the varying of new information, there was stability in the team's action of collective cognition (Weick, Sutcliffe and Obstfeld, 1999). Thus, no new knowledge was created (foresight). Two pathologies associated with the sensemaking configuration contributed to these misalignments.

**Pathology 1. Lack of a collective memory and values** Much of the new information that was brought into firm was achieved by adding newly acquired business unit managers to the executive team. This process provided the team with diversity in expertise but with little shared memories, stories, and valuing of the firm's processes and leadership. This lack of common memories and values contributed to large diversities in sensemaking. For example, the external cues (Weick, 1995) that triggered sensemaking for the information technology manager were not the same as those for the more conservative government accounts managers. These views were not bad – in fact, they were desirable – however, the team was unable to reflect on the information's (cues') relative value to forming collective foresight. It was not sufficient for the team to agree on an abstract future that was characterized by generalities such as "customer responsiveness" and "product flexibility," because such generalities did not provide the detailed framework to make sense of the new information. Over time, this led to the collective ignoring of the cues and inappropriate scanning actions (Daft and Weick, 1984).

**Pathology 2. Collective inquiry avoidance**    The executive team did not inquire into members' basic assumptions and values concerning existing knowledge of their external environment. This reluctance to reflect spilled over to a lack of inquiry about themselves as members of a leadership team. The team members silently colluded with this avoidance (Morrison and Milliken, 2000; Schein, 1992). They saw dialog, debate, and even discussion as a reflection of inefficient and non-executive behavior. This type of interaction would have surfaced conflicts, and they "knew" that conflict was negated by the CEO's conception of a "unified and loyal" executive team. Team cultural assumptions were not identified, let alone queried (Schein, 1992).

Team members saw critical discussions and reflection as being a "waste of time." This became a rationale for avoidance of retrospective inquiry (Weick, 1995). They did not realize that it is through these types of interactions that foresight can be created, or that previous knowledge can be confirmed or rejected. A "pass-through" of information without any reflection resulted from the team's overly structured meeting agendas that did not allow inquiry or other acts of foreseeing (Barker, 1993; Guzzo and Shea, 1992). This pathological behavior results in all new information's being equivocal and being passed on to the rest of the firm as new knowledge or equivocal foresight. This leads to organizational confusion concerning the future and – of course – the operational paths to the future.

## Pathological Relationship between Collective Foreseeing and Structuring

The actions of the team to integrate information and knowledge within the team and across the firm's units were hampered by a "traditional" organizational differentiation by "product line." Information flowed and knowledge was created within units, but never across units. The nature of this structure was emulated at the executive-team level and inhibited its ability to foresee. This is similar to the results obtained from Gioia and Thomas's (1996) study of academia in which they found interpretive processes were influenced by team context (structure). Two pathologies contributed to the misalignment of the new information and structuring configurational patterns (Table 5.4) and to the team's general inability to adjust their actions to enhance their collective cognitive capacity.

**Pathology 3. Executive team design** The "traditional" nature of the executive team design led to the devaluing of interactions for anything other than coordination and control of the firm's short-term operational objectives. These traditional aspects were reinforced by meetings' and offsite retreats' being chaired by the CEO, structured agendas to achieve efficiency, limited "outsider participation," and secretive deliberations directed at policy setting for the firm (Kim and Mauborgne, 1998; Knight et al., 1999).

The one-on-one relationships of the managers with either the CEO or COO (never with both) created competition and an atmosphere of distrust among the ELT members (Nadler, 1997) the unique product focus of the units within the firm did not require cross-unit collaboration to achieve success. This led to a set of norms for the team and its members that did not encourage the sharing of information and knowledge (Kim and Mauborgne, 1998). In fact, the managers' reward system was structured around their respective units' output and not the output of the executive team. This structuring reinforced non-collaboration at the executive-team level and within the organization.

Unlike action learning (Marquardt, 1999), the executive team's design did not allow for experimentation. The firm's historical norms of "conservatism" and "paternalism" allowed little tolerance for failure and led to actions based on accuracy rather than plausibility (Weick, 1995). New members of the team (managers of recently acquired units) came with norms that reflected greater risk taking. These differences were manifested in the conflicting actions of the CEO/COO and team members with respect to intrusion into the external environment (Daft and Weick, 1984).

**Pathology 4. Inappropriate team role definition** Service Corp.'s CEO held implicit expectations for the team members to participate in a critical inquiry process that would yield foresight. However, these expectations were never made explicit (Cohen and Bailey, 1997). The reluctance to make these expectations clear to the members may have emanated from the role-confusion between CEO and COO and their mixed expectations of the team members' readiness for participation (Nadler, 1997). Contributing to this lack of clarity were the latent effects of the firm's culture, which was based on a "family" model requiring paternal leadership (Edmondson, 2002). This allowed the members of the team to default to their traditional management roles governed by norms of controlling and directing rather than facilitating and enabling (Weick, 1979).

Another dimension of the team member role is its relative status within the context of the team. The Service Corp. team was characterized by large differences in position, status, and power between the CEO, COO, and the other members (e.g., the salary differential between the CEO/COO and others was a factor of 16) (Ocasio, 1994; Pfeffer, 1981). These large differences reinforced implicit structuring norms that influenced the members' actions and willingness to participate in critical inquiry within the context of the team.

Organizational foresight emerges as a critical product of collective knowledge creation. Because of the collective nature of foresight, to understand its emergence requires understanding the social actions and context of the collective. This means that the dynamic interaction of human collective phenomena such as leadership, power, communications, roles, and values can determine the ability of a collective to create useful knowledge and foresight. In the case of Service Corp., these dynamics worked against the cognitive capacity of the executive team.

## Conclusions

This chapter focused on the collective foresight capability of an executive team. Using a sociological approach, the study revealed that the internal dynamics associated with executive teams prevented the team from developing a capacity to collectively foresee "what must happen." Four pathologies further delineated the dysfunctional relationship between team actions and collective cognition. The misalignment between the team's new information orientation and it's structuring and sensemaking orientation prevented the creation of useful knowledge.

The Service Corp.'s interchange media configurations were, in a short-timeframe perspective, effective for performance. However, the Service Corp. executive team was tasked with creating foresight for the firm. To be successful, the team would have had to change its actions and resulting configurational patterns to reflect collective cognition. Unfortunately, the pathology of its failure was not recognized – the team had no foresight of its own situation.

In general, the team was not able to overcome the social dynamics associated with the collective sensemaking required to transform external information into useful knowledge. This prevented them from employing a social structure to reflect on that information, and, finally, make critical judgments concerning the plausibility of the information as it related to the future of the firm. The complexity of team dynamics led to the failure of collective cognition and the inability to create foresight. The four pathologies discussed result in a set of conclusions concerning the dynamic nature of collective foreseeing:

1  Executive team may not be the best "collective" for generating foresight. The dynamics associated with the team may suppress foresight or may cause it to regress to a "mutually acceptable mean" that satisfies the social dynamics but might lead to a less than optimum future.

2  The members of the collective must develop the skills of critical inquiry at a level that facilitates the questioning of the premises of new information and existing knowledge. This applies to both technical knowledge and knowledge of team's social actions. The criteria for membership in collective foreseeing activities must include expertise, experience, some common values, some uncommon values, involvement in organizational leadership, creative imagination, and appropriate heterogeneity of the top management team (TMT) (Bantel, 1993; Bantel and Jackson, 1989).

3  Special attention must be directed at structuring the context of the collective so that inquiry and common experiences are not blocked by human power differen-

tials, organizational norms, and structures that may emphasize performance at the expense of learning.

4  Roles of the members must be defined explicitly and negotiated to diminish the effects of participant's actions defaulting to previously learned skills. Actions of directing, relying on routines, and problem solving must be supplemented with actions of dialog, experimentation, and facilitation.

Organizational foresight emerges as a critical product of collective knowledge creation. Because of the collective nature of foresight, to understand its emergence requires understanding the social actions and context of the collective. This means that the dynamic interaction of human collective phenomena such as leadership, power, communications, roles, and values can determine the ability of a collective to create useful knowledge and foresight. Future research in foresight should focus on its relationship to collective learning and knowledge creation. These approaches should incorporate and mix methodologies from multiple sources to ensure they capture the complexity of this phenomenon.

## REFERENCES

Axelrod, R. and Cohen, D. (2000) *Harnessing Complexity: Organizational Implications of a Scientific Frontier*, New York: Free Press.

Bantel, K. (1993) Top team, environment, and performance effects on strategic planning formality, *Group and Organization Management*, 18, 436–58.

Bantel, K. (1994) Strategic planning openness: The role of top team demography, *Group and Organization Management*, 19(4), 406–24.

Bantel, K. A. and Jackson, S. E. (1989) Top management and innovation in banking: Does the composition of the top team make a difference?, *Strategic Management Journal*, 10, 107–24.

Barker, J. R. (1993) Tightening the iron cage: Concertive control in self-managing teams, *Administrative Science Quarterly*, 38(3), 408–37.

Berger, P. L. and Luckman, T. (1966) *The Social Construction of Reality*, Garden City, NY: Doubleday and Company.

Berthon, P., Pitt, L. F., and Ewing, M. T. (2001) Corollaries of the collective: The influence of organizational culture and memory development on perceived decision-making context, *Journal of the Academy of Marketing Science*, 29(2), 135–50.

Burrell, G. and Morgan, G. (1979) *Sociological Paradigms and Organizational Analysis: Elements of the Sociology of Corporate Life*, Portsmouth, NH: Heinemann.

Cohen, S. and Bailey, D. (1997) What makes teamwork?: Group effectiveness research from the shop floor to the executive suite, *Journal of Management*, 23(3), 239–90.

Daft, R. L. and Weick, K. E. (1984) Toward a model of organizations as interpretation systems, *Academy of Management Review*, 9(2), 284–95.

Eden, C. and Ackermann, F. (1998) *Making Strategy: The Journey of Strategic Management*, London: Sage.

Edmondson, A. C. (2002) The local and variegated nature of learning in organizations: A group-level perspective, *Organizational Science*, 13(2), 128–46.

Giddens, A. (1996) *Introduction to Sociology*, 2nd edn., New York: W. W. Norton and Company.

Gioia, D. A. and Chittipeddi, K. (1991) Sensemaking and sensegiving in strategic change initiation, *Strategic Management Journal*, 12(6), 433–48.

Gioia, D. A. and Pitre, E. (1990) Multiparadigm perspectives on theory building, *Academy of Management Review*, 15(4), 584–602.

Gioia, D. A. and Thomas, J. B. (1996) Identity, image, and issue interpretation: Sensemaking during strategic change in academia, *Administrative Science Quarterly*, 41, 370–403.

Gupta, A. K. and Govindarajan, V. (2000) Knowledge flows within multinational corporations, *Strategic Management Journal*, 21, 473–96.

Guzzo, R. and Shea, G. (eds.) (1992) *Group Performance and Intergroup Relations in Organizations*, (vol. 3), Palo Alto, CA: Consulting Psychologists Press.

Guzzo, R., Yost, P., Campbell, R., and Shea, G. (1993) Potency in groups: Articulating a construct, *British Journal of Social Psychology*, 32, 87–106.

Hackman, J. (1990) *Groups that Work (and Those That Don't)*, San Fransico: Jossey-Bass.

Hambrick, D. C. and Mason, P. A. (1984) Upper echelons: The organization as a reflection of its top management, *Academy of Management Review*, 9(2), 193–206.

Hansen, M. T. and von Oetinger, B. (2001) Introducing T-shaped managers: Knowledge management's next generation, *Harvard Business Review Onpoint Collection*, April.

Huff, A. S. (1990) Mapping strategic thought. In A. S. Huff (ed.), *Mapping Strategic Thought*, Chichester: John Wiley, pp. 11–49.

Jehn, K. (1997) A qualitative analysis of conflict types and dimensions in organizational groups, *Administrative Science Quarterly*, 42, 530–57.

Katzenbach, J. R. (1997) The myth of the top management team, *Harvard Business Review*, 75(6), 82–92.

Kim, W. and Mauborgne, R. (1998) Procedural justice, strategic decision making, and the knowledge economy, *Strategic Management Journal*, 19(Special Issue April), 323–38.

Knight, D., Craig, L., Smith, K., Olian, J., Sims, H., Smith, K., and Flood, P. (1999) Top management team diversity, group process, and strategic consensus, *Strategic Management Journal*, 20(5), 445–65.

Lumsdon, K. (1995) Will nursing ever be the same?, *Hospitals and Health Networks*, (December 5), 31–5.

Makin, E., Ford, N., and Robertson, A. M. (1996) Cataloguing in special libraries in the 1990s, *Information Research*, 2(3), December.

Marquardt, M. J. (1999) *Action Learning in Action: Transforming Problems and People for World-class Organizational Learning*, Palo Alto: Davies-Black.

Meyer, A. D., Tsui, A. S., and Hinings, C. R. (1993) Configurational approaches to organizational analysis, *Academy of Management Journal*, 36(6), 1175–95.

Morrison, E. and Milliken, F. (2000) Organizational silence: Barriers to change and development in a pluralistic world, *Academy of Management Review*, 25(4), 706–25.

Nadler, D. (ed.) (1997) *Executive Teams*, San Francisco: Jossey-Bass.

Nadler, D. A. and Ancona, D. G. (1989) Top hats and executive roles: Designing the senior team, *Sloan Management Review*, 24–5.

Nadler, D. A. and Spencer, J. L. (1997) *Executive Teams*, San Francisco: Jossey-Bass.

Ocasio, W. (1994) Political dynamics and the circulation of power: CEO succession in US industrial corporations, *Administrative Science Quarterly*, 44, 384–416.

OED (1991) *The Compact Oxford English Dictionary*, 2nd edn., New York: Oxford University Press Inc.

Parsons, T. (1975) Social structure and the symbolic media of interchange. In P. Blau (ed.), *Approaches to the Study of Social Structure*, New York: Free Press, pp. 94–100.

Parsons, T. and Shils, E. A. (eds.) (1952) *Toward a General Theory of Action*, Cambridge, MA: Harvard University Press.

Pfeffer, J. (1981) *Power in Organizations*, Marshfield, MA: Pitman.

Quinn, R. E. (1988) *Beyond Rational Management: Mastering the Paradoxes and Competing Demands of High Performance*, San Francisco: Jossey-Bass.

Schein, E. H. (1990) Organizational culture, *American Psychologist*, 45(2), 109–19.

Schein, E. H. (1992) *Organizational Culture and Leadership*, 2nd edn., San Francisco: Jossey-Bass.

Schein, E. H. (1996) Three cultures of management: The key to organizational learning, *Sloan Management Review*, Fall, 9–20.

Schwandt, D. R. (1997) Integrating strategy and organizational learning: A theory of action perspective. In J. P. Walsh and A. S. Huff (eds.), *Organizational Learning and Strategic Management* (vol. 14), Greenwich, CT: JAI Press Inc.

Schwandt, D. R. and Marquardt, M. J. (2000) *Organizational Learning: From World-class Theories to Global Best Practices*, New York: St Lucie Press.

Shen, W. and Cannella, A. (2002) Power dynamics within top management and their impacts on CEO dismissal followed by inside succession, *Academy of Management Journal*, 45(6), 1195–206.

Smith, K. K. and Berg, D. N. (1987) *Paradoxes of Group Life*, San Francisco: Jossey-Bass.

Taylor, J. R. and Van Every, E. J. (2000) *The Emergent Organization: Communication as its Site and Surface*, Mahwah, NJ: Lawerence Erlbaum Associates.

Tsoukas, H. (1996) The firm as a distributed knowledge system, *Strategic Management Journal*, 17(Special Issue – Winter), 11–26.

Weick, K. (1979) *The Social Psychology of Organizing*, 2nd edn., New York: McGraw-Hill.

Weick, K. E. (1993) Sensemaking in organizations: Small structures with large consequences. In J. K. Murnighan (ed.), *Social Psychology in Organizations: Advances in Theory and Research*, Englewood Cliffs, NJ: Prentice Hall.

Weick, K. E. (1995) *Sensemaking in Organisations*, Thousand Oaks, CA: Sage.

Weick, K. E. and Sutcliffe, K. M. (2001) *Managing the Unexpected: Assuring High Performance in an Age of Complexity*, Ann Arbor: Jossey-Bass.

Weick, K. E., Sutcliffe, K. M., and Obstfeld, D. (1999) Organizing for high reliability: Processes of collective minds. In B. M. Straw and L. L. Cummings (eds.), *Research in Organizational Behavior*, vol.21, Greenwich, CT: JAI Press Inc., pp. 81–123.

West, M. and Anderson, N. (1996) Innovation in top management teams, *Journal of Applied Psychology*, 81(6), 680–93.

Wiersema, M. and Bantel, K. (1993) Top management team turnover as an adaptation mechanism: The role of the environment, *Strategic Management Journal*, 14, 485–504.

# Chapter Six

# Retrospective Sensemaking and Foresight: Studying the Past to Prepare for the Future

*Raanan Lipshitz, Neta Ron, and Micha Popper*

## Introduction

This chapter relates Weick's theory of sensemaking in organizations (Weick, 1995) to a specific organizational routine, post-flight reviews in the Israel Defense Force Air Force (IDFAF). The purpose of this exercise is threefold:

1 to elucidate after-action or post-project reviews with insights obtained from Weick's theory;
2 to elaborate the theory through the empirical investigation of a prevalent organizational learning mechanism (Lipshitz et al., 2002); and
3 to explore how retrospective sensemaking can contribute to foresight and preparing for the future.

Linking post-flight reviews to Weick's theory is interesting because post-flight reviews constitute a form of retrospective sensemaking that was not treated by Weick, in which the issue of accuracy, which Weick downgrades in favor of plausibility, looms large. Exploring the relationship between retrospective sensemaking and foresight is intriguing because the former involves gaining insights about the past, while the latter is designed to prepare for an uncertain future. As we will argue, studying the past contributes to preparing for the future by improving people's ability to improvise when unanticipated contingencies arise.

The chapter is divided into four parts: a review of Weick's theory; a description of a benchmark example of post-flight reviews in an Israel Defense Force fighter squadron (Ron et al., 2004); a discussion of both in light of one another; and a discussion of the relationship between after-action or post-project reviews and organizational foresight.

## Weick's Theory of Sensemaking

Sensemaking is the process through which people construct an image of their situation and act on the basis of this image thereby affecting the nature of the situation. Weick proposes seven defining characteristics for sensemaking. According to Weick sensemaking is grounded in identity construction; retrospective; enactive of sensible environments; social; ongoing; focused on and by extracted cues; and driven by plausibility rather than accuracy. We will present each of these briefly:

- *Grounded in identity construction*: Sensemaking is both driven by self-image and a factor that shapes this image:

  > [People] make sense of whatever happens around [them], by asking what implications these events may have on who [they] will be. What the situation will have meant to [them] is dictated by the identity they adopt in dealing with it, [which, in turn] is affected by what they think is occurring. What the situation means is defined by who [they] become while dealing with it or what and who they represent. (Weick, 1995, pp. 23–4)

- *Retrospective*: Weick's emphasis that people necessarily notice and make sense of that which has already passed is arguably the most distinguishing characteristic of his conceptualization of sensemaking: "The act of attention presupposes an elapsed passed-away experience" (Schutz quoted in Weick, 1995, p. 25). Two corollaries of this characteristic are that sensemaking is hampered by equivocality (multiplicity of meaning of available information) and uncertainty (lack of information), and that people make sense of their actions in light of their actions, as neatly captured by Weick's favorite adage "How can I know what I think until I hear what I say?"
- *Enactive of sensible environments*: Environments are enacted rather than being out there in two ways. First, people make sense of their situations by investing them with meanings that make sense to them. In addition, people are partly responsible for the environment that they encounter – self-fulfilling prophecies being one prototype of sensemaking. Sensemaking goes, therefore, beyond interpretation in two important respects: It pertains to the creation of that which is interpreted as well as to the act of interpretation, and it "keeps cognition and action together" (Weick, 1995, p. 30) inasmuch as action both begets interpretation and is contingent on interpretation. "Enactment is first and foremost about action in the world, and not about conceptual pictures of the world" (Weick, 1995, p. 36).
- *Social*: Organizations are social systems. As a corollary, sensemaking in organizations is a social phenomenon. It is made in the presence of others, is steeped in shared conceptual categories, and translated into messages and actions that are understood by others.
- *Ongoing*: People engage in sensemaking continuously because the world around them never stands still. Ongoing does not imply uniformity. The amount of attention allocated to sensemaking is regulated by "shocks" that interrupt the

ongoing flow of events (Weick, 1995, p. 85). These shocks are "incongruous events that violate perceptual frameworks" (Starbuck and Milliken, 1988, p. 52, quoted in Weick, 1995, p. 100) such as problems (gaps between desired and obtained states), goal conflicts, ambiguity (openness to multiple interpretations) and uncertainty (lack of information).

- *Focused on and by extracted cues*: People make sense of their situation based on cues that they extract – and embellish – from it. Because the process of extraction is swift and effortless, studying sensemaking requires instances of prolonged sensemaking such as people encountering novel situations.
- *Driven by plausibility rather than accuracy*: To the extent that the goal of sensemaking is to generate action, accuracy is nice to have but not a necessity. What action requires is a feeling (not necessarily valid) of "order, rationality and clarity" (Weick, 1995, p. 29). The unique aspect of the sensemaking carried out in post-flight reviews in the Israel Defense Force Air Force (IDFAF), to which we now turn, is that accuracy is not regarded as "nice to have" but as a constitutive aspect of the process. Our analysis of post-flight reviews is based on Ron et al. (2004).

## Post-flight reviews in the IDFAF

Every operational or training mission in the combat squadrons of the IDFAF is followed by a process of post-flight reviews (debriefing). The two phases of this process are the formation and the daily post-flight reviews (pilots also tend to engage in self-debriefing as they walk from the plane to the debriefing room). The methodology in both is to review flight films recorded by the VCR which is mounted in the cockpit and which provides accurate information on the pilot's and airplane's behavior during the mission.

The formation and daily post-flight reviews are conducted in different forums and focus on different issues. Formation post-flight reviews are attended by the two to eight pilots (or pilot-navigator teams) who flew in formation and are facilitated by the formation leader. Their focus is on the *process* of flying, i.e., what happened during the sortie and how each pilot flew his plane and performed in combat. Every pilot's video record is reviewed meticulously, with particular attention paid to errors (typically inappropriate actions), causes of error, and potential remedies (e.g., alternative actions). Daily post-flight reviews are attended by all the pilots (or pilot-navigator teams) who participated in the day's flight activities and are facilitated by the squadron commander or one of his deputies. They focus on the *output* of flying (i.e., mission accomplishment), the functioning of the formations as units, and errors with general relevance owing to their pervasiveness and risk potential or because they involve rule infraction necessitating disciplinary action. Pilots select their own films for review based on these criteria.

Ron et al. (2004) conducted a study of post-flight reviews in an F-16 squadron of the IDFAF. Based on observations of post-flight review sessions and semi-structured interviews with 13 pilots and navigators, which were transcribed and analyzed using thematic analysis, they developed a model of the post-flight review process that captured its functions, psychological and interpersonal dynamics, and culture, which is of particular interest to the present discussion.

The atmosphere in the post-flight reviews is highly critical – no stone is left unturned while participants debate the errors, which they identify, and their causes and remedies. Rank does not count; everyone is free to comment on the pilot's performance. The daily post-flight reviews are more formal and less supportive than the formation post-flight reviews. The number of participants and the presence of the squadron's commander make the daily post-flight review less intimate and a relatively more judgmental experience.

The formation and the daily post-flight reviews are embedded in what Lipshitz et al. (2002) identified as a learning culture, consisting of five shared values that facilitate productive learning: transparency (exposing one's thoughts and actions to others in order to receive feedback), integrity (giving and receiving full and accurate feedback without defending oneself and others), issue-orientation (focusing on the relevance of information to the issues regardless of the social standing, e.g., rank, of recipient or source), inquiry (persisting in a line of inquiry until a satisfactory understanding is achieved), and accountability (assuming responsibility both for learning and for implementing lessons learned). Table 6.1 presents the behavioral manifestations of these values in the post-flight reviews that Ron et al. (2004) identified and illustrative interviewee reports on which they based their derivations.

Applying Weick's theory to the post-flight reviews is interesting because the kind of retrospective sensemaking practiced by pilots in them is atypical from the standpoint of the theory. While Weick focuses on sensemaking that is practiced online inseparably from action, post-flight reviews are conducted away from the action and may be considered as a secondary level sensemaking of the online sensemaking that guided past actions. The next section considers, therefore, the applicability of Weick's model to this type of sensemaking.

## Post-flight Reviews as Retrospective Sensemaking

When asked to explain what post-flight reviews are all about, pilots and navigators often use a three-part mantra that can show that post-flight reviews are quintessentially a retrospective sensemaking activity: "What happened? What went wrong? How can we do better next time?" (Figure 6.1). Thus, it is interesting to analyze them in terms of Weick's seven defining characteristics, grounded in identity construction; retrospective; enactive of sensible environments; social; ongoing; focused on and by extracted cues; and driven by plausibility rather than accuracy. Our analysis will show that the first four characteristics fit post-flight reviews to Weick's theory, the last three set them apart in a way that is interesting to both Weick's theory and the usefulness of retrospective sensemaking for organizational foresight, understood as preparing organizations and their members for future contingencies.

*Grounded in identity construction*: The F-16 pilots interviewed by Ron et al. (2004) were an extremely competitive lot, striving to excel in everything that they did. The way to achieve this goal, they believed, was to answer the three magic

**Table 6.1**    Behavioral manifestations of learning values in post-flight review interviews

| Value | Reported behavioral manifestations | Illustrative text |
|---|---|---|
| Inquiry | Persistent search for causes of and remedies for sub-optimal performance. | We always check what we have done and ask how we can improve. Always ask questions and never take anything for granted. |
| Integrity | Accounting for one's errors in a frank and convincing fashion. | The biggest benefit from the post flight review is that it forces you to recognize your errors for yourself in order in order to be able to account for them in public. I have yet to meet a pilot who lied in the post-flight review. |
| Transparency | Honest reporting of one's actions and reasoning; non-defensive acceptance of feedback from others. | Because of the VCR, the post-flight review is an act of mental striptease. People who admit that "That was an error, I need to improve here" are highly regarded. |
| Issue orientation | Ignoring rank and personal relationships but not differential experience in the process of learning. | I know that my opinion counts, and if I think that it's relevant I will say it even to the commander of the Israel Defense Force Air Force or the world's number one ace. The opinions of someone with more flying hours under his belt count more though. |
| Accountability | Conscientious participation in the post-flight review process; implementing the post-flight review's lessons-learned. | Because post-flight reviews are essential we show them respect: we arrive on time, ready to review the videos and make comments, and all data sheets are properly filled beforehand. When the post-flight review ends, lessons-learned are left hanging for the picking. Some pilots do so, either because the lessons meet their needs, or because the learning culture is ingrained in them. Others leave without using the opportunity to learn that came their way. |

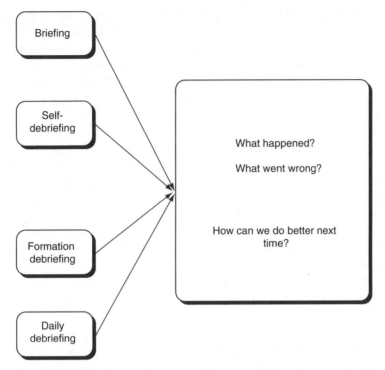

**Figure 6.1** Post-flight reviews: Systematic retrospective sensemaking where accuracy matters

questions "What happened? What went wrong? How can we do better next time?" after every activity in which they engaged, be it at work (e.g., flying), at home (e.g., putting the children to sleep) or in sport (learning to surf). Thus, debriefing becomes second nature to a pilot through a long process of socialization. Adhering to the strict informal code of proper post-flight reviews behavior (e.g., admitting error and receiving feedback non-defensively) turns them into occasions for affirming one's identity as a pilot, occasions equal in importance to excelling in the air.

*Retrospective*: Post-flight reviews are retrospective by definition, as pilots and navigators make sense of their past performances by reviewing their video records. The fact that post-flight reviews are performed away from action and the availability of objective input from VCRs mean that one type of uncertainty that afflicts sensemaking, "What's going on?" (or, to be more attuned to Weick, "What has *just* gone on?") is greatly reduced. The problem of equivocality remains and is dealt with by vigorous argumentation over what was wrong, or which action should have been taken in the reviewed situation.

*Enactive of sensible environments*: This characteristic of sensemaking has a passive facet of interpreting one's situation, and an active facet of contributing to its coming into being. Both facets are present in the post-flight reviews. Considering the former, participants in post-flight reviews work at devising reasonable explanations for their own and others' actions and the alternatives that they propose. The active facet is more interesting. Pilots claim that they learn to "fly the post-flight review." Conscious of the presence of the VCR and the impending post-flight review, they manage the mission in a way that will obtain them "high grades" in the review. Thus, the institutionalization of the post-flight reviews creates a beneficial cycle where performance reviews beget good performances followed by additional reviews and so on and so forth.

*Social*: The social nature of sensemaking in post-flight reviews in the IDFAF has several manifestations. (1) Post-flight reviews are performed in the presence of others. This helps pilots to notice errors which they may otherwise miss, ignore, or misinterpret, and to learn vicariously by observing the errors of others. (2) Post-flight reviews fulfill several social functions including discipline, socialization, and social comparison. Post-flight reviews also serve as a ritual that allows pilots to celebrate their communal membership, similar to the "tribe gathering around the camp fire" (a metaphor that was used by one of Ron et al.'s, 2004, interviewees). (3) Post-flight reviews owe their effectiveness as learning mechanisms to the fact that they are embedded in a learning culture consisting of the five values identified by Lipshitz et al. (2002). (4) These values help participants to satisfy the difficult normative requirements of proper conduct during post-flight reviews: detecting and admitting error in public without covering up or rationalizing, withstanding severe criticism without defensiveness, drawing plausible conclusions, and remaining focused on the issues (Ron et al., 2004).

*Ongoing*: Weick (1995) derived this characteristic of sensemaking from the fact that "people are always in the middle of things, which become things, only when those same people focus on the past from some point beyond it" (p. 43). Quoting Winograd and Flores (1986), Weick suggested that two properties of sensemaking are that people cannot step back and reflect on their actions and that they lack a stable representation of the situation. Pilots certainly engage in this type of *online* sensemaking during their missions. Post-flight reviews, however, are deliberately set up to support a different kind of sensemaking, one that is removed from the action to which it pertains and that relies on technology to protect pilots from the time pressure and operational stress that distort their sensemaking online.

*Focused on and by extracted cues*: The key notion of this characteristic of sensemaking is that people create full-blown images of their situations by embellishing those stimuli offered by the environment that they extract. The notion of embellishment is nicely captured by the expression "terrace stories" which pilots use to describe the period prior to the advent of the cockpit-mounted VCR. During that period post-flight reviews had to rely on pilots' unaided reports which were often inaccurate, partly because of willful concealment of mistakes and violation of rules of flight security, and partly owing to the objective difficulty of comprehending what happened in the air (pilots often understand what actually happened in the air only by reviewing their films). The truth would come out in informal conversations on the terrace of the officer's club; hence the derogatory label "terrace stories" which expresses the pilots' distrust of unaided reconstruction of events – regardless of their plausibility – that are based on the embellishment of hastily noticed cues.

*Driven by plausibility rather than accuracy*: Weick (1995) claims provocatively that "a reasonable position to start from in studies of sensemaking is to argue that accuracy is nice, but not necessary" (p. 56); "sensemaking is about plausibility, pragmatics, coherence, reasonableness, creation, invention, and instrumentality" (p. 57); and "speed often reduces the necessity for accuracy in the sense that quick responses shape events before they have crystallized into a single meaning. A fast response can be an influential response that enacts an environment" (p. 58). To buttress this claim Weick relates the story of a Hungarian military detachment, lost in the Alps, that overcame fear and inertia and worked its way back from the wilderness aided by a map that was later discovered to be of the Pyrenees. The map was helpful, despite its inaccuracy, because it instilled in the troops a hope that galvanized them into action that produced further cues that allowed them to reach their destination.

Contrary to Weick's proposition, accuracy is paramount in post-flight reviews. Tremendous resources are invested by the IDFAF in electronic hardware (the VCRs being one prominent example) to ensure that the question "What happened?" is answered accurately. This is not to say that plausibility does not play a role in post-flight reviews. The answers to the questions "What went wrong?" and "How can we do better next time?" are judged by their plausibility. Accuracy, though, is paramount because inaccurate answers to "What went wrong?" entail irrelevant or destructive answers to "What went wrong?" and "How can we do better next time?"

Sensemaking, as conceptualized by Weick, and sensemaking, as practiced during post-flight reviews, differ, therefore, in their attitude to accuracy. Weick downplays accuracy because he construes sensemaking primarily as means for mobilizing action. Air combat puts pilots in situations in which survival depends on their ability to assess a situation and in a split second choose the right action to take. The margin of error is so slim that taking just any odd action will not do. Post-flight reviews prepare pilots to act effectively under these conditions by creating conditions in which the stories of their missions can be reconstructed accurately by arguing vigorously over what the video records reveal. Interestingly, stories and argumentation or, "debative cooperation," are two principal forms of organizational sensemaking in Weick's theory.

## Retrospective Sensemaking and Foresight

The three-part mantra "What happened? What went wrong? How can we do better next time?" shows that post-flight reviews are about the future as much as the past. Pilots have to prepare for time-constrained situations that are inherently unpredictable (according to pilots, air combat is challenging because unanticipated contingencies frequently arise), and in which the cost of error is high and the margin for error is slim.

To understand how post-flight reviews and other forms of systematic retrospective sensemaking that emphasize accurate reconstruction and rigorous interpretation (e.g., British Petroleum's post-project assessments, Prokesch, 1997), can improve the effectiveness of future action, consider Figure 6.2, which presents a schematic representation of situation-assessment based action as discussed, for example, by Cohen et al. (1996), March (1994), and Klein (1998).

Figure 6.2 presents three generic modes of situation-assessment based decision making: (1) sizing up the situation – developing a situation awareness – acting; (2) sizing up the situation – constructing a story – developing a situation awareness –

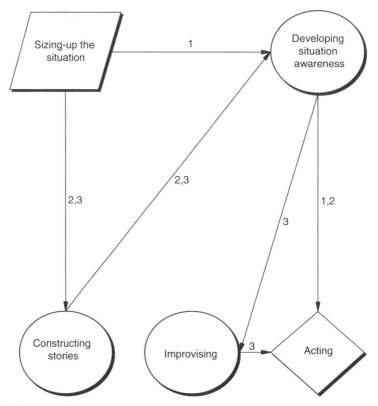

**Figure 6.2**    Varieties of situation-assessment based action

acting; and (3) sizing up the situation – constructing a story – developing a situation awareness – improvising – acting.

1   *Sizing up the situation – developing a situation awareness – acting*: This simple rule-based action, prevalent in well-rehearsed situations, can be performed either automatically or relatively deliberately, depending on factors such as the decision maker's proficiency and time pressure. Post-flight reviews help pilots improve this mode of action by (1) enriching their repertoire of familiar situations through listening to, or actively participating in, the analysis of the experience of others; (2) pruning their repertoire of situation–action matching rules through the unlearning of ineffective situation–action matching rules; and (3) learning new situation–action matching rules either through direct experience followed by corrective feedback or through vicarious learning.

2   *Sizing up the situation – constructing a story – developing a situation awareness – acting*: When situations are too ambiguous for simple rule-based action, decision makers develop situation awareness by collecting additional information, and by constructing plausible stories based on available stories that produce reasoned understanding of how past causal factors produced the present situation and where the situation is likely to go (Cohen et al., 1996; Klein, 1998; Tsoukas

and Hatch, 2001). Participants of post-flight reviews enrich their repertoire of such action-guiding stories by engaging in composing and analyzing alternative stories of each pilot's mission that explain (1) what happened most plausibly, and (2) how the mission could have been accomplished in the most effective and efficient fashion.

3  *Sizing up the situation – constructing a story – developing a situation awareness – improvising – acting*: This mode is required when the situation calls for responding with a course of action that is not available in the decision maker's repertoire. The assertion that studying the past can help decision makers in such situations raises a basic puzzle with respect to the relevance of retrospective sensemaking to foresight: How can studying the past prepare for the future given that the future is problematic because it is uncertain, and that this uncertainty – and decision-makers' difficulties and need for assistance – increase as a function of the *dissimilarity* between the past (and the present) and the future? The puzzle disappears once we realize that one method for coping with unanticipated situations is to improvise, and that one's ability to improvise is crucially dependent on the richness and complexity of what one already knows. As Charlie Mingus put it "You can't improvise on nothing. You gotta have somethin'" (Barret and Peplowski, 1998, p. 558).

Although improvisation is inherently the opposite of foresightedness in the sense of foreseeing the future (Weick, 2001), it is indispensable for foresightedness in the sense of being prepared for the unforeseen, unanticipated, and unprovided-for situations. In the case of musicians, embellishments, variations, and improvisations begin with a given tune or theme. In the case of decision makers they begin with the information at hand and the repertoire of situation and action schemas in their heads. Improvisation lies on one end of a continuum in which routine performance lies on the other, and embellishment and variation lying in between these poles (Weick, 2001). Thus, "to improve improvisation, is to improve memory, whether it be organizational (Walsh and Ungson, 1991), small group (Wegner, 1987), or individual" (Neisser and Winograd, 1988; Weick, 2001, p. 547). Post-flight reviews, similar to other forms of institutionalized retrospective sensemaking methods such as British Petroleum's post project assessment (Prokesch, 1997), are designed to fulfill Weick's advice. As a final illustration of the contribution of learning from the past to future response flexibility, consider how Dennis Rodman, a comparatively short player in the NBA, "watches game films of opponents' shooting, charts the direction and angles of their misses, and monitors what types of defensive plays throws them off their game . . . [combining study and experience with practical flexibility and elbowing], to become the premier rebounder in the game" (Mirvis, 2001, p. 587).

## REFERENCES

Barrett, F. and Peplowski, K. (1998) Minimal structures within a song: An analysis of "All of Me," *Organization Science*, 9, 558–61.

Cohen, M. S., Freeman, J. T., and Wolf, S. (1996) Meta-recognition in time-stressed decision making: Recognizing, critiquing and correcting, *Human Factors*, 38, 206–19.

Klein, G. (1998) *Sources of Power: How People Make Decisions*, Cambridge, MA: MIT Press.

Lipshitz, R., Popper, M., and Friedman, V. (2002). A multi-facet model of organizational learning, *Journal of Applied Behavioral Science*, 38, 78–98.

March, J. G. (1994) *A Primer on Decision Making: How Decisions Happen*, New York: Free Press.

Mirvis. P. (2001) Practice improvisation, *Organization Science*, 9, 586–92.

Neisser, U. and Winograd, E. (eds.) (1988) *Remembering Reconsidered: Ecological and Traditional Approaches to the Study of Memory*, Cambridge UK: Cambridge University Press.

Prokesch, S. E. (1997) Unleashing the power of learning: An interview with British Petroleum's John Browne, *Harvard Business Review*, 75(5), 147–68.

Ron, N., Lipshitz, R., and Popper, M. (2004) *Post-flight Reviews in an F-16 Fighter Squadron: An Empirical Test of a Multi-facet Model of Organization Learning*. Revision submitted to Organization Studies, Haifa, Israel: University of Haifa.

Tsoukas, H. and Hatch, M. J. (2001) Complex thinking, complex practice: The case for narrative approach to organizational action, *Human Relations*, 54, 979–1013.

Walsh, J. P. and Ungson, G. R. (1991) Organizational memory, *Academy of Management Review*, 16, 57–91.

Wegner, D. M. (1987) Transactive memory: A contemporary analysis of the group mind. In B. Mullen and G. R. Goethals (eds.), *Theories of Group Behavior*, New York: Springer-Verlag, pp. 185–208.

Weick, K. E. (1979) *The Social Psychology of Organizing*, Reading, MA: Addison Wesley.

Weick, K. E. (1995) *Sensemaking in Organizations*, Thousand Oaks, CA: Sage.

Weick, K. E. (2001) Improvisation as a mindset for organizational analysis, *Organization Science*, 9, 543–55.

Winograd, T. and Flores, F. (1986) *Understanding Computers and Cognition: A New Foundation for Design*, Norwood, NJ: Ablex.

# Chapter Seven

# Can Illusion of Control Destroy a Firm's Competence? The Case of Forecasting Ability

*Rodolphe Durand*

## Introduction

Precise forecasts of industry evolutions are of utmost importance for the work of managers and market analysts (Baghai et al., 1999; Einsenhardt and Brown, 1998; Eliasson, 1976; Porter, 1980). Understanding how (in)accurate estimates influence performance becomes central to understanding resource allocations (McNamara and Bromiley, 1999; Mosakowski, 1998). Most of the contributions have empirically examined, at the individual or group level, the effects of an accurate perception on performance (Das et al., 1998; Starbuck and Mezias, 1996; Sutcliffe, 1994). A paradox emerges from this literature. Some authors assume that errors in forecasts lead to under-performance (Makadok and Walker, 2000). Others offer an opposite view, showing that positive errors in forecasts (i.e. optimistic assessment) motivate an organization's members, and become parts of the "self-fulfilling prophecy" effect leading to improved firm performance (Simon et al., 2000b).

Research on cognitive biases has flourished up until now and has provided scholars with a range of warning indicators signaling organizational dysfunctions at forecasting (Barnes, 1984; Clapham and Schwenk, 1991; Kahneman and Tversky, 1984; Simon et al., 2000a; Durand, 2003). The main drivers of errors are overconfidence and inflated self-perception, which are caused by illusion of control (Das and Teng, 1999; Schwenk, 1984). Illusion of control causes firms to overlook negative signals, pursue their paths of action independently of external events, overestimate the likelihood of intended actions, and eventually fail (Ocasio, 1997; Staw and Ross, 1987; Tripsas and Gavetti, 2000). However, research has rarely studied the influence, at the organizational level, of illusion of control on the forecasting ability–performance relationship.

Therefore, the raison d'être of this chapter is to determine the relationship between a firm's forecasting ability, its illusion of control, and its performance (King and Zeithaml, 2001). We use a representative sample of 785 firms from 36 manufacturing industries to test our hypotheses. Our core finding is that forecast errors are positively related to performance but that organizational illusion of control interacts negatively with a firm's forecasting ability to such an extent that overall it cancels out the moderately positive effect of optimistic estimations. By shedding light on the influences of forecasting accuracy on performance, we contribute to: (1) the definition of an organizational competence; (2) the contextualization of organizational competences – this study shows that organizational factors like illusion of control may ruin the hypothesized or empirical benefits of a competence; and (3) the explanation of a firm's strategic behaviors (Mosakowski, 1998).

## Background and Hypothesis

## *Positioning the Research: Organizational Forecasting Ability and Performance*

To work and grow, modern economic life needs accuracy in forecasts emanating from firms. Recent scandals have shed a dull light on investors' confidence in firms' forecasting ability about their industry evolution as well as about their capability to accurately evaluate their own internal performance. Large errors in forecasts undermine stakeholders' morale (employees and stockholders) and ruin trust so essential to economic life and development.

In this chapter, we define organizational forecasting ability (OFA) as an organization's capability to deliver to its internal and external stakeholders an accurate estimation about market evolutions. OFA presents two noteworthy particularities. First, OFA is an interesting unit of analysis, since it raises the measurement problem that face both the resource-based and competence-based view of the firm. A competence is a set of resources and capabilities, mobilized and combined in such a manner that a firm is at a rent-earning advantage *vis-à-vis* its competitors. In the case of OFA, the existence of such a competence is directly observable through the result of its implementation, i.e. through the magnitude of the forecasting error. Firms that are accurate in evaluating a future change have a high OFA. OFA is an organizational competence that leads to a result, namely accuracy, that reveals the presence of OFA (Makadok and Walker, 2000).

This chapter also explores the effect of forecasting ability on performance at the organizational level of analysis. So far, most of the research on forecasting ability has been done at the individual or group levels of analysis. However, according to Sutcliffe and Huber's (1998) study of top management team (TMT) perceptions, belonging to the same organization significantly shapes top executives' common perception on five environmental dimensions: instability; munificence; complexity; hostility; and controllability. Firm affiliation significantly accounts for a great deal of the variance in these five characteristics, especially for controllability (in absolute values from the results provided in table 2 of Sutcliffe and Huber, 1998, p. 800). Therefore, the perception and estimation capabilities of organizational members is severely influenced by the fact they belong to a particular organization and not to another. Therefore, the study of OFA goes far beyond studying individual evaluations of environmental indicators. OFA concerns the whole organization in terms of engaged resources and commitment to stakeholders. Organizational dimensions are likely to impact on the direct relationship between OFA and performance.

As evidenced by other researches, every organization has a unique history that accounts for intra-firm commonalities and inter-firm differences. Firms keep on building a paradigm on how they perceive and assess the environment through their successful and unsuccessful actions (Prahalad and Bettis, 1986). Several studies have shown that organizational idiosyncratic characteristics affect the relationship between perceptions, beliefs, forecasts, and performance. Sixteen years ago, Staw and Ross (1987) illustrated the "escalation of commitment" syndrome, when exogenous information is not transformed in timely warning signals by an organization because of the organization's non-absorptive capacity. Garud and Rappa (1994) have shown how organizational cognition, inertial representations, and interorganizational settings relate in explaining the anticipated evolution of the cochlear implant industry. Recently, Tripsas and Gavetti (2000) showed how Polaroid's top management's beliefs were constraining Polaroid's market position more than traditional path-dependent capability phenomena (Teece, Pisano, and Shuen, 1997). These elements imply that the organization is a critical level of analysis for distinctive competences, such as OFA, which result in forecast accuracy (Durand, 2003).

In summary, this research investigates the direct effect of OFA (operationalized forecasting errors, assuming that a high error reveals an absence of OFA) on a firm's performance, and the moderating influence of an important organizational factor, organizational illusion of control, on this OFA–performance relationship. It is noteworthy that firms are supposed to estimate favorable factors from their perspective (such as growth), and the proposed hypotheses should be reversed in case of estimating adverse factors (like recession).

## Alternative Views on the Relationship Between Accuracy and Performance

There is a debate about the direct effect of OFA on firm performance. On the one hand, OFA, expressed by accurate forecasts, can help build stakeholders' trust and commitment. Therefore, OFA should be positively related to firm performance. The results of Makadok and Walker (2000), one of the rare studies on forecasting ability led at the organization level and tested in the money market mutual funds industry, confirm the importance of OFA as a distinctive competence. They "provide unequivocal evidence that, in the vast majority of cases, forecasting ability is an organizational not an individual-level competence ... Our regression analysis also indicates that the more adept organizations experience both higher levels of discretion over their income and stronger growth" (Makadok and Walker, 2000, p. 862). Forecasting ability is a distinctive organizational competence, and forecasting errors are negatively associated with firm performance. However, Makadok and Walker study an industry in which forecasting accuracy is directly connected with financial performance through direct investment positions in financial markets, which may not be the case for manufacturing industries.

On the other hand, OFA, expressed by accurate forecasts may appear to be counterproductive in a sense that it would better to slightly overestimate positive changes in order to sustain employees' motivation and stockholders' interest. According to this view, OFA, expressed by accurate forecasts, would not be positively related to performance. Rather, there should be a positive effect of forecast errors on performance, due to the "self-fulfilling prophecy" effect. Testing the competing views of optimism on the performance of product introductions, Simon et al. (2000b) show that while overconfidence could lead to faulty assumptions, enactment can prove these assumptions to be true. Indeed, this mechanism of enactment does not chiefly concern the mutual fund industry (for which accuracy *is* performance) but manufacturing industries (for which a small positive forecast error can represent an incentive to do better and reach ambitious objectives). Overall, we have an alternative set of hypotheses:

- H1a: Organizational forecasting errors are negatively related to firm performance
- H1b: Organizational forecasting errors are positively related to firm performance

## Organizational Forecasting Ability and Illusion of Control

For 20 years, research on forecasting has evidenced the conditions of forecasting efficiency. Forecast specialists distinguish between objective forecasts and judgmental forecasts. The former concerns statistical methods that provide results based on time series data. The latter corresponds to a human agent estimating future values of indicators, either based on objective data or not. To account for judgmental estimates, Fildes (1985) has shown that it is critical to make the theoretical model developed by the decision maker explicit. Moreover, an important condition for improving accuracy in estimates is the independence of forecasters relative to their forecasts (Shamir, 1986). Studies show that when experts use an implicit judgmental process to make real forecasts, the resulting forecasts are more accurate than those produced by quantitative models alone. This is because experts use additional information that cannot be fixed in quantitative models, such as incidental or unusual events which have been called "broken leg" cues (Blattburg and Hoch, 1990; Bunn and Wright, 1991).

To render explicit judgmental models and to enforce expert-forecast independence are means to reduce the experts' illusion of control on the environment on which they express assessments. The illusion of control argument states that the higher the perception of control on a situation, the higher the likelihood to underestimate the risks associated with a situation (Schwenk, 1986). In other words, if a manager has positive misconceptions on the control she has on her resources, she will over-value the ratio of success for a task.

Several works have dealt with the illusion of control bias at the organizational levels (among others: Barnes, 1984; Clapham and Schwenk, 1991; Coff, 1999; Greve, 1998; Kahneman and Tversky, 1984; Simon et al., 2000a). In one of the seminal work on organizational biases, Schwenk (1984) presents the biases associated with illusion of control:

1 partial representativeness of events leads to inaccurate prediction of consequences by falsely associating a current situation with past events (Tversky and Kahneman, 1974);
2 a devaluation of partially described alternatives leads to the rejection of strong but poorly presented alternatives (Yates et al., 1978); and
3 illusion of control entails an inaccurate assessment of risks (Langer, 1975).

According to Hayward and Hambrick (1997), one main source of illusion of control is the organizational self-perception. How a firm perceives itself, relative to its competitors, on the dominant factors and activities creating value in an industry is deeply related to its organizational illusion of control. For instance, a company that claims to have relative advantages in the key activities of its industry is likely to have a high self-perception, since this organization assumes being perfectly aligned with environmental selection conditions (Powell, 1992). We state that this favorable self-perception enhances the firm's illusion of control (Matute, 1996). We assume as a consequence that organizations with high perceived advantages will be prone to exaggerate their situation, which leads to inappropriate decisions and a reduced performance (Clapham and Schwenk, 1991; Coff, 1999; Duhaime and Schwenk, 1985).

- Hypothesis 2. The higher a firm's illusion of control, the lower the firm's performance

## Interacting Forecasting Ability and Illusion of Control

Organizations may be good or bad at forecasting. Arguments indicate that OFA is a competence (i.e. improves performance) and others assume that positive forecast errors are better incentives than accuracy for performance achievements. Illusion of control reduces the perception of risks and biases the information selection during the forecast process. Interestingly enough, illusion of control counters the natural tendency for forecasters to seek to reduce ex post errors by announcing a forecast slightly lower than what they actually estimated (Langer, 1975). When producing estimates, individuals and organizations behave as if they preferred to reduce ex post error, thus tending to underestimate positive information and overestimate negative information (Schweitzer and Cachon, 2000). Illusion of control inactivate this defence mechanism by disinhibiting forecasters, and therefore reduces the likelihood of negative errors (pessimism). However, it increases the likelihood of committing positive errors. In absence of vigilance and attention (Ocasio, 1997), through inflated optimism, illusion of control tends to reduce negative errors and increase positive errors. Assuming a negative relationship between errors and performance (H1a), illusion of control moderates the negative impact of pessimism but increases the negative impact

of optimism. Assuming a positive relationship between positive errors and performance (H1b), illusion of control increases overconfidence and the size of errors to such
an extent that forecasts become unrealistic and that the negative impact of illusion of
control on performance (H2) dominates the potentially self-fulfilling prophecy effect
of forecasting errors. Therefore, depending on the branch of the forecasting errors-
performance alternative:

- H3a. Illusion of control moderates the negative effect of forecasting errors on
  performance
- H3b. Illusion of control moderates the positive effect of forecasting errors on
  performance

## Methods

### *Data*

The Bank of France, the French central bank, provided the data used in this study.
Initiated in 1993, a data collection project called Sesame has enabled the Bank of
France to complement its financial databases with more qualitative and strategic
information. This project is part of the public policy mission of the French central
bank and there is no merchant or power relations whatsoever between the
central bank and the interviewed companies. Econometricians from the Bank of
France consult a representative sample of firms operating in manufacturing industries
each year. In conformity with the characteristics of the French economic landscape,
the great majority of firms in the survey are small to medium-sized. In 1996, the year
of the survey used in this paper, 90 percent of the 2,145 firms surveyed had a size of
30 to 1,500 employees. The database represents a very reliable sample of French
manufacturing industries and has been used in several previous empirical studies
(Amburgey and Dacin, 1997; Cool and Henderson, 1998).

### *Sample Selection*

In the sample for this study, we selected only 4-digit industries for which there were
at least 15 firms (using the European classification of industries, called NACE,
comparable to the American SIC codes). This procedure enabled us to minimize
the presence of outliers and to be able to compare a firm's situation with its industry
average situation (notably for the variable "illusion of control"). This selection
procedure has been widely used, and especially in previous studies having used the
Bank of France dataset (Cool and Henderson, 1998). 1,750 firms representing
84 industries remained after this first selection.

We chose future industry growth as the factor to be forecast by organizations.
Industry growth presents several advantages: it is a non-ambiguous variable, important for a firm's decision making, available for each respondent, and not likely to be

influenced by the respondents' personal judgments. One may argue that CEOs gave the estimates, and not the organization per se. However, the survey does not ask a personal estimate but a firm's estimate, since the question appears in a section where all the information relates to the firm's industry characteristics. Also, the question in itself does not raise any issue that would entice the CEO to dissociate her personal judgment from her role as the head of a firm – as ethical questions, opinion, or advice could imply. Therefore, the use of subjective data is valuable in this study as it is for the evaluation of strategic issues (Hambrick, 1981; 1982; Starbuck and Mezias, 1996). Unfortunately, additional data that could have improved the precision of estimate were not available.

There was a need to check the presence of intra-industry commonality of perception before testing our hypotheses. It is recognized that cross-sectional studies bear the risk of including in industry categories firms which share SIC-codes but do not really belong to the same industry clusters (Lubatkin et al., 2001). If firms are part of the same industry code while not being competitors, they will diverge in their growth estimates due to sample construction reasons. Therefore, to reduce this risk, we selected industries for which firms are likely to be competitors by controlling their agreement on the nature of their industry structure. For each of these 84 industries, we calculated kappa-statistics on inter-firm agreements when assessing industry variables: bargaining power of suppliers, bargaining power of customers, barriers to entry, industry rivalry, and threat of substitutes.[1] If the firms agree on these structural characteristics, they likely belong to the same industry clusters. By selecting firms that agree about their industry structure, we can be sure that their divergences in industry growth estimates proceed from internal factors and not from exogenous causes. Therefore, their industry growth forecast can be compared and potentially explained by OFA and illusion of control.

The "Kappa-statistics measure of agreement" is a coefficient scaled to be 0 when the amount of agreement is what would be expected to be observed by chance and 1 when there is perfect agreement among evaluators. Landis and Koch (1977) suggest that above 0.20, kappa-statistics represent a fair level of agreement among observers. Therefore, we disregarded industries for which kappa-statistics based on firm estimations were less than 0.20. The final sample consisted of 36 industries and 785 firms. At each step of the data process, we tested whether we introduced a selection bias. No significant bias appeared.

### *Dependent Variable: Performance Indicators*

We chose two different performance indicators to test our hypotheses. First, we selected a traditional accounting performance measure, return on sales (ROS). ROS has been calculated as a 3-year average (1996–98). ROS is a performance indicator that deals with the firm's economic exchanges, and as such it is less liable to be modified by extraneous financial and exceptional operations than net profit or stock-based indicators for instance. Second, we chose the quick ratio, a liquidity ratio, as a measure of performance. The quick ratio corresponds to the 3-year average annual difference between current assets and inventory, divided by current liabilities. Quick ratio measures the ability of a firm to meet its short-term obligations without selling its current inventory. This ratio is interesting in a context of forecasting errors in industry growth. Indeed, the price, sales, purchases, and inventory strategies are influenced by the growth forecasts. Therefore, quick ratio seems well-suited to our test.

## *Independent Variables*

**Forecasting errors**   As mentioned before, in 1996, CEOs were asked by the Bank of France to evaluate the 1997 SIC-4 industry growth. Next, we collected data from national statistics on actual industry growth rates that occurred in 1997 for the industries of the sample. "Forecasting error" is the difference between each firm's estimates and actual 1997 industry growth rates.

**Illusion of control**   For illusion of control, we used the sum of a firm's perceived strengths on factors identified by the firm as key success factors weighted relatively to the other firms' assessment within the industry. This variable contains characteristics common to formerly used metrics. First, industry key success factors are similar to previous studies on top management teams (Beyer et al., 1997; Chattopadhyay et al., 1999) and consist of cost, quality, technical performance, reputation, responsiveness, services, and proximity (see Appendix). The method used to calculate this item consists of a sum of the respondents' grade, controlled for variability (e.g., see Knight et al.'s (1999) study on consensus or, in the same spirit while applied to a different construct, the weighted average of the individual-level complexity measures used in McNamara et al. (2002)). Here, we control for inter-firm agreement on industry key success factors. The illusion of control variable is maximum when responses on the relative strength of the firm versus its competitors does not coincide with inter-firm recognized industry key success factors.

## *Control Variables*

Many other factors contribute to firm performance. In order to control for both a firm's resource endowment and industry structure effects on performance, we included a series of firm-level and industry-level control variables.

**Firm-level controls**   First, we introduced three resource variables, measured relative to industry averages: technical resource, marketing resource, and knowledge resource. Technical resource is the difference between a firm's R&D expenditures expressed as a percentage of sales and the average percentage of R&D expenditures at the industry level. Marketing resource is the difference between a firm's marketing expenditures and the average percentage of marketing expenditures at the industry level. Finally, knowledge resource is the difference between a firm's investments in education and training (expressed as a percentage of overall salary expenses) and the average corresponding expenditures at the industry level. Each of these firms' relative resource endowment is supposedly positively related to performance indicators.

Second, we added three more firm-level controls which may impact a firm's performance. First, "Past-Prod" corresponds to the increase in firm production over the last two years (in percentage). A high increase in production may increase a firm's ROS through inventory selling, but diminish the quick ratio (since the numerator of quick ratio is current assets minus inventory). "Size" is the logarithm of a firm's 3-year average number of employees. Finally, "diversified" is a dichotomous variable, which equals 0 when the firm has more than 90 percent of its sales coming from one business – and 1 otherwise. These last two variables control for firm structural characteristics.

**Industry controls** We also introduced control variables at the industry level, i.e. an evaluation of the five forces: customer bargaining power, supplier bargaining power, threat of new entrants, threat of substitutes, and internal rivalry (see Appendix for details on variables used). According to Porter's model, the five industry forces pressure a firm and negatively influence firm performance.

## Data Analysis Procedures

In our analyses, we control for the direct effect of a firm's resource endowment on performance. However, we must pay attention to the fact that a firm's relative level of resource investment (in R&D, marketing, and knowledge) can also influence a firm's accuracy in industry growth estimates, i.e. forecasting error. Therefore, in order to correctly estimate the impact of forecasting errors on performance, we must include in the set of equations to be tested the resource-forecast effect. Also, the forecast error depends on each industry, which may be more or less fluctuant, namely easy to forecast. Therefore, in order to get a robust estimate of the effect of forecasting error on performance in the main equation, we have to control for these effects on forecasting error in another equation. Thus, we use a two-equation model, as follows:

$$\text{Performance} = \alpha_0 + \beta_{1,2,3} \ \textit{Resources} + \beta_{4,5,6}.$$
$$\text{Firm Controls} + \beta_{7,8,9,10,11}. \ \text{Industry Controls} +$$
$$\beta_{12}.\text{Forecasting error} + \beta_{13}.\text{Illusion of Control} +$$
$$\beta_{14}.\textit{Illusion} \ \text{of Control} \times \text{Forecasting error} + \varepsilon \qquad (7.1)$$

$$\text{Forecasting error} = \alpha_1 + \chi_{1,2,3}.\text{Resources} + \chi_4 \ \text{Difficulty in Forecast} + \varepsilon_1 \quad (7.2)$$

In order to assess an ex ante industry difficulty in forecasting ("Difficulty in Forecast"), we used $\varepsilon$ from the following equation, calculated for each of the 36 industries:

$$IG_{i,t} = \alpha + \beta\ IG_{i,t-1} + \varepsilon_{i,t} \tag{7.3}$$

where IG = industry growth, $i$ indexes the industry (i = 1, ..., 36), and $t$ indexes the years 1995 to 1997. The residual $\varepsilon$ represents that portion of industry growth not explained as a function of the industry growth rate ($\alpha$ and $\beta$ coefficients). "Difficulty in Forecast" is the absolute value of $\varepsilon$ (since a high $\varepsilon$ indicates a large deviation).

Equations 7.1 and 7.2 form a simultaneous equation system that can be estimated using a three-stage-least-square estimator (3SLS model). Ordinary least squares (OLS) estimates of IGE would be biased because of the responsiveness of forecasting ability to the resource and "Difficulty in Forecast" variable. Three-stage least square is one of the most common system methods. System estimating methods estimate all the identified structural equations together as a set, instead of estimating the structural parameters of each equation separately (Kennedy, 1998). It has been recognized that 3SLS estimators are asymptotically more efficient than the 2SLS estimator. The superiority of 3SLS is specifically relevant when the sample size is large, a situation which matches our case (Pindyck and Rubinfeld, 1981; Theil, 1971). Therefore, the 3SLS model is used to test our hypotheses.

## Results

Table 7.1 presents the descriptive statistics and correlation matrix of the variables used in the models. No variable exhibits distribution or correlation problems.

Table 7.2 shows the results. Two general models are provided. Model 1 uses ROS as the dependent variable in eqn. 7.1 while model 2 presents the tests on quick ratio. Each model presents first the controls alone, the controls plus the effect of forecasting error, and the complete model (controls, forecasting error, illusion of control, and the interaction between forecasting error and illusion of control).

H1a postulates that the forecasting error reduces performance whereas H1b assumes the opposite. Results from models 1 and 2 show that the forecasting error has a positive and significant impact ($p < .001$) on both performance indicators (ROS and quick ratio). The addition of forecasting error to eqn. 7.1 increases significantly the performance variance (2.7 percent for ROS and 0.6 percent for quick ratio) over the baseline model. This gives support to H1b. Firms that overestimate industry growth have a better ROS and quick ratio than more accurate firms.

H2 anticipated that a illusion of control lowers performance. The coefficients are negative in model 1 and 2, but significant only for model 2 ($p < .01$). H2 receives partial support. Since H1b has found support in our results, we expect for H3 that illusion of control moderates the positive effect of forecasting errors on performance (H3b). Our results show that for each performance indicator, the coefficient of the interaction term is negative and significant, confirming H3b ($p < .05$ for model 1, and $p < .01$ for model 2).

However, to be exhaustive, we need to consider in detail the conditional effects of illusion of control. Indeed, it seems that high illusion of control moderates the influence of forecasting error on performance But, more precisely, the impact of a

**Table 7.1** Correlation matrix

| Variable | Mean | Std Dev | 1 | 2 | 3 | 4 | 5 | 6 | 7 | 8 | 9 | 10 | 11 | 12 | 13 | 14 | 15 |
|---|---|---|---|---|---|---|---|---|---|---|---|---|---|---|---|---|---|
| 1 ROS | 0.067 | 0.057 | 1.00 | | | | | | | | | | | | | | |
| 2 Quick ratio | 0.182 | 0.224 | **0.19** | 1.00 | | | | | | | | | | | | | |
| 3 Forecasting error | −0.13 | 0.61 | **0.15** | 0.07 | 1.00 | | | | | | | | | | | | |
| 4 Illusion of control | 11.82 | 1.70 | 0.02 | −0.02 | −0.03 | 1.00 | | | | | | | | | | | |
| 5 Technical resource | 0.06 | 1.99 | 0.03 | 0.06 | 0.03 | 0.04 | 1.00 | | | | | | | | | | |
| 6 Marketing resource | 0.15 | 4.64 | 0.04 | −0.02 | 0.02 | −0.03 | 0.04 | 1.00 | | | | | | | | | |
| 7 Knowledge resource | 1.75 | 4.40 | −0.06 | **0.10** | **−0.24** | **0.20** | 0.06 | 0.04 | 1.00 | | | | | | | | |
| 8 PastProd | 5.02 | 13.64 | **0.16** | −0.02 | **0.33** | 0.04 | 0.03 | −0.05 | **−0.29** | 1.00 | | | | | | | |
| 9 Size | 4.67 | 0.90 | 0.01 | −0.01 | **0.13** | **−0.12** | **0.10** | **0.13** | **−0.10** | 0.04 | 1.00 | | | | | | |
| 10 Diversified | 0.27 | 0.44 | −0.02 | 0.01 | 0.00 | −0.04 | 0.02 | **0.08** | **−0.13** | 0.03 | 0.02 | 1.00 | | | | | |
| 11 Difficulty in forecast | 2.02 | 1.04 | 0.05 | **0.08** | **0.12** | −0.03 | −0.04 | −0.01 | **−0.31** | **0.10** | 0.04 | 0.06 | 1.00 | | | | |
| 12 Customer power | 4.39 | 1.05 | **−0.21** | **−0.14** | 0.01 | 0.01 | 0.03 | −0.01 | −0.03 | −0.03 | **0.11** | −0.02 | −0.04 | 1.00 | | | |
| 13 Supplier power | 2.95 | 1.34 | −0.04 | 0.02 | 0.05 | **−0.09** | 0.03 | −0.03 | 0.06 | **−0.12** | 0.02 | 0.00 | 0.05 | −0.08 | 1.00 | | |
| 14 BTE | 3.49 | 1.19 | **0.08** | 0.02 | **0.08** | **0.09** | 0.05 | −0.03 | −0.06 | **0.14** | 0.07 | −0.02 | −0.05 | 0.03 | −0.05 | 1.00 | |
| 15 Substitutes | 49.57 | 34.90 | −0.07 | −0.02 | 0.05 | **−0.17** | −0.09 | 0.01 | **−0.26** | **0.10** | **0.10** | 0.03 | −0.08 | −0.09 | **−0.10** | −0.04 | 1.00 |
| 16 Rivalry | 2.26 | 1.43 | **0.09** | 0.02 | **0.09** | −0.06 | **0.08** | 0.11 | −0.11 | 0.08 | 0.07 | 0.05 | −0.04 | 0.00 | −0.06 | −0.08 | −0.01 |

Significant Pearson correlations at the 5% level are shown in bold

**Table 7.2**  Results of 3SLS analyses

| N = 785 | Model 1 | | | Model 2 | | |
|---|---|---|---|---|---|---|
| *Equation 1* | *ROS* | | | *Quick ratio* | | |
| Intercept | 0.115*** (7.31) | 0.116*** (7.36) | 0.127*** (5.83) | 0.767*** (8.92) | 0.775*** (8.98) | 0.980*** (8.72) |
| Technical resource | 0.134*** (3.96) | 0.099** (2.68) | 0.105** (2.98) | 0.030 (0.86) | 0.008 (0.26) | 0.012 (0.36) |
| Marketing resource | −0.037 (−1.13) | −0.034 (−1.16) | −0.044 (−1.28) | −0.019 (−0.55) | −0.016 (−0.49) | −0.019 (−0.55) |
| Knowledge resource | 0.070* (2.07) | 0.075* (2.10) | 0.123** (3.00) | 0.086** (2.46) | 0.134*** (3.57) | 0.163*** (4.26) |
| PastProd | 0.175*** (5.30) | 0.174*** (5.28) | 0.175*** (5.10) | −0.059+ (−1.68) | −0.059+ (−1.73) | −0.059+ (−1.73) |
| Size | 0.069+ (1.69) | 0.052 (1.46) | 0.046 (1.23) | −0.031 (−0.82) | −0.038 (−0.99) | −0.037 (−0.99) |
| Diversified | 0.021 (0.66) | 0.021 (0.64) | 0.033 (0.96) | −0.036 (−0.90) | −0.036 (−1.06) | −0.031 (−0.90) |
| Customer power | −0.207*** (−6.16) | −0.205*** (−6.08) | −0.200*** (−5.70) | −0.238*** (−6.70) | −0.234*** (−6.59) | −0.230*** (−6.53) |
| Supplier power | −0.158*** (−4.84) | −0.159*** (−4.87) | −0.162*** (−4.79) | −0.146*** (−4.24) | −0.147*** (−4.27) | −0.148*** (−4.35) |
| BTE | 0.018 (0.54) | 0.014 (0.40) | 0.016 (0.47) | 0.030 (0.82) | 0.024 (0.65) | 0.030 (0.40) |
| Substitutes | −0.188*** (−5.38) | −0.185*** (−5.23) | −0.151*** (−3.83) | 0.011 (0.30) | 0.014 (0.39) | 0.028 (0.74) |
| Rivalry | 0.095** (2.89) | 0.093** (2.81) | 0.083* (2.38) | −0.136*** (−3.92) | −0.140*** (−4.00) | −0.153*** (−4.42) |
| Forecasting error | 0.209*** (5.72) | | 2.197** (2.43) | 0.140*** (3.68) | | 0.885*** (3.39) |

**Table 7.2** Results of 3SLS analyses (*Cont'd*)

| | Forecasting error | | | Forecasting error | | |
|---|---|---|---|---|---|---|
| Illusion of control | | | −0.029 (−0.82) | | | −0.100** (−2.89) |
| Forecasting error × Illusion of control | | | −1.923* (−2.08) | | | −0.726** (−2.79) |

*Equation 2*

| | Forecasting error | | | Forecasting error | | |
|---|---|---|---|---|---|---|
| Intercept | 0.179*** (3.87) | 0.205*** (4.39) | 0.208*** (4.45) | 0.184*** (3.92) | 0.210*** (4.50) | 0.210*** (4.50) |
| Difficulty in forecast | 0.112*** (3.23) | 0.134*** (3.81) | 0.136*** (3.88) | 0.116*** (3.31) | 0.137*** (3.92) | 0.137*** (3.92) |
| Technical resource | 0.172*** (5.28) | 0.170*** (5.24) | 0.170*** (5.24) | 0.171*** (5.26) | 0.170*** (5.22) | 0.170*** (5.22) |
| Marketing resource | −0.023 (−0.66) | −0.023 (−0.71) | −0.023 (−0.71) | −0.022 (−0.67) | −0.023 (−0.71) | −0.023 (−0.71) |
| Knowledge resource | −0.314*** (−9.00) | −0.306*** (−8.76) | −0.305*** (−8.73) | −0.313*** (−8.95) | −0.304*** (−8.72) | −0.304*** (−8.72) |
| System weighted $R^2$ | 17.6% | 20.3% | 21.2% | 15.2% | 15.8% | 16.6% |
| $\Delta R^2$ | | 2.7%*** | 0.8%** | | 0.6%** | 0.8%** |

a: all β, χ, and δ are standardized coefficients. In parentheses, T values

*** p < .001, ** p < .01, * p < .05, and + p < .1

change in illusion of control is given by the derivative of eqn. 7.1 with respect to illusion of control:

For ROS:          d[Equation 7.1] / d Illusion of control = $-.029 - 1.923$ Forecasting error

For Quick ratio:  d[Equation 7.1] / d Illusion of control = $-.100 - .726$ Forecasting error

If Forecasting error is $-0.03$ (average observed value), a one unit change in illusion of control increases ROS by 0.02 and reduces quick ratio by $-0.08$. The range of values for Forecasting error goes from minimum $= -3.36$ to maximum $= 3.63$. At the minimum value for forecasting error (i.e. a very pessimistic industry growth estimate), the direct and indirect influence of illusion of control is therefore 6.43 for ROS and 2.34 for quick ratio. At the maximum value of forecasting error, the total influence of illusion of control is $-7.00$ for ROS and $-2.73$ for quick ratio. Therefore, illusion of control contributes to increasing performance for pessimistic firms (for which forecasting error is negative) but reduces performance for optimistic firms (for which forecasting error is positive).[2] The influence of illusion of control is close to zero for accurate forecasts, becomes increasingly negative with increase in positive forecasting errors, and becomes increasingly positive with increase in negative forecasting errors.

Concerning the reciprocal effects (eqn. 7.2), difficulty in forecasting significantly increases the forecasting error in forecasts. Higher investment in technical capabilities tend to inflate estimates (increase forecasting error) while higher investments in knowledge tend to reduce estimates (reduce lower estimates). Marketing investments does not significantly reduce the forecasting errors.

Focusing on control variables at the firm level, results show a positive relationship between an advantage in terms of technical and knowledge resource and performance (ROS). For the quick ratio, the main influence proceeds from knowledge resource investments. Size is hardly significant, and diversification not significant. Past production enables to foster ROS (through sales) but impairs quick ratio (since past production is likely to be related to higher inventories).

Concerning industry controls, two of the industry variables impact significantly both performance indicators ($p < .001$): customer and buyer bargaining powers. Next, rivalry seems to significantly foster ROS, while undermining quick ratio. Finally, the threat of substitutes reduces ROS.

## Discussion

This research focuses on OFA as an intriguing competence. The presence of this competence can be operationalized ex post through observation and calculated differences between forecast and actual changes. The general philosophy about OFA is to associate it with performance: to be accurate reduces perceived uncertainty and should reinforce performance. However, our results open two interesting discussion points. First, positive biases in forecasts are positively related to ROS and quick ratio. Hence, not being "competent" seems better than being competent in forecasts. Therefore, what is really the strategic value of a competence? There may exist competences that, on their own, do not positively impact performance. Being excellent in one task or domain needs a complementary set of conditions (an organizational context) to deliver rents and imply performance (Durand, 2002).

Second, we must take a firm's competence in its organizational context. When introducing recognized dimensions that alter performance, like illusion of control in this research, the strategic value of the competence (i.e. its impact on performance) changes. Without the contextual effect of illusion of control, a slight error of industry growth forecast by +1 percent gives you on average a 0.88 improved quick ratio. However, with the same error in forecast and a high illusion of control, the impact on quick ratio becomes negative. Foresight is not good in absolute, but must include in its process the effects on the forecast ability–performance relationship of as many contextual biases as possible.

Theoretically, this chapter bridges the resource-based view of the firm and decision theory. As explained elsewhere, a firm's resource endowment matters for creating rents, appropriating growth opportunities, and fostering performance (Barney, 1991; Dierickx and Cool, 1989). Once inter-firm resource differences are accounted for, complementary competencies remain to be identified, like forecasting ability, that contribute to the explanation of firm performance. Being able to define appropriate goals depends on a firm's evaluation of opportunities, and the cumulated result of past investments (Mosakowski, 1998). Moreover, organizational traits influence the exercise of complementary competences. This study gives evidence of one trait (illusion of control) that, on top of its direct negative influence on performance, alters the benefits of an organization's forecasting ability. As Priem and Butler's (2001) state in conclusion of their debate with Barney (2001) on the resource-based view, there is a need to go beyond the artificial separation between firm resources and competitive environment. This study is a modest attempt to formalize "an elaborative, evolving, and emerging process that works toward solutions by addressing the core *connections* between resources and the environment" (Priem and Butler, 2001, p. 64). One of the core connections may be the particular role played by the interaction between distinctive competencies (source of competitive advantage) and organizational traits (that reduce the likelihood of an organization to be a capable organization), and their impact on performance (Durand, 2002). Durand (2002) formalized a simple model of firm performance that uses the conjunction of competitive advantage and a capable organization. In the context of this research, a capable organization is an organization that is able to comprehend and integrate its own self-perception into decision-making processes.

Empirically, this study is a primary response to Starbuck and Mezias: "To find out whether [perceptions may be very inaccurate], researchers need to investigate the larger or smaller errors and of different biases. Nevertheless, surprisingly little research focuses on the accuracies of perceptions. Studies comparing subjective with objective data may be rare because it is so difficult to design good questionnaires, to obtain good 'objective' data and to obtain enough suitable respondents" (Starbuck and Mezias, 1996, p. 115). This chapter tries to overcome these difficulties through:

1 observing forecast errors and associating inaccuracy with the absence of OFA competence;
2 careful sample selection to reduce ex-ante sample heterogeneity at the industry-code level;
3 controling for systemic effects of resource endowment on forecasting errors;
4 controling for direct effects of firm resources and industry structure on firm performance; and
5 testing the relationships on two performance variables.

However, the findings of this study present some limitations. We used secondary data to test our hypotheses. Although previous studies have indeed shown that using subjective data can be valuable in the evaluation of strategic issues (Hambrick, 1981; 1982; Starbuck and Mezias, 1996), this may nevertheless be damaging to the validity of our research. As the Bank of France has increased the reliability of its survey over the years, using well-trained interviewers and specialists in econometrics to insure the quality of the data, we are rather confident that our results can be generalized (see preceding studies by Cool and Henderson, 1998). However, we regret the absence of additional questions that could have enabled us to test the external validity of our constructs. We controled for respondents' biases from the outside of the organization (through the Kappas). However, it was not possible to have an internal cross-evaluation of the organizational perceptions – which is an intrinsic but regretful limitation of studies using secondary data.

The results of this study can also lead to other extensions. First, an organization's estimates of industry growth influence its performance. We might extend this statement to other elements for which firms have to estimate the future potential value, like a resource itself. Organizational illusion of control may also affect the processes that lead firms to generate divergent estimation of the strategic value of a resource. Several factors have been acknowledged to distort the objective judgement made by firms. Effects of bounded rationality, the role of dominant logic, or the strength of organizational paradigms have all been related to internal decision processes and tested at the individual level. However, organizational illusion of control increases the likelihood of overestimating the firm's resource value and underestimating a competitor's resource value, and its effects should be tested on other variables like the choice of technical standards, the decision to diversify, and so forth.

Second, previous studies have shown that national culture can impact how individuals and organizations respond to strategic issues. Notably, Schneider and de Meyer (1991) found that Latin European managers when compared with other managers were more likely to negatively interpret environmental changes (in their case, a deregulation). A replication of this study in different national contexts or in multicultural contexts will help shed more light on the interactions between individual, organizational, and cultural influences on forecasting abilities and illusion of control.

Third, it would be interesting to extend the analysis of the relationships between organizational traits and forecasting ability, in order to uncover the chain of causes and effects from resource endowment, organizational traits, forecasting ability, and performance. Notably, organizational attention appears to be an important trait that enables firms to focus (or not) on relevant signals (Ocasio, 1997). Organizational attention and other traits (like structure or compensation characteristics) could therefore be added to the future models.

As far as management is concerned, this study shows that top managers must be aware of the influence of the organization they belong to when they have to deliver estimates and build scenarios for decision-making. This chapter does not allow us to suggest explicit recommendations in terms of investment in resources for reducing illusion of control. However, it suggests that beyond the technical recommendations drawn from the forecasting literature, many actions may improve a firm's estimation resource and corollary decisions. These management actions presumably deal with organizational balance (in terms of the team(s) in charge of forecasts and estimates), organizational diversity (in terms of education, background, culture within and across teams), and organizational governance (in terms of vested interests, opportunism, and agency relationships). Altogether, these factors may help a firm better estimate its environmental conditions, realize the reality of its own resourcefulness, and improve its performance.

## NOTES

1   One may suspect the validity and reliability on these measures as single items. However, while independently of each other these variables would be suspect of such liabilities, we use them in this research in two specific ways that reduce significantly the reach of their defects. First, they are used all together as descriptors of the industry in order to assess each firm's perception of the industry structure. In this case, it is the set of variables which matter, and not each one individually, to select out industries with high heterogeneity of firm's perceptions. Second, they are introduced as control variables in the model and not as explanatory variables. We acknowledge that the results of a research using these single indicators as independent variables would be doubtful. However, in the context of this study, they are only proxies that control for the industry effects on a firm's performance. As such, they do a good job, since the results seem coherent with Porter's model and alone explain about 15 percent of the firm's performance.

2   To be precise, the inflexion points varies slightly for ROS and quick ratio: for ROS the inflexion point is $-.015$ and for quick ratio $-.137$.

## REFERENCES

Amburgey, T. and Dacin, T. (1997) Event count analysis and strategic management. In M. Ghertman, J. Obadia, and J.-L. Arregle, (eds.), *Statistical Models for Strategic Management*, Boston: Kluwer Academic Publishers, pp. 29–45.

Baghai, M., Coley, S., and White, D. (1999) *The Alchemy of Growth*, New York: Perseus Books.

Bandura, A. (1977) Self-efficacy: Toward a unifying theory of behavioral change, *Psychological Review*, 84(2), 191–215.

Barnes, J. H. (1984) Cognitives biases and their impact on strategic planning, *Strategic Management Journal*, 5, 129–37.

Barney, J. (1991) Firm resources and sustained competitive advantage, *Journal of Management*, 17, 99–120.

Barney, J. B. (2001) Is the resource-based "view" a useful perspective for strategic management research? Yes, *Academy of Management Review*, 26(1), 41–56.

Beyer, J., Chattopadhyay, P., George, E., Glick, W. H., and Pugliese, D. (1997) The selective perception of managers revisited, *Academy of Management Journal*, 40, 716–37.

Blattburg, R. C. and Hoch, S. J. (1990) Database models and managerial intuition: 50% model + 50% manager, *Management Science*, 36, 887–99.

Bourgeois, L. J. (1985) Strategic goals, perceived uncertainty, and economic performance in volatile environments, *Academy of Management Journal*, 28, 548–73.

Bunn, D. and Wright, G. (1991) Interaction of judgmental and statistical forecasting methods: Issues and analysis, *Management Science*, 37, 501–18.

Chattopadhyay, P., Glick, W. H., Miller, C. C., and Huber, G. P. (1999) Determinants of executive beliefs: Comparing functional conditioning and social influence, *Strategic Management Journal*, 20, 763–89.

Clapham, S. E. and Schwenk, C. R. (1991) Self-serving attributions, managerial cognition, and company performance, *Strategic Management Journal*, 12, 219–29.

Coff, R. W. (1999) How buyers cope with uncertainty when acquiring firms in knowledge-intensive industries: Caveat emptor, *Organization Science*, 10, 144–61.

Cool, K. and Henderson, J. (1998) Power and firm profitability in supply chains: French manufacturing industry in 1993, *Strategic Management Journal*, 19(10), 909–26.

Corner, P., Kinicki, A., and Keats, B. (1994) Integrating organizational and individual information processing perspectives on choice, *Organization Science*, 5(3), 294–309.

Daft, R. and Weick, K. (1984) Toward a model of organizations as interpretation systems, *Academy of Management Review*, 9(2), 284–95.

Das, S., Levine, C., and Sivaramakrishnan, K., (1998) Earnings predictability and bias in analysts' earnings forecast, *The Accounting Review*, 73, 277–94.

Das, T. K. and Teng, B. S. (1999) Cognitive biases and strategic decision processes: An integrative perspective, *Journal of Management Studies*, 36, 757–78.

Dierickx, I. and Cool, K. (1989) Asset stock accumulation and sustainability of competitive advantage, *Management Science*, 35, 1504–11.

Duhaime, I. and Schwenk, C. (1985) Conjectures on cognitive simplification in acquisition and divestment decision making, *Academy of Management Review*, 10, 287–95.

Durand, R. (2002) Competitive advantages exist: A response to Powell, *Strategic Management Journal*, 23(9), 867–72.

Durand R. (2003) Predicting a Firm's Forecasting Ability – The Role of Organizational Illusion of Control and Organizational Attention, *Strategic Management Journal*, 24(9), 821–38.

Eisenhardt, K. and Brown, S. L. (1998) Time pacing: Competing in markets that won't stand still, *Harvard Business Review*, March, 59–71.

Eliasson, G. (1976) *Business Economic Planning: Theory, Practice and Comparison*, Swedish Industrial Publication.

Fildes, R. (1985) Quantitative forecasting – The state of the art: Econometrics models, *Journal of the Operational Research Society*, 36, 549–80.

Garud, R. and Rappa, M. (1994) A socio-cognitive model of technology evolution: The case of cochlear implants, *Organization Science*, 5(3), 344–62.

Greve, H. (1998) Managerial cognition and the mimetic adoption of market positions: What you see is what you do, *Strategic Management Journal*, 19, 967–88.

Halman, J. and Keizer, J. (1994) Diagnosing risk in product innovation projects, *International Journal of Project Management*, 12(2), 75–81.

Hambrick, D. C. (1981) Strategic awareness within top management teams. *Strategic Management Journal*, 2(2), 153–73.

Hambrick, D. C. (1982) Environmental scanning and organizational strategy, *Strategic Management Journal*, 3(2), 159–74.

Hayward, M. L. and Hambrick, D. C. (1997) Explaining premium paid for large acquisitions: Evidence of CEO hubris, *Administrative Science Quarterly*, 42(1), 103–27.

Kahneman, D. and Tversky, A. (1984) Choice, values, and frames, *American Psychologist*, 39, 341–50.

Kennedy, P. (1998) *A Guide to Econometrics*, Cambridge: MA: MIT Press.

King, A. W. and Zeithaml, C. P. (2001) Competencies and firm performance: Examining the causal ambiguity paradox, *Strategic Management Journal*, 22, 75–99.

Knight, D., Pearce, C. L., Smith, K. G., Olian, J. D., Sims, H. P., Smith, K. A., and Flood, P. (1999) Top management team diversity, group process, and strategic consensus, *Strategic Management Journal*, 20, 445–65.

Landis, R. J. and Koch, G. G. (1977) The measurement of observer agreement for categorical data, *Biometrics*, 33, 159–74.

Langer, E. J. (1975) The illusion of control, *Journal of Personality and Personal Psychology*, 32(2), 311–28.

Lubatkin, M., Schulze, W., Mainkar, A, and Cotterill, R. W. (2001) Ecological investigation of firm-effect in horizontal mergers, *Strategic Management Journal*, 22, 335–57.

Makadok, R. and Walker, G. (2000) Identifying a distinctive competence: Forecasting ability in the money fund industry, *Strategic Management Journal*, 21, 853–64.

Matute, H. (1996). Illusion of control: Detecting response-outcome independence in analytic but not in naturalistic conditions, *Psychological Science*, 7(5), 289–99.

McNamara, G. and Bromiley, P. (1997) Decision making in an organizational setting: Cognitive and organizational influences on risk assessment in commercial lending, *Academy of Management Journal*, 40(5), 1063–88.

McNamara, G. and Bromiley, P. (1999) Risk and return in organizational decision making, *Academy of Management Journal*, 42(3), 330–9.

McNamara, G., Luce, R. A., and Tompson, G. H. (2002) Examining the effect of complexity in strategic group knowledge on firm performance, *Strategic Management Journal*, 23(2), 153–70.

Mosakowski, E. (1998) Managerial prescriptions under the resource-based view of strategy: The example of motivational techniques, *Strategic Management Journal*, 19(12), 1169–82.

Ocasio, W. (1997) Towards an attention-based view of the firm, *Strategic Management Journal*, 18, 187–206.

Pindyck, R. S. and Rubinfeld, D. L. (1981) *Econometric Models and Economic Forecast*, New York: McGraw-Hill Book Company.

Porter, M. E. (1980) *Competitive Strategy*, New York: Free Press.

Powell, T. P. (1992) Organizational alignment as competitive advantage, *Strategic Management Journal*, 13, 119–34.

Prahalad, C. K. and Bettis, R. (1986) The dominant logic: A new linkage between diversity and performance, *Strategic Management Journal*, 7, 485–502.

Priem, R. L. and Butler, J. E. (2001) Tautology in the resource-based view and the implications of externally determined resource value: Further comments, *Academy of Management Review*, 26(1), 57–66.

Schneider, S. C. and de Meyer, A. (1991) Interpreting and responding to strategic issues: The impact of national culture, *Strategic Management Journal*, 12, 307–20.

Schweitzer, M. and Cachon, G. (2000) Decision biases in the newsvendor problem with a known demand distribution: Experimental evidence, *Management Science*, 46, 404–20.

Schwenk, C. R. (1986) Information, cognitive biases, and commitment to a course of action, *Academy of Management Review*, 11, 298–310.

Schwenk, C. R. (1984) Cognitive simplification processes in strategic decision-making, *Strategic Management Journal*, 5, 111–28.

Shamir, J. (1986) Pre-election polls in Israel: structural constraints on accuracy, *Public Opinion Quarterly*, 54, 609–26.

Simon, M., Houghton, S. M., and Aquino, K. (2000a) Cognitive biases, risk perception, and venture formation: How individuals decide to start companies, *Journal of Business Venturing*.

Simon, M., Houghton, S. M., and Savelli, S. (2000b) The effects of overconfidence on the performance of product introductions: Evidence from an exploration field study, paper presented at the Academy of Management, Toronto.

Starbuck, W. H. and Mezias, J. (1996) Opening Pandora's box: Studying the accuracy of managers' perceptions, *Journal of Organizational Behavior*, 17, 99–117.

Staw, B. M. and Ross, J. (1987) Behaviors in escalation situations: Antecedents, prototypes, and solutions. In L. G. Cummings and B. Staw (eds.), *Research in Organizational Behavior*, Greewich, CT: JAI Press, pp. 39–78.

Sutcliffe, K. M. (1994) What executives notice: Accurate perceptions in top management teams, *Academy of Management Journal*, 37, 1360–78.

Sutcliffe, K. M. and Huber, G. P. (1998) Firm and industry as determinants of executive perceptions of the environment, *Strategic Management Journal*, 19(8), 793–807.

Teece, D. J., Pisano, G., and Shuen, A. (1997) Dynamic capabilities and strategic management, *Strategic Management Journal*, 18(7), 509–53.

Theil, H. (1971) *Principles of Econometrics*, New York: John Wiley and Sons.

Tripsas, M. and Gavetti, G. (2000) Capabilities, cognition, and inertia: Evidence from digital imaging, *Strategic Management Journal*, 21, 1147–61.

Tversky, A. and Kahneman, D. (1974) Judgement under uncertainty: Heuristics and biases, *Science*, 185, 1124–31.

Wood, R. E. and Bandura, A. (1989) Impact of the conceptions of ability on self-regulatory mechanism and complex decision making, *Journal of Personality and Social Psychology*, 56, 407–15.

Yates, J. R., Jagacinski, C. M. and Faber, M. D. (1978) Evaluation of partially described multiattribute options, *Organizational Behavior and Human Performance*, 21, 240–51.

# Appendix

## *Independent Variables*

**Forecasting error:** Straight difference between a firm's forecast 1997 industry growth and accurate 1997 industry growth.

**Illusion of control:** Illusion of control corresponds to a weighted average of a firm's perceived strength on identified success factors:

$$\text{Illusion of Control}_{i,j} = \Sigma_n[\text{Strength}_i \times (KSF_i/\Sigma(KSF_j/j))]$$

where i stands for a firm, and j for the number of different firms in an industry, and n for 7 for the industry factors below. KSF stands for key success factors.

*Strength* is the answer to the following questions: Among the following factors, indicate your relative strength *vis-à-vis* your competition on (5 point scale):

1  cost/price
2  quality
3  technical performance
4  reputation
5  delays, responsiveness
6  services
7  proximity

KSF is the answer to the question: Among the following variables, indicate those which are the most valorized in your industry (multiple binary answers):

1  cost/price
2  quality
3  technical performance
4  reputation
5  delays, responsiveness
6  services
7  proximity

$KSF_i/\Sigma(KSF_j/j)$ indicates that we weight the perceived KSF of a firm by the interfirm (and intra-industry) average acknowledgment of the factor as a key success factor.

## Firm Control Variables

**Technical resource:** Firm R&D expenditures (percentage of sales) minus industry average R&D expenditures (NACE 4 digit level).

**Marketing resource:** Firm marketing expenditures (percentage of sales) minus industry average marketing expenditures (NACE 4 digit level).

**Knowledge resource:** Firm education and training expenditures (percentage of overall salary expenses) minus industry average education and training expenditures (NACE 4 digit level).

**Past Prod:** "Over the last 2 years, your production has increased by (percent)?"

**Size:** logarithm of the 3-year average number of employees.

**Diversified:** binary variable: 1 if the firm has diversified activities, 0 otherwise.

## *Industry Control Variables*

**SupplierPower:** Your main suppliers have a high bargaining power that enable them to negotiate contracts:

strongly disagree       strongly agree
1      2      3      4      5

**CustomerPower:** Your customers have a high bargaining power that enables them to negotiate contracts:

strongly disagree       strongly agree
1      2      3      4      5

**BTE:** Barriers to Entry (BTE) comprises the average answers to the following questions:

1  The difficulties for new competitors in reaching a sufficient plant size are:
weak                    strong
1      2      3      4      5
2  The difficulties for new competitors in reaching a sufficient cumulated volume of production are: (same scale)
3  difficulties for new competitors in having access to your production technologies are: (same scale)
4  The difficulties for new competitors in finding equivalent conditions of raw material or component access are: (same scale)
5  The difficulties for new competitors in reaching a similar labor productivity level are: (same scale)

**Substitutes:** "What is the percentage of standardized products in your activity?" is used as a proxy for the threat of substitutes, with the idea that the higher the percentage of standardized products, the higher the likelihood of substitution.

**Rivalry:** Companies in your industry modify frequently their offering (every 2 years):
strongly disagree       strongly agree
1      2      3      4      5

# Part Three

## Developing Foresightful Organizations

# Chapter Eight

# Time Traveling: Organizational Foresight as Temporal Reflexivity[1]

*Miguel Pina E. Cunha*

## Introduction

Strategic foresight has long been considered a crucial feature of the competent business manager (Fayol, 1949). In this chapter, it is argued that temporal reflexivity may be viewed as an essential ingredient of strategic foresight. This happens because new competitive landscapes demand high-velocity planning and opportunity grabbing as necessary predicaments for organizational survival (e.g. Eisenhardt and Martin, 2000). Thus, looking at the future must be complemented with strategizing in the present and learning fast from the past.

When facing high-speed competitive landscapes, organizations have to make an effort to anticipate which events may turn out to be significant enough to challenge their competitive position. But they also need to develop the capacity to improvise, i.e. to act without the benefit of prior planning, in order to take advantage of unexpected opportunities or to neutralize significant threats. In other words, they need to focus on both the future and the present. But more than considering these as independent efforts, organizations need to manage temporal articulation. In this sense, organizational foresight, instead of being focused exclusively on the future, may refer to managing the links between the past, present, and future. Hence the double suggestion that organizational foresight may be thought of as time traveling and that time traveling may be considered as an instantiation of temporal reflexivity, or the awareness of "the human potential for reinforcing and altering temporal structures" (Orlikowski and Yates, 2002, p. 698) through action. This chapter contributes to the organizational and foresight literatures by stressing the importance of temporal reflexivity. Such importance is illustrated by the multiplicity of "time travels" in which organizations engage in their daily practice. To limit foresight to an extrapolation of the past to the future is to ignore the significance of temporal reflexivity.

The chapter is organized as follows. The initial section discusses the major theoretical issues underlying "time traveling." Then, the traditional view of foresight as prediction is introduced. According to this perspective, organizations should try to anticipate the shape of the future in order to adjust. Recent developments in the field of complexity science have suggested, however, that the assumptions upon which the "foresight as prediction" perspective rests, are possibly untenable. Based upon complexity theory, the prediction perspective is then critically analyzed. Its limitations lead to the consideration of an alternative view. This alternative is discussed in the "foresight as invention" section. Here, foresight is not taken as an attempt to devise what will happen in the future, but rather as an effort for articulation between past experiences, today's realities and possible trajectories. The "foresight as invention" perspective draws upon the concept of emergence and views the future as the unpredictable outcome of myriad interactions between complex agents. Despite the agentic nature of organizational behaviors (Bandura, 2001), and even in the face of genuine efforts for prediction, the influence of previous learning, the need to solve pressing problems immediately, the complexity of causal chains, and the fortuitous small interactions that end up producing significant consequences, all deem prediction efforts insufficient to make accurate anticipations. Through emergence, organizations invent their futures. These "inventions" are the result of the interaction between multiple time horizons: paths inherited from the past, possibilities of the present and visions of the future. These time horizons are not easy to separate and distinguish. People often blend them, circulating from one to another. Organizational foresight may, as such, be analyzed as time traveling. In these travels, as will be discussed in the following section, every kind of combination between past, present, and future is admissible. To grasp the complexities of foresight, then, one possibly needs to understand how the future is a product of the synthesis of multiple temporal landscapes construed through temporal reflexivity.

## Travels in Time: Prediction or Invention?

It is argued here that organizational foresight may be approached from two major paradigms, one which is close to the foresight-as-prediction view, the other to the foresight-as-invention perspective.

The first paradigm lies at the heart of the forecasting discipline. It views time structures as objective and, as such, predictable. The rigor of predictions may then be understood as the result of the availability of reliable technical instruments. As a consequence, traditional research in the domain of forecasting has been directed basically towards the development of analytical tools aimed at improving the potency of prediction. This orientation is evident, for example, in Makridakis and Wheelwright's (1982a) handbook of forecasting, mostly devoted to the development of analytical methods such as ARIMA (autoregressive integrated moving average) models, Bayesian forecasting, single equation regression models, simultaneous system models, and so forth (Fildes, 1982). In this perspective, a forecast is "an estimate of the future based on the past, as opposed to subjective prediction" (p. 572). It could then be assumed that the future is an extrapolation of the past and that, with the adequate statistical methods, such extrapolation could be produced with a reasonable accuracy.

A result of the application of the adequate tools is as follows: "Consider the following illustrative scenario about company X. Through 1971 a regression model explaining companywide sales with real GNP performed well both statistically and as a general guide to individual product line performance. During the 1973–75 period, sales were affected by a number of unusual changes in the environment" (Beckenstein, 1982, p. 261). This view, then, takes organizational foresight as a subfield of the management discipline dominated by statistical methods applied to historical data. People, including forecasters, acted within the context of these structures.

A second foresight paradigm views organizational foresight as the interaction between the way people simultaneously construe and are constrained by the temporal structures that are both enacted and changed through practice. This view draws in Giddens' (1984) theory of structuration. It has been applied to the study of organizations by Orlikowski and Yates (2002), for example. These authors suggest that, through practice, people sustain and change the temporal structures that are the context of their action. In this perspective, foresight is not as much a matter of prediction ("there is a future out there, waiting to be predicted"), as a matter of invention ("how are human agents inventing their futures through practice?").

The implications, theoretical and practical, of these two paradigms, are significant. Under the first paradigm, foresight is a matter of statistical forecasting; under the second paradigm, forecasting is a matter of interpretation. Foresight as prediction means traveling from the past to the future on the basis of statistical analysis; foresight as invention means analyzing all relations between the past, present, and future, in order to cultivate awareness of the role of time. Some authors have called these efforts of temporal reflexivity as "operations of fantasy" (Weick and Sutcliffe, 2001) or time stretching (Tsoukas and Hatch, 2001). It is argued here that it is possible to integrate both paradigms under the perspective of time traveling. Such a perspective, then, may have as much in common with statistical analysis as with Jules Verne fantasy journeys.

Several reasons may be advanced to justify the integration of both perspectives. These include the limits of human agents in both the production and reading of forecasts. Cognitive limitations and biases, and political interests were presented as obstacles to the implementation of forecasting (Makridakis and Wheelwright, 1982b). Developments in complexity theory and in the interpretive literature on organizations, however, exposed the limits of the statistically based causal analysis and the existence of an objective world, which could be analyzed independently of human agency. If there are clear limits to prediction, foresight may be as much a matter of prediction as well as a matter of interpretation. Extrapolating the future from the past may be wise, but it can also be wise to explore complementary time travels. The exploration of multiple relationships may thus help to understand the human potential to act upon temporal structures through praxis. It is argued, then, that organizations need to operate within both paradigms and play with the multiple combinations of time. The following sections develop the foresight as prediction and as invention paradigms. The discussion then turns to time travels as instances of temporal reflexivity.

## Foresight as Prediction

This section critically discusses the traditional view of foresight as prediction. According to this perspective, organizations should try to anticipate the shape of the future in order to adapt. Traditional views of organizational foresight are aimed at predicting the future as reflected in Fayol's (1949, p. 43) maxim, that "managing means looking ahead." This perspective is still attractive today, as illustrated by the subtitle of Laermer's (2001) book: "Think forward, get ahead, and cash in on the future." The most respected means to formalize this look ahead is through strategic planning. Such formalization may be deemed unnecessary, however, if a brilliant visionary is in command. As that does not seem to be the case in most organizations, planning became a fundamental part of the manager's job. The appeal of the great designer, however, is still alive and revives on those occasions when an organization shows above-normal returns. In most cases, that tends to be associated with a brilliant CEO, able to balance discipline and imagination, the two recurrent ingredients of strategy making (Szulanski and Amin, 2001).

This chapter, however, is focused on the role of strategic planning as discipline. Discipline, as Ackoff (1970) put it, may refer to the design of a desired future and the means to attain it. Planning, thus, is closely linked with the capacity to conduct accurate forecasts. Accurate forecasts, according to models of rational actors, are a matter of collecting information, developing alternatives, and picking the best alternative. The period during which a firm can make accurate forecasts, "plus or minus 20 percent" (Ansoff, 1964, p. 64), is called its planning horizon. Under the rational actor model, plans and forecasts may be a matter of rationality, consistency, and systems, of eliminating avoidable errors, and treating information adequately.

The problem with planning horizons in contemporary business environments is that they have become too short too quickly. Effective planning depends on accurate forecasts, but long-range forecasts tend to be inaccurate. Therefore, planning activities must accept the limitations inherent in long-range forecasts. The obviousness of these limitations attracted criticism to the planning perspective. Brown (2001, p. 113) offered a good example of this criticism when stating that "plans, in short, are easy. Planning is impossible."

From this, one can conclude that the discipline of organizational forecasting faces a paradoxical situation. This paradox can be shown in many ways, including the following:

- Foresight exists to help managers in making accurate predictions; its experts, however, warn prospective users of the impossibility of obtaining accurate long-term predictions.
- Formal analytical tools, such as those offered by strategic planning, help to overcome the flaws of unaided human judgment; plans, however, may stimulate the "wishful thinking" they intended to avoid in the first place.

Given the impossibility of reliable prediction, the foresight area has "repositioned," approaching the emerging field of organizational learning. Efforts of prediction have been substituted by the analysis of trends, characterized by Drucker (1997) as the future that has already happened, and scenarios, which aim to identify and describe a set of possible future states. Scenarios will be useful to the extent that they stimulate the organization in its efforts of learning, providing a more informed reading of possible future(s), and helping to make sense of the desired end state at a given moment in time. They help the organization to reflect about possible futures and may be considered useful independently of their accuracy. Scenarios are important because they circumvent the insurmountable obstacles to accurate forecasts. These obstacles include the facts that the future cannot be anticipated except under the form of regular and general patterns; and that, given the influence of cycles of positive feedback, organizational ecosystems may move towards non-equilibrium. Moreover, as demonstrated by complexity theorists, evolution from a present state to a future one, seems to be less a sequential process controlled by the organization, and more the product of a number of interactions between events that take the organization into new and sometimes unexpected directions (Fonseca, 2002). As such, when trying to respond to uncertain events and attempting to influence the environment in a certain way, organizations are contributing to the creation of a dynamic that they cannot control. Examples of the emergence of complex dynamics are available in the literature, exposing the possibility of both beneficial and harmful dynamics – from the organization's point of view. The unfolding of a vicious circle has been discussed by Perrow (1984), who showed that the succession of free-will actions may escalate to become what he called a normal accident. The case of Honda's dominance of the US motorcycle market provides an eloquent example of a virtuous cycle, with the company reaping unexpected outcomes from an unplanned strategy (Pascale, 1990).

It is not possible, though, to assume that the future can be read as an extension of the past, but as an outcome of the competitive moves of complex, multi-agent systems. As argued by Stacey (1996), foresight efforts are only reliable when, in a given system, a cause produces a limited number of effects and the relationships between causes and effects can be followed over a long period of time. The practical problem is that, in most complex systems, such as organizations and their environments, there are too many causes and effects to allow close scrutiny. The lack of accuracy aggravates the fact that significant effects may be caused by the accumulation of a great number of small and apparently negligible causes. Small causes may amplify and end up producing large-scale effects. The impossibility of considering all potential small causes, as well as the interactions among them, qualifies any attempt of accurate prediction as fallible. The more the organization's environment changes, the more this inaccuracy will be exposed.

When we take organizations as complex responsive systems that compete in changing environments, it becomes clear that environments are moving targets, whose characteristics are in constant flux, while agents interact with other agents that are, themselves, complex and responsive (Stacey, 1996). Many of these interactions can appear to an external observer as trivial, but they may nevertheless escalate and produce major consequences. The impact of "small causes" that combine with one another leads to the creation of surprising and unpredictable futures in an emergent fashion (Thiétart and Forgues, 1997). In other words, through their actions, organizational actors create contexts. These contexts, in turn, develop a dynamic of their own, which escapes their control. The future then, cannot be predicted and organizational foresight techniques should not aim at prediction, but at the facilitation of learning about the major trends, framing the debate on how the organization may deal with the changing states of the world. The irrevocable unpredictability of organizational systems should invite the organization to create competencies for dealing with changes at the moment in which they occur, i.e. helping them to plan in real-time and to influence the future through action. The role of foresight may then be less of prediction and more of invention through action, as will be discussed in the following section.

## Foresight as Invention

We now consider the foresight-as-invention perspective. In this case, foresight is not taken as an effort to devise what will happen in the future, but as an attempt of articulation between past experiences, today's realities, and possible trajectories. The foresight-as-invention perspective is based upon the concept of emergence and conceives the future as the unpredictable outcome of endless interactions between agents. As Eisenhardt and Bhatia (2002) have pointed out, in many industries efforts of adaptability imply the loss of control and the recognition of unpredictability as a given. This stimulates discovery through practice.

The perspective of foresight as invention argues that organizations cannot be fully described by traditional theories and approaches, which are based upon a Newtonian, mechanistic view of the world. Under this view, the future could be anticipated with reasonable accuracy, provided that the organizational foresight system received a proper input and conducted the foresight process in a technically adequate manner. As such, the future could be discovered through analysis and technique. Recent developments tend to relax the Newtonian script and to emphasize the non-deterministic nature of organizations and their environments. Strategy can then be conceived, among other possibilities, as guided evolution (Lovas and Ghoshal, 2000). Organizational complexity scholars rejected the former linear view and pointed out the role of emergence: the future cannot be predicted, because it is being constructed through interaction (Tsoukas and Chia, 2002). Under this view, organizations may be thought of as complex feedback systems that co-evolve into an open-ended evolutionary space. These complex systems are indeterministic and impossible to "capture" in formal plans, regardless of how carefully prepared. When the speed of change increases and competitive effects spread quickly, the evolution of business landscapes seems to escape human agency. Expressions like "viral marketing" or "viral organizing" have been coined to match these new realities and to reflect the emergent ethos of organizational and environmental change.

The impact of the concept of emergence on the field of organizational foresight is noteworthy. It shows that there are features of organizing and of organizational foresight that the traditional mechanistic mindsets and instruments do not allow us to grasp. Recent research suggests that two concepts may be central to this nascent view of foresight: *improvisation* and *temporal reflexivity*. These are now discussed and their potential usefulness to the theory of organizational foresight is analyzed.

## *Improvisation*

Organizations improvise when they contract planning and action, i.e. when they plan in real-time with the available resources (Cunha et al., 1999; Miner et al., 2001). Improvisation is an emerging topic in the organizational field. Its conceptual discovery is related to criticisms of traditional planning modes (Mintzberg, 1994) and to the recognition that, in high-velocity environments, occurrences take place at a rate of change that allows little time for planning. This is especially evident in the information technology sector (e.g. Bourgeois and Eisenhardt, 1988), but may also be crossing other industries as well, due for example to the exploration of e-business models (Kanter, 2001), where speed and innovation are major features.

While improvising, people and organizations learn from real events and test imagined solutions on the spot. In this way, improvisation facilitates the synthesis between learning and imagining, two essential components of organization development (Calori, 2002). Improvisation has also been shown to develop intuition (Bourgeois and Eisenhardt, 1988), interrupt simplification (Miller, 1990) and favour discovery (Weick, 1990). The bias for action and for reflecting-while-doing, which is central to the concept of improvisation, is important because it aptly deals with the impossibility of accurate prediction. If, as pointed out by Godet and Roubelat (1996), certainty is death, then to deal with uncertainty, improvisation is vital. Therefore, and as it is impossible to predict the future – it is open-ended – techniques for foresight and prospective analysis are of limited value. Thus, efforts at prediction should be combined with stimulus for discovery-driven action. Action and sense-making, in turn, may help to shape the future while it unfolds.

In this sense, to improvise is to conduct "real-time foresight." This paradoxical suggestion is a consequence of the observation that people in organizations improvise when they must act immediately, in order to take advantage of unexpected opportunities or to neutralize threatening moves from competitors. Through improvisation, organizations invent unplanned futures. That is why Kanter (2001, p. 132) pointed out that "a culture oriented toward tomorrow is a culture of improvisation." The invention perspective is greatly influenced by a developed sensitivity to the importance of small, local events. These events are often unpredictable and, sometimes, must be tackled immediately. Organizational improvisation, thus, alters foresight's time horizon: it suggests that a focus on the future must be complemented with attention to the present. The focus on the future will be useless unless the organization shows its ability to deal with here-and-now challenges. The future and the present are therefore inextricably linked. The future, being a continuation of the present, builds upon it. As such, present and future should be articulated instead of detached. It is then needless to say that the past is critical when deciding what to do in the present. O'Shea (2002, p. 119) observed that "both the past and the future are important not as determined or deterministic points but as what may enable, and be realizable through, action in the present moment." In conclusion, foresight may have more to do with temporal articulation than with the prediction of the future. The crucial issue of temporal reflexivity through articulation is introduced below.

## Temporal Reflexivity

Organizational improvisation must not be equated with short-term thinking. In fact, improvisation suggests that the articulation between past, present, and future is possible, as demonstrated by Brown and Eisenhardt (1997) in their empirical research with computer firms. These authors identified several mechanisms of temporal articulation that may have more to do with foresight and temporal reflexivity than is usually acknowledged. One of the most relevant of those mechanisms is the creation of rigid time intervals for launching new products. These intervals, once internalized, influence the rhythms of the organization in such a way that they get "entrained" (i.e. enmeshed, articulated) with the pace of other organizational processes.

Internalized and pressing organizational rhythms limit the possibility of musing around the future, and invite the organization to think about it as a dynamic and palpable projection of the present. In other words, given the iterations between successive generations of products or projects, the future is not separated from the present, but is taken as the sequence and consequence of it. In this case, knowledge and action flow from one project to the next, and the future should not be understood as independent of the present. The future, in fact, is created through reflection-in-action, or the articulation between past knowledge and events, present circumstances, and imagined possibilities. The future, therefore, is the result of the integration of present-focused action and future-centered interaction.

Future-centred interactions involve a set of agents that will potentially help in devising open ways. These agents may be insiders or outsiders to the organization. Inside agents include people involved in contacts with customers (e.g., front-line employees, salesmen), R&D, project leaders, and other potential "vision-shapers." Outside agents may include futurists, lead users, and technology experts. All these agents may help the organization in its effort to make sense of the future. The future, thus, is not conceived as an abstraction, i.e. as something independent of present action, but as the outcome of multiple organizational interactions, some them taking place in the present and aiming to solve local and immediate problems, others trying to materialize a strategy, vision, or intent (see, e.g. Hamel and Prahalad, 1994).

The articulation between the past, present, and future, should then be thought of as reflection (e.g. strategic planning), but also as action (aimed at solving local problems), and reflection-in-action (making sense of the present, reflecting on how the past can be extrapolated to the future). Instead of exclusively focusing on the future, organizational foresight may thus be viewed as rooted in the capacity to understand how multiple time horizons interact and eventually merge, in the sense that every future is destined to become past. The importance of temporal articulation for the practice of foresight has been pointed out, for example, in Drucker's (1997) view of foresight as a synthesis of future and past. This merging of time horizons will be discussed in the next section, in order to explore its implications for organizational foresight.

## Time Travels: Foresight's Temporal Landscapes

Through action, organizations invent their futures. Invented futures are, as such, an outcome of the interaction between multiple time horizons: lessons from the past, possibilities of the present, and visions of the future. These time horizons are not easy to separate and distinguish. As indicated by Bradbury and Mainemelis (2001), the experience of organizational transformation involves elements of action and reflection in a dialectical relationship. People and organizations, through action and reflection, combine the past, present, and future – circulating from one to another. Organizational foresight may, as such, be viewed as time traveling. During time travels, every kind of combination between past, present, and future is possible. To grasp the complexities of foresight, then, is to understand how the invention of the future is a product of the combination of multiple temporal landscapes.

One of the potential contributions of the concepts of improvisation and emergence to the organizational foresight literature is to show how the separation of time, so common in the forecasting literature, may cause more harm than good. Improvisation, while taking place in the present, synthesizes time to plan and time to act (Crossan et al., 2002). It provides an example of how, as reflected in Table 8.1, past, present, and future may be intertwined in all possible combinations or "time travels." These temporal relationships, which operate within both foresight-as-prediction and foresight-as-invention paradigms, will be discussed next. Only brief sketches of each case will be presented for the purpose of illustration.

### Past to Past

Many organizational actions have taken place in the past and will not recur. Routines that were once useful may lose their value for several reasons. One of the more

**Table 8.1**  Travels in time: Foresight's temporal landscapes

| *Past* | | *Present* | *Future* |
|---|---|---|---|
| Past | Past-Past (e.g. Former practices) | Past-Present (e.g. Organizational memory) | Past-Future (e.g. Organizational retrieval) |
| *Present* | Present-Past (e.g. Declining practices) | Present-Present (e.g. Improvisations) | Present-Future (e.g. Planning) |
| *Future* | Future-Past (e.g. Intuition) | Future-Present (e.g. Scenario planning) | Future-Future (e.g. R&D) |

powerful reasons is the evolution of technology cycles, which may introduce significant changes in organizations and whole industries (Tushman and O'Reilly, 1997), rendering old routines obsolete. Episodic improvisations used for solving non-habitual problems may vanish once the problem is solved. Experimental behaviors may be forgotten because they have not worked well enough to be kept active. Thus, many organizational behaviors may simply "die" after having been used, either successfully or unsuccessfully (Cunha, Kamoche and Cunha, 2003).

## Past to Present

It is possible that some past behaviors may be transferred to the present. This process of transference may display both positive and negative effects. Some of these effects will be discussed in this "travel," which leads people to see the past in the present (Gilovich, 1981). This happens, for example, when a solution that worked well in the past is perceived as adequate for solving a current problem. Organizational knowledge is then stocked in memory and retrieved when necessary (Walsh and Ungson, 1991). Another influence of the past in the present is the development of experience-based interpretive schemas that inform individuals about how to act in a given circumstance (Ford, 1996).

Other effects of the past-present influence include the development of frames of thought and action. Frames of habitual thought and action narrow the range of likely behaviors in familiar organizational settings (Gioia and Poole, 1984). This tendency tends to be reinforced by the fact that schemas, once "validated" in the organizational or institutional contexts, are likely to be applied as standard procedures. The perception of competency that they entail may increase an organization's vulnerability to competency traps, with more experience with an inferior procedure leading to a growing desire to use it, instead of learning different and more adequate procedures (Levitt and March, 1988). This pervasive and harmful influence of previous knowledge on present results has also been documented by Miller's research on the Icarus paradox (e.g. Miller, 1990), or the over-commitment to known and tested courses of action.

## Past to Future

Some knowledge used in the past may be considered so valuable for a potential future that a proactive effort is made to keep it available in some form. In this case, knowledge was originally developed to deal with an existing problem. For one reason or another, this knowledge became unnecessary. For example, medical or technological advances may have rendered some knowledge or practices obsolete. The possibility, however, remains that they may be needed in the future. The eradication of a disease may render knowledge on it irrelevant. But a possible resurgence of the disease as a consequence of terrorist intentions or natural reasons may suggest the need to protect existing knowledge. In this case, organizations create ways to protect and encode such knowledge, in order to retrieve it if and when it should become necessary. Davenport and Prusak (1998) mention this practice as an instance of knowledge management.

## Present to Past

Some organizational practices may be taking place in the present, having already started their journey to the past. This may be due to obsolescence or organizational change. While making a present decision, managers may find themselves recalling a previous situation with similar characteristics (George, 2000) or returning to "tried and trusted" paths. Travels from the present to the past are often due to the fact that people who have successfully used a certain method are not likely to readily switch to another one. They tend to search out the roots of present decisions in past successes.

To make sense of the present, people often return to the past. The past provides experience, tested assumptions, and valuable learning. But it may also lead to errone-ous cause–effect associations, superstitious learning and illusory perceptions of psychological safety. The advantages of this "time travel," thus, may not be enough to ensure the quality of present decisions. It is this web of effects that led Schoemaker (1995) to say that looking at the past is a double-edged sword. Other examples of travels from present to past include the use of a discredited and passing organizational fad or fashion, or what has been called organizational nostalgia, a "time travel" that leads people to look for safe psychological havens in a golden past that contrasts with a less bright present. As Gabriel (1993) has remarked, nostalgia tells us more about today's discontents than about yesterday's contents.

## Present to Present

This corresponds to ongoing improvisation: an action is taken to solve a problem that is important and pressing enough to invite people to tackle it while it is occurring, and for which there is no established or tried solution. "Pure" improvisations are not taken with the intention of learning for the future, but simply for the sake of immediate problem solving (Cunha, Kamoche and Cunha, 2003). They exist in the present due to some present problem. Most of them will possibly be forgotten and travel back to the past. Practitioner-orientated literature is starting to explore some implications of this type of approach under such labels as real-time strategy (Bein-hocker and Kaplan, 2002) or just-in-time strategy (Bryan, 2002).

## Present to Future

Traditional foresight issues are concerned mainly with this case: how can an organiza-tion prepare for the future in the present? As discussed, the capacity to transfer the present to the future has been described as a distinguishing feature of the competent manager. This skill has received several names, such as planning or strategic intent: the art of anticipating the future in the present. Its benefits have been and still are vigorously presented by management scholars (e.g. Kim and Mauborgne, 2002). Planning, involving the systematic study of issues, may help organizations to make better, more informed decisions. As such, despite its limits, the practice of planning, more than the art of making plans, can be of enormous value to organizations. This does not preclude the possibility of making poor use of the planning process. Langley (1995) provides several examples of how the misuse of planning may lead to negative consequences, including the symptoms that the author aggregated under the label "paralysis by analysis" (e.g. paper fights and decision vacuums).

Other travels from present to future are identifiable. One is the situation that Weick (1993) described as *vu jadé*, which occurs when one is confronted, in the here and now, with a completely novel situation that transports him/her to what can be thought of, by analogy and through the collapse of previous knowledge, as an unknown and unimagined future. This instantaneous leap from the present to the future forces the person to make an extra effort of sensemaking, in order to comprehend what is going on in the present.

## Future to Past

Future-past traveling may occur when, while scanning possible futures, organizational foresight leads to situations of *déjà vu*: there is a pattern, whose contours are recognizable in advance. Time may elapse momentarily, with past and future becoming one and the same thing. Pattern recognition or previous experience is certainly important, because organizational cycles repeat. This is also why intuition is so valuable: it instantaneously blends a projected future with accumulated knowledge (e.g. Mintzberg and Westley, 2001). The tacit knowledge it rests upon is an important, but often ignored, ingredient of organizational foresight.

## Future to Present

This is a classic of time traveling. Ackoff (1981), for example, urged managers to be "future-oriented" by imagining the direction of the company and working backward from that future. Perhaps the best-known strategy for bringing the future into the present is scenario planning (e.g. Kleiner, 1994; Wack, 1985). In this case, the organization makes an effort to put itself in the future in the present. The effort may be more valuable for the learning that ensues than from the real capacity to anticipate what occurrences will materialize. It can depart from a future perfect (Rura-Polley et al., 2000) or from a multiple scenario approach, but the learning output is a fundamental part of the process. In the above-mentioned or any other forms, scenarios become one of the more prominent developments in the field of organizational foresight. They show how important the art of planning-in-reverse may be for traveling from the future to the present.

Another form of traveling from the future to the present is through "stimulational marketing," which refers to the creation of a positive demand for a product where none currently exists. The introduction of the pocket-sized transistor radio by Sony, provides a good illustration of stimulational marketing in action: the company imagined a product that did not exist at the time, and started to create demand for this through imagination. The initial users were Sony salesmen, whose shirts had pockets slightly larger than normal pockets. These were perfect to slip the "pocket-sized" radio into until technological advance allowed for the manufacture of truly pocketable radios (Varadarajan et al., 1992).

## Future to Future

Some organizational practices always have an eye on the future. In this sense, they are in the future looking for an even more distant future. This is the case of R&D activities. These are important for their long-term impacts, not for immediate consequences. Research activity, while cumulative and past-dependent, is always forward-looking. When an issue is solved, another will arise. R&D thus represents the future looking forward.

## Beyond Binary Time Travels

Organizations may actually be involved in more complex moments of temporal coordination than the above division suggests. This may occur, for example, when the three temporal sections are present at the same time. The use of learning histories, as discussed by Kleiner and Roth (1997), constitutes an example. Learning histories are written narratives of past critical episodes. These episodes are retrieved in order to help people move forward. This is expected to happen due to the uncovering of the underpinnings of a particular situation. In this case, people re-experience an event together, learn its meaning, and apply the lessons learned in forthcoming episodes. Learning histories are powerful learning processes because they allow time stretching. As noted by Tsoukas and Hatch (2001), narratives are temporally sensitive and allow multiple connections of events across time. They synthesize psychological time and clock time, accommodate multiple temporalities, introduce a component of "complication" that is absent from propositional thinking and connect what Weick and Roberts (1993) described as longer stretches of time. As these authors have noted, connections between the past, the present, and the future complicate the collective mind. If, as noted by Tsoukas and Hatch (2001, p. 1007), "our understandings of complex systems and their properties will always be grounded in the narratives we construct about them," narratives poor in temporality will not give rise to rich understandings of complex systems.

Examples of complicated time travels can be taken from Gioia and Chittipeddi (1991) and Isabella (1990). In their study of strategic change in a public university, Gioia and Chittipeddi concluded that the initiation of the change process involves both sensemaking (traveling to the past in order to ascribe meaning to relevant information) and sensegiving (traveling to the future on the wings of a vision derived from the previous process of sensemaking). These two processes took place in an iterative, sequential, and reciprocal fashion. Isabella's research on evolving interpretations of managers during a change process also contributes to an understanding of the role of temporal reflexivity. The author concluded that managers initially construed change analogically (by drawing on past experiences) and, as change unfolded, symbolically (their guide for the future being the symbols coming from senior management).

## Implications

The emergent nature of organizational environments, the inseparability of time horizons and the fallibility of human judgment provide a setting for the study of organizational foresight that differs significantly from that generally portrayed in the literature. Some implications, theoretical and managerial, arising from the perspective developed in this chapter, which is informed by the perspective of temporal reflexivity, are significant and will be briefly presented in this section.

A first implication is that the past is an inescapable presence in the present. Therefore, its influence needs to be explicitly managed, in order to avoid the organization repeating its actions over and over. The past provides experience and perhaps valuable learning. But when the past is taken too seriously, an organization risks becoming a prisoner of organizational memory and incurring single loop learning (Argyris, 1992; Moorman and Miner, 1998).

The risks of being trapped by the present are well captured in the cognitive phenomenon of availability bias. The availability bias (Tversky and Kahneman, 1973) suggests that people may attribute an excessive importance to available information simply because it is available. Given the difficulty of envisioning how the future may unfold, people may overemphasize what is going on in the present. Thus, the organization may make a certain decision not because it results from a reflected choice, but as the outcome of a process of cognitive overconfidence (Russo and Schoemaker, 1992).

Another implication has to do with the likely consequences of dreams of the future. It is certainly important for an organization to consider where it wants to go, or what vision it intends to enact. Beautiful visions of the future, however, should not distract the organization from the conditions of the present. Therefore, it is as important to prepare the future as to create conditions for aptly responding to the challenges of the present.

Several remedies have been proposed to deal with the problems discussed above. Most of them have to do with the need to develop time-mindful, complicated understandings (Bartunek et al., 1983; Cunha, Cunha and Cabral-Cardoso, forthcoming; Weick and Sutcliffe, 2001). Complicated understandings refer to the voluntary avoidance of automatic and mindless perspectives, through the analyses of an issue from multiple points of view. Means for developing complicated understandings that may contribute to avoiding time traps, include the distinction between experience and learning (observing that time breeds experience but not necessarily learning), considering that organizational memory is both friend and foe, not taking good old recipes as adequate for new situations, actively searching for potentially positive as well as negative consequences of strategic decisions, and taking visions as stimulus for action, not as pauses for reflection. These examples are nothing more than a sample of possibilities for avoiding the negative consequences of the inter-action between different temporal horizons. It should be noted, however, that it is as important to reap the positive consequences of temporal coordination as it is to avoid the negative ones.

## Conclusion

This chapter discussed organizational foresight as temporal reflexivity. The concepts of emergence, improvisation – a concept that takes emergence seriously – and temporal coordination, or the necessity to articulate the past, present, and future, have been related. Foresight was then presented as a field that deals with "time travels," more than with the "simple" anticipation of the shape of the future. By taking foresight as time traveling and accepting that sometimes it is necessary to look back to see ahead (Brown, 2001), an alternative view of foresight emerges: foresight as the need to understand how the past, present, and future interact, merge, and constrain each other. This perspective enriches the study of foresight by articulating reflection and action, prediction and comprehension, anticipation, and sensemaking. In this sense, the chapter contributes to the literature on the emergent side of organizing. This change in perspective does not mean that traditional approaches to foresight were wrong or that planning has become useless. In fact, recent empirical evidence suggests otherwise, i.e. that firms perceive a growing pressure to plan (Harris, 2001).

The foresight-as-time-travel perspective suggests that, as recent developments in the organizational sciences have pointed out, the path towards the future may be impossible to understand unless the exploration of the future is deeply rooted in past learning and present action. This chapter has offered a preliminary glimpse of a possible theoretical future through the reading of past research.

## NOTE

1 I am grateful to the participants in the session of the "Probing the Future" conference (Glasgow, July 11–13, 2002), where a preliminary version of this chapter was presented, for their valuable comments and suggestions. Support from *Instituto Nova Forum* is gratefully acknowledged.

## REFERENCES

Ackoff, R. (1970) *A Concept of Corporate Planning*, New York: Wiley.
Ackoff, R. (1981) *Creating the Corporate Future: Plan or Be Planned For*, New York: Wiley.

Ansoff, H. I. (1964) A quasi-analytical approach of the business strategy problem, *Management Technology*, 4(1), 67–77.

Argyris, C. (1992) *On organizational Learning*, Cambridge, MA: Blackwell.

Bandura, A. (2001) Social cognitive theory: An agentic perspective, *Annual Review of Psychology*, 52, 1–26.

Bartunek, J. M., Gordon, J. R., and Weathersby, R. P. (1983) Developing "complicated" understanding in administrators, *Academy of Management Review*, 8, 273–84.

Beckenstein, A. R. (1982) Forecasting and the environment: The challenges of rapid change. In S. Makridakis and S. C. Wheelwright (eds.), *Handbook of Forecasting. A Manager's Guide*, New York: Wiley, pp. 259–72.

Beinhocker, E. D. and Kaplan, S. (2002) Tired of strategic planning? *McKinsey Quarterly*, special issue, 49–57.

Bourgeois, L. J. and Eisenhardt, K. M. (1988) Strategic decision processes in high velocity environments: Four cases in the microcomputer industry, *Management Science*, 34, 816–35.

Bradbury, H. and Mainemelis, C. (2001) Learning history and organizational praxis, *Journal of Management Inquiry*, 10, 340–57.

Brown, S. (2001) *Marketing – The Retro Revolution*, London: Sage.

Brown, S. L. and Eisenhardt, K. (1997) The art of continuous change: Linking complexity theory and time-paced evolution in relentlessly shifting organizations, *Administrative Science Quarterly*, 42, 1–34.

Bryan, L. L. (2002) Just-in-time strategy for a turbulent world, *McKinsey Quarterly*, special issue, 17–27.

Calori, R. (2002) Organizational development and the ontology of creative dialectical evolution, *Organization*, 9, 127–50.

Crossan, M., Cunha, J. V., Vera, D., and Cunha, M. P. (2002) Time and organizational improvisation: Kairos meets Chronos, paper presented at the "Dynamic Time and Creative Inquiry in Organizational Change" Conference. Cape Ann, MA, June 18– 21.

Cunha, M. P., Cunha, J. V. and Cabral-Cardoso, C. (forthcoming) Looking for complication: Four approaches to management education, *Journal of Management Education*.

Cunha, M. P., Cunha, J. V. and Kamoche, K. (1999) Organizational improvisation: What, when, how and why, *International Journal of Management Reviews*, 1, 299–341.

Cunha, M. P., Kamoche, K. and Cunha, R. C. (2003). Organizational improvisation and leadership: A field study in two computer-mediated settings, *International Studies of Management and Organization*, 33(1), 34–57.

Davenport, T. and Prusak, L. (1998) *Working Knowledge*, Boston, MA: Harvard Business School Press.

Drucker, P. F. (1997) The future that has already happened, *Harvard Business Review*, 75(5), 20–4.

Eisenhardt, K. M. and Bhatia, M. H. (2002) Organizational complexity and computation. In J. A. C Baum (ed.), *Companion to Organizations*, Oxford: Blackwell, pp. 442–66.

Eisenhardt, K. M. and Martin, J. A. (2000) Dynamic capabilities: What are they? *Strategic Management Journal*, 21, 1105–21.

Fayol, H. (1949) *General and Industrial Management*, London: Pitman.

Fildes, R. (1982) Forecasting: The issues. In S. Makridakis and S. C. Wheelwright (eds.), *Handbook of Forecasting. A Manager's Guide*, New York: Wiley, pp. 83–104.

Fonseca, J. (2002) *Complexity and Innovation in Organizations*, London: Routledge.

Ford, C. (1996) A theory of individual creative action in multiple domains, *Academy of Management Review*, 21, 1112– 42.

Gabriel, Y (1993) Organizational nostalgia. In S. Fineman (ed.), *Emotion in Organizations*, London: Sage, pp. 118–41.

George, J. M. (2000) Emotions and leadership: The role of emotional intelligence, *Human Relations*, 53, 1027–55.

Giddens, A. (1984) *The Constitution of Society: Outline of a Theory of Structure*, Berkeley, CA: University of California Press.

Gilovich, J. (1981) Seeing the past in the present: The effect of associations to familiar events on judgments and decisions, *Journal of Personality and Social Psychology*, 40, 797– 808.

Gioia, D. A. and Chittipeddi, K. (1991) Sensemaking and sensegiving in strategic change initiation, *Strategic Management Journal*, 12, 433–48.

Gioia, D. A. and Poole, P. P. (1984) Scripts in organizational behavior, *Academy of Management Behavior*, 9, 449–59.

Godet, M. and Roubelat, F. (1996) Creating the future: The use and misuse of scenarios, *Long Range Planning*, 29(2), 164–71.

Hamel, G. and Prahalad, C. K. (1994) *Competing for the Future*, Boston, MA: Harvard Business School Press.

Harris, L. C. (2001) Getting professionals to plan: Pressures, obstacles and tactical responses, *Long Range Planning*, 33, 849–77.

Isabella, L. A. (1990) Evolving interpretations as a change unfolds: How managers construe organizational events, *Academy of Management Journal*, 33, 7–41.

Kanter, R. M. (2001) *Evolve. Succeeding in the Digital Culture of Tomorrow*, Boston, MA: Harvard Business School Press.

Kim, W. C. and Mauborgne, R. (2002) Charting your company's future, *Harvard Business Review*, June, 77–83.

Kleiner, A. (1994) Creating scenarios. In P. M. Senge, C. Roberts, R. Ross, B. Smith, and A. Kleiner (eds.), *The Fifth Discipline Fieldbook: Strategies and Tools for Building a Learning Organization*, New York: Currency/Doubleday.

Kleiner, A. and Roth, G. (1997) How to make experience your company's best teacher, *Harvard Business Review*, 75(5), 172–77.

Laermer, R. (2001) *Trendspotting: Think Forward, Get Ahead, and Cash in on the Future*, New York: Perigee.

Langley, A. (1995) Between "paralysis by analysis" and "extinction by instinct," *Sloan Management Review*, Spring, 63–76.

Levitt, B. and March, J. G. (1988) Organizational learning, *Annual Review of Psychology*, 14, 319–40.

Lovas, B. and Ghoshal, S. (2000) Strategy as guided evolution, *Strategic Management Journal*, 21, 875–96.

Makridakis, S. and Wheelwright, S. C. (eds.) (1982a) *Handbook of Forecasting. A Manager's Guide*, New York: Wiley.

Makridakis, S. and Wheelwright, S. C. (1982b) Introduction to management forecasting: Status and needs. In S. Makridakis and S. C. Wheelwright (eds.), *Handbook of Forecasting. A Manager's Guide*, New York: Wiley, pp. 3–12.

Miller, D. (1990) *The Icarus Paradox: How Exceptional Companies Bring About Their Own Fall*, HarperCollins: New York.

Miner, A. S., Bassoff, P., and Moorman, C. (2001) Organizational improvisation and learning: A field study, *Administrative Science Quarterly*, 46, 304–37.

Mintzberg, H. (1994) *The Rise and Fall of Strategic Planning*, Hemel Hempstead: Prentice-Hall.

Mintzberg, H. and Westley, F. (2001) Decision making: It's not what you think, *Sloan Management Review*, 42(3), 89–93.

Moorman, C. and Miner, A. (1998) The convergence between planning and execution: Improvisation in new product development, *Journal of Marketing*, 62, 1–20.

O'Shea, A. (2002) The (r)evolution of new product innovation, *Organization*, 9, 113–25.

Orlikowski, W. J. and Yates, J. (2002) It's about time: Temporal structuring in organizations, *Organization Science*, 13, 684–700.

Pascale, R. T. (1990) *Managing on the Edge*, London: Penguin.

Perrow, C. (1984) *Normal Accidents: Living with High Risk Technologies*, New York: Basic Books.

Rura-Polley, T., Pitsis, T., and Clegg, S. R. (2000) Future perfect tense?, paper presented at the Academy of Management Meeting, Toronto.

Russo, J. E. and Schoemaker, P. J. H. (1992) Managing overconfidence, *Sloan Management Review*, Winter, 7–17.

Schoemaker, P. J. H. (1995) Strategic planning: A tool for strategic thinking, *Sloan Management Review*, Winter, 25–40.

Stacey, R. D. (1996) *Strategic Management and Organisational Dynamics*, 2nd edn., London: Pitman.

Szulanski, G. and Amin, K. (2001) Learning to make strategy: Balancing discipline and imagination, *Long Range Planning*, 34, 537–56.

Thiétart, R.A. and Forgues, B. (1997) Action, structure and chaos, *Organization Studies*, 18, 119–43.

Tsoukas, H. and Chia, R. (2002) On organizational becoming: Rethinking organizational change, *Organization Science*, 13, 567–82.

Tsoukas, H. and Hatch, M. J. (2001) Complex thinking, complex practice: The case for a narrative approach to organizational complexity, *Human Relations*, 54, 979–1013.

Tushman, M. L. and O'Reilly, C. A. (1997) *Winning Through Innovation*, Boston. MA: Harvard Business School Press.

Tversky, A. and Kahneman, D. (1973) Availability, A heuristic for judging frequency and probability, *Cognitive Psychology*, 5, 207–32.

Varadarajan, P. R., Clark, T., and Pride, W. M. (1992) Controling the uncontrollable: Managing your market environment, *Sloan Management Review*, Winter, 39–47.

Wack, P. (1985) Scenarios: Uncharted waters ahead, *Harvard Business Review*, 64(1), 72–89.

Walsh, J. P. and Ungson, G. R. (1991) Organizational memory, *Academy of Management Review*, 16, 578–91.

Weick, K. E. (1990) Cartographic myths in organizations. In A. S. Huff (ed.), *Mapping Strategic Thought*, New York: Wiley, pp. 1–10.

Weick, K. E. (1993) The collapse of sensemaking in organizations: The Mann Gulch disaster, *Administrative Science Quarterly*, 38, 628–52.

Weick, K. E. and Roberts, K. H. (1993) Collective mind in organizations: Heedful interrelating on flight decks, *Administrative Science Quarterly*, 38, 357–81.

Weick, K. E. and Sutcliffe, K. M. (2001) *Managing the Unexpected*, San Francisco: Jossey Bass.

# Chapter Nine

# The Concept of "Weak Signals" Revisited: A Re-description From a Constructivist Perspective

*David Seidl*

## Introduction

Scanning the environment for potential threats and opportunities is one of the most important occupations of contemporary organizations. Organizations try to register threats and opportunities as early as possible in order to be able to react to them in time. However, often it isn't even enough to register threats and opportunities when they actually arise, but they have to be foreseen, in order for the organization to have enough time to react. This ability to foresee developments becomes more and more important in a time in which the speed with which changes occur is increasing while, simultaneously, the time necessary for reaction is increasing. In this sense, the viability of an organization depends to a great extent on its ability to *foresee* future events.

How can we conceptualize this ability to foresee future events? The classical answer to this question is that organizations can register *other* events that *indicate* future events. Ansoff (1975, 1976, 1980, 1984) speaks of so-called "weak signals" which point to "strategic discontinuities." From this perspective organizations possess the ability for strategic foresight to the extent that they are able to receive, interpret, and act on such weak signals. In this chapter we revisit this classical notion of "weak signals," as it still offers an interesting perspective. Yet, in its original form it rests on naive epistemological assumptions, according to which cognitions are conceptualized as direct representations of the external world. By slightly modifying the concept, however, we can put it on a more sophisticated epistemological foundation. We try to demonstrate how the concept can be re-described from the perspective of a (radically) constructivist framework, which assumes that the world as one sees it is entirely one's own construction. On this basis, strategic foresight wouldn't be directed at the development of the environment, but at the development of one's *constructions* of it. Weak signals accordingly would have to be conceptualized as experiences with one's current constructions, which in some way or other point at future problems.

The chapter is organized in five sections. We first elaborate on the concept of weak signals as it can be found in the literature. We aim at portraying and explaining the logic of the ideas *as they are presented there*. In the second part we focus on the epistemological assumptions made in the literature showing their limitations and fallacies. In the third part we will present the central elements of our (radically) constructivist framework. This will serve as a background against which we then try to *re-describe* the concept of weak signals. In the last section we will illustrate our argument with two examples of organizational features that could contribute to strategic foresight.

### The Concepts of "Strategic Discontinuity," "Strategic Surprise," and "Weak Signals"

One of the first and most important contributions to the conceptualization of strategic foresight came from Igor Ansoff (1975, 1976, 1980, 1984).[1] He argued that the traditional forms of forecasting, which are heavily based on "historically familiar raw data," failed in face of strategic discontinuities in the development of the environment. Organizations were caught unawares by such discontinuities and were thus faced with strategic surprises. Strategic surprises, he defined, are "sudden, urgent, unfamiliar changes in the firm's perspective which threaten either a major profit reversal or loss of a major opportunity" (Ansoff, 1976, p. 131). Ansoff argued that the probability of such strategic surprises could be minimized if the available information was properly made use of. In other words even a strategic discontinuity could be foreseen so "that by the time it strikes, [it] has lost its suddenness, urgency and unfamiliarity" (1976, p. 131) – and in this way would not constitute a surprise.

Ansoff gives the example of the "petroleum crises" of the 1970s, which confronted most firms with a major discontinuity. These crises had caught even large and important firms completely unawares. This discontinuity, though, could have been foreseen, as there had been many signals that had pointed at them. However, these signals had not been properly taken notice of. Reports on Arab action had been publicly available long before the events and had even found their way onto the desks of those managers who were later on surprised by the events. Such information, however, wasn't acted upon, as it constituted what Ansoff calls "weak signals" – in contrast to "strong signals." A signal is weak if its information content is unstructured, ambiguous, and unclear. In concrete terms this means that the signal is not "adequate for estimating the impact on the firm, for identifying specific responses, and for estimating the potential profit [or performance] impact of these responses" (Ansoff, 1976, p. 133). Thus, what can be said so far is that in advance of strategic discontinuities there usually exists information in the environment that makes it possible in principle to foresee the discontinuity. This information, however, is normally not really picked up and put to good use, as it doesn't fit the standard structures of information processing.

Ansoff (1976) argues that organizations would be able to foresee many strategic discontinuities, if their modes of information processing were compatible with a systematic analysis of weak signals. In order to better understand his concept of weak signals we have to differentiate between organizational and environmental phenomena. The (strategic) discontinuity takes place in the *environment*; the qualification as "strategic," however, refers to the *organization*. That is to say, the discontinuity is strategic with regard to its implications for the *organization*. Discontinuities, Ansoff argues, are usually preceded by other *environmental* events that are (directly or indirectly)[2] causally connected with (the possibility of) later discontinuities. If an *organization* observed these events and understood their (direct or indirect) causal relation properly, it could foresee the (potential) later discontinuity. In this sense the preceding environmental event is conceptualized as a "signal" for (potential) discontinuities, which merely has to be picked up. The signal can be said to be weak to the extent that the *organization* cannot deduce a picture of the future discontinuity that is clear enough for taking decisive action.[3]

In Figure 9.1 we have represented the argument graphically. On the one side we have organizational and on the other environmental phenomena. We start with the environment side. First we have an event X – the preceding event – taking place in time t = 1. This event is *causally* connected to a *later* event Y – the environmental discontinuity – taking place in time t = 2. In time t = 1 the organization notices the event in its environment. In this sense we have on the organization side an information about the occurrence of event X in t = 1 – formally: $I_{(t=1) X}$. This information about event X is *at the same time* interpreted as information about an (impending) environmental event Y. Thus, in time t = 1 we can distinguish *two* information values: information about the occurrence of event X – formally: $I_{(t=1) X}$ – *and* information about the (more or less probable) future occurrence of event Y in time t = 2 – formally: $I_{(t=1) Y}$.

There are two possible reasons for the weakness of a signal: an environmental one (having to do with the causal connection between X and Y; see straight arrow on the right hand side in Figure 9.1) and an organizational one (having to do with the interpretation of the information about the occurrence of X; see straight arrow on the left hand side in Figure 9.1). In the first case the preceding event is only *weakly* connected to the later discontinuity; or in Weick's words (Orton and Weick, 1990): the preceding event and the discontinuity are only loosely coupled. That is to say, the preceding event is likely to be, but *not necessarily,* followed by the discontinuity (cf. e.g. Berg, 1979, p. 136). In the second case there may be a strong connection between

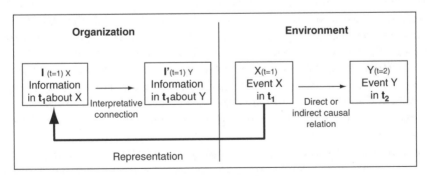

**Figure 9.1**   The relation between actual event and internal representation

preceding event and later discontinuity, but the organization doesn't *see* the strong connection (cf. e.g. Kirsch, 1997a, pp. 52ff). Both cases are usually considered when discussing possibilities for making better use of weak signals for forecasting.

We start with the environmental side of the issue.[4] A single event might be only weakly connected to a later discontinuity. However, as time proceeds usually further events will take place which either *themselves*, or *in combination* with the other events, are more strongly connected to the impending discontinuity. We take Ansoff's example of the petroleum crises. The initial talks between some Arab oil producing countries, in which they discussed vague ideas on concerted actions, were only weakly linked to the later oil crises. But as time proceeded and the talks became more concrete, the stronger they were connected to the impending crises. For the organization this means that the closer it gets to the discontinuity, the more events can be observed that – on their own or together with other events – are progressively more strongly connected to the discontinuity. On the basis of this part of the argument an organization would possess strategic foresight to the extent that the registration of a weakly linked event – i.e. the reception of a weak signal – stimulates an "environmental awareness" (Ansoff, 1976) with regard to possible other events pointing in the same direction. The registration of a weak signal would have to trigger efforts at monitoring particular aspects of the environment in contrast to a mere unfocused scanning (Liebl, 1994; Krystek and Müller-Stewens, 1993, pp. 175ff). For example, when the organizations registered the first talks between the oil producing countries, they would have had to be alert to further Arab interactions. In this way they would have increased the chances of registering later events that were strongly linked to the impending crises, i.e. events that could have been interpreted as (relatively) stronger signals; e.g. a meeting in which a binding decision on concerted action was made. An environmental awareness on its own, however, might not be enough where no qualitatively different events take place, i.e. if all preceding events *on their own* are only weakly linked to the impending crisis. In such a case the organization would also have to be able to see the different events *in relation* to each other. While the different events on their own might be only weakly linked, the events taken together might be strongly linked to the impending crises.

On the other side, a signal may be weak because the organization does not see the (existing) strong connection between the preceding event and the ensuing discontinuity. Thus the organization increases its ability of strategic foresight by optimizing its mode of information processing alone. There are first of all the classical information pathologies or intelligence failures – one can distinguish between structural, psychological, and doctrinal failures (Kirsch, 1997a; Kirsch and Klein, 1977; Kirsch and Trux 1978, 1983; Wilensky, 1967) – which might impede the extraction of all the, in principle, available, relevant information from an observed (preceding) event. Due to these failures weak signals are either not properly registered or not passed on to the relevant people or positions. To improve the ability of strategic foresight would mean minimizing such failures.

The most important events in an organization's environment are *social* events. In order to understand how social events are connected to each other and what social events are likely to follow each other, one has to understand the meaning of these events. These social events can be interpreted by organizations as signals to the extent that the organization can interpret their meaning and thus their reference to, and in this sense, connection with, later social events. These signals are weak to the extent that the organization attributes merely an ambiguous or unclear meaning to these events. Kirsch (1997a, pp. 52ff.) argues that the weakness of a signal might have something to do with the *context* in which the signal is received. He explains that a person (in the environment of the organization) may communicate a message in a specific, well-defined communicative context, in which the information value of that message is clearly defined. For another person (in the organization), however, the information value of that message becomes ambiguous and unclear, if he interprets it in a different, incompatible context. For example, the message contained in a statement of a diplomat may seem ambiguous or unclear unless one interprets it according to the "codes" of diplomatic speech. In this sense, the message (as environmental event) might be strictly coupled to an impending discontinuity, but the organization sees only a weak connection, since the context in which it puts the message (i.e. the observed event) differs from the original context in which it has taken place. In other words, the signal may be weak, because the context of the recipient does not match the one of the sender. The signal, however, might also be weak in the sense that one does not know in which context to put it (Kirsch, 1997a, pp. 56ff.). One might possess many different contexts in which the message has different meanings. The signal thus seems ambiguous.[5] Kirsch (Kirsch, 1997a, pp. 56ff.; Kirsch and Trux, 1979, p. 54) argues that one can never know for sure whether one is using the right context for one's interpretation. Because of that it might be rational to try out different contexts when analysing signals.

So far we have described the environmental and the organizational side to the problem of weak signals. In both cases the ability of strategic foresight ultimately would mean to get *systematically* and *quickly* from a weak signal to a strong signal. However, the mechanisms for that are somewhat different. In the first case the signal can be made stronger only by monitoring the environment for *other* events and relating the observations to each other. In the second case the (initially weak) signal itself can be made stronger through the way it is processed as information.

Apart from the mechanisms for dealing with weak signals that have been received by the organization, the ability of strategic foresight has also something to do with the ability to register (weak) signals at all. Generally, the better (both quantitatively and qualitatively) an organization is able to register relevant events the better its ability to foresee strategic discontinuities. What is suggested is a comprehensive scanning and issue-related monitoring of the environment (Krystek and Müller, 1993, pp. 175ff.). Kirsch and Trux (1979, p. 60) in this sense write that this usually means an increase in the number of "sensors" or "probes": "If one wants to receive weak signals, one usually has to increase the 'surface' for reception and one has to make sure that every point on the surface is connected to the information center" (my translation).

So far our description of the concept of strategic foresight has been based on the existing literature on this topic. We have tried to explain the logic of the ideas *as they are presented there*. In the following, however, we want to critically analyze the underlying epistemological assumptions.

## The Epistemological Assumptions of Ansoff's Concept of Weak Signals

Ansoff's classical concept of weak signals and the literature it sparked rests on particular epistemological assumptions. These are not explicitly stated but can be clearly reconstructed from most of the texts. What we find is a fairly naive representationalist belief. Cognitions are conceptualized as direct representations of the outside world; outside "reality" and internal cognitions are perceived as directly related. According to this view the only two relevant questions, then, are:

1  Is something that exists in the outside world also represented in the cognitive system? and
2  If it is represented, is it a true representation?

Along these lines the literature on weak signals is primarily focused on whether signaling events in the environment are represented in the cognitive system – and in the right places, as it were. And furthermore, if so, are they represented in the right way, i.e. are they understood as signals for (potential) impending strategic discontinuities. This view, however, is naive and contradicts most of what is common knowledge about the essentially constructed nature of our cognitions. This does not, of course, mean that there is not anything beyond cognitions, but merely that there is no direct correspondence or "pairing off" between cognitions and "chunks of reality." As Tsoukas (2000, p. 533), based on Rorty (1991; 1989), writes, "the world causes us to have beliefs, but it cannot tell us what to believe." It is ultimately the cognitive system that determines what it makes of the outside world and there is no way of comparing the cognitions with the outside world as such – as it would presuppose for the cognitions to get beyond the cognitive domain. A theoretically sound study of foresight thus would have to deal with the problem that a cognitive system has no access to any reality beyond its own cognitions. Ultimately it would have to deal with the relation of cognitions to each other rather than with relations between cognitions and any reality beyond (cf. Tsoukas, 2000). Going back to Figure 9.1 the problem rests in the large arrow connecting organization and environment: Weak signals do not exist as such in the outside environment waiting to be picked up by the (members of the) organization. Rather they have to be conceptualized cognitively, i.e. as cognitive phenomena, determined by the structures of the cognitive system.

## A (Radically) Constructivist Framework

In the following section we present a constructivist framework based on insights from new systems theory – in particular: Luhmann's version of autopoiesis theory. This framework will then serve us as a background for a re-description of the original concept of weak signals.

According to autopoiesis theory cognitive systems have to be conceptualized as *operatively closed* systems that reproduce their cognitions in a *self-referential* manner

(Maturana and Varela, 1980; 1992 Luhmann, 1990b; 1993; 1995; Von Foerster, 1981; see also Von Krogh et al., 1994; Von Krogh and Roos, 1995). That is to say, the cognitions (i.e. the operations) of a cognitive system can neither get out of the cognitive system nor can anything outside the cognitive system enter into it and become a cognition – in this sense the system is said to be *operatively* closed. If we, for example, take the psychic system as a system consisting of thoughts, we can say that the system is operatively closed as no thought can leave the psychic system and enter into the environment; nor can anything outside the system enter into the psychic system and become a thought. Rather than coming from outside the system, the cognitions of a cognitive system are self-referentially produced through the inter- action of the cognitions in the system. Thus, what thoughts are thought at a concrete moment depends on the thoughts and thought processes that are already in place. In other words, thoughts are produced in the interaction of the cognitive system with itself. Consequently, in order to understand concrete thought operations, one has to focus on the internal interactions between thought operations – and not on the outside world.

The internal interactions between the operations of a cognitive system are usually guided by cognitive *structures*, e.g. cognitive schemata and scripts. These structures determine what cognitions can connect with, or lead to, what other cognitions. The important point, however, is that these structures are themselves a product of cognitive operations. The cognitive processes bring forth the cognitive structures, which then are recursively reproduced. Von Foerster (1981, pp. 304–5; 1993), in this sense, speaks of a second closure of a cognitive system – in addition to the operative closure – on the level of its structures: not only are the operations closed off from the environment, but also so are the structures. In other words, cognitive structures must not be understood as imported from the environment of the cognitive system, but as its own constructs developed in the interaction of its operations with themselves. For example, the recurrent occurrence of certain new thought processes might lead to the establishment of new thought structures. This double closure for the cognitive system means that it has no point of reference for its operations other than its *own* operations and structures.

Speaking of double closure of cognitive systems, however, is not to deny the relevance or even existence of the environment – as Luhmann (1993, p. 40) says: "There is no doubt that an external environment exists" (my translation). Operative closure does not mean that the environment does not have an impact on the cognitive system; it rather means that how environmental events affect the cognitive processes is determined by the system itself (its structures and processes). Cognitive systems interact with their environments, but it is the cognitive system – and not the environment – that determines how and in what way it interacts. The environment can merely (negatively) restrict the possibilities of interaction but cannot itself (positively) select them.

Against this background one cannot speak of cognitions being more or less true or correct. Instead, cognitions (or better cognitive structures) can only be said to be more or less *viable*; i.e. they either work or they do not. This again is not determined by the outside world as such, but by other cognitions and cognitive structures within the system. In other words, cognitive structures are viable if they can be sustained within the context of other cognitive processes. If a cognitive structure is in conflict with other cognitive structures, paralyzing the cognitive processes, it becomes non-viable and needs to be changed.

Luhmann (1986; 1995) argues that social systems, analogously to psychic systems, can be conceptualized as operatively closed systems, which construct their environment in a self-referential manner. Their operations are not, however, thoughts as in the case of psychic systems but communications. Social systems are conceptualized as networks of "communications, which are recursively produced and reproduced by the network of communications and which cannot exist outside of such a network" (Luhmann, 1986, p. 174). These communications are the "cognitions" of the social system. That is to say, in the same way as psychic systems construct their world in the form of thoughts, social systems construct their world in the form of communications. Due to their operative closure – i.e. what communications come about is determined by the network of communications and not from outside – a social system has no other point of reference for judging its communications than other communications.[6] For example, if an organization (as a type of social system) wants to review its strategy (conceptualized as a specific communication structure), it can only compare it with other communications (or communication structures) in the organization, for example, its financial report. Like the psychic system a social system has no possibility of judging the correspondence of its communications with anything outside its communications, as that would require communications to get beyond the domain of communications. Ultimately a social system can only communicate about its communications and it depends on these communications what other communications come about.

Social systems are not only closed with regard to operations other than communications, but they are also closed with regard to the communications of *other* social systems (Luhmann, 1995). For example, an organization clearly distinguishes between its own communications (in particular its own decision communications)[7] and those of other organizations; a decision of another organization will never become a decision of the own organization. Unless a social system communicates about the communication of another system – in other words, unless it produces its *own* communication about the communication of another system – the communication of the other system is irrelevant for it. That is to say, communications in other systems have no significance for a particular system, if they do not trigger communications in that system. Whether, and what kind of, communications are triggered in a particular system by external communications is determined entirely by the system itself.

According to Luhmann (1995, chapter 8) the (communication) structures of social systems can be conceptualized as expectations. They are expectations about what communications can come about and what communications can connect with what other communications. For example, a hierarchy in an organization is an expectation about what types of communication are communicated between what types of position; and strategies are expectations about how to communicate about the competitive environment and what types of decision are to be communicated.

So far we have explained our constructivist framework. What should have become clear is that psychic systems as well as social systems are operatively closed; they can only construct their environment in the form of their own operations (thoughts or communications), which they can only judge in relation to their own operations (thoughts or communications).

This proposed understanding of organizations as "cognitive" systems, which process communications, has affinities with the conceptualization of organizations as inquiring systems suggested by Churchman (1971), Mason and Mitroff (1981), and others. In this sense Luhmann (2000, p. 57) writes: "All operations of the system [organization] are operations of information processing" (my translation). Some authors (e.g. Courtney, 2001, p. 25) have suggested that the fundamental self-referentiality and operative closure expressed by autopoiesis theory resemble the Leibnizian inquirer (Churchman, 1971, pp. 34–5). This is true to the extent that in autopoiesis theory *internal* consistency/inconsistency is the only criterion for evaluating the information produced. It is, however, wrong to the extent that autopoiesis theory does not deny the influence of the environment on the internal processes. Autopoietic systems are not completely self-contained, but reproduce themselves *in (self-determined) interaction* with their environment. In this sense, autopoiesis theory has also been classified by some authors (Courtney et al., 1998) as describing a Lockean inquirer (Churchman, 1991, pp. 126–7). Ultimately however, autopoiesis theory is compatible with all of Churchman's five types of inquirer. Based on an understanding of organizations as autopoietic systems, Leibnizian, Lockean, Kantian, Hegelian and Singerian organizations would be conceptualized as different types of *structurings* of an organization. In this sense, the same autopoietic organization might change from a "formal, highly structured, rigidly organized, and strictly operated" one, representing the Leibnizian organization (Courtney et al., 1998) to one that encourages debate between opposing views, displays dialectical planning systems (Mason, 1969) and the like, representing the Hegelian organization. Thus, we have to distinguish between on the one hand, the conceptualization of organizations as autopoietic systems reproducing themselves self-referentially; and, on the other hand, the concrete form in which the self-reproduction is structured. In the following section we focus on the former and discuss the consequences of it for conceptualising strategic foresight.

## A Re-description of the Concept of Weak Signals From a (Radically) Constructivist Perspective

On the basis of our (radically) constructivist framework one is inclined to argue that strategic foresight or foresight in general is impossible. If a cognitive system, be it a psychic or social system, cannot "see" the world as it is – but can only produce its own constructions of it – it can of course neither fore-see it. Any effort at foreseeing future events ultimately would just produce a construction of the future; of which one could not even say whether it were true or false, once the future has become the present. In this respect Ansoff's concept of foresight with its focus on the observation of *environmental* events seems completely inadequate. The strategic discontinuities in the environment would be something the organization has no cognitive access to; organizations could not even tell whether certain strategic events have taken place or not. An organization could even less observe the events preceding the strategic discontinuities.

From our constructivist perspective strategic foresight might seem not only impossible but also unnecessary. We have argued that social systems consist of communications that reproduce communications and that, furthermore, that it is the communications – not the environment – that determine whether and how the system is reproduced.[8] Thus, predicting the development of the external environment seems unnecessary as the system itself determines what role the environment plays in its communications. And even if certain ways of communication became impossible due to changes in the environment, the system just had to change its structures of communication – in other words it, just had to communicate about something else.

These two arguments about foresight being impossible and unnecessary are both correct and incorrect. It is correct that it is unnecessary for an organization – even if possible – to know exactly what events will take place in its external environment, as the organization is self-determined and not determined by its external environment. This, however, does not mean that an organization is completely in control of itself (i.e. its communications) and could deliberately change its structures. Rather, an organization can only change its (communication) structures on the basis of its existing structures. In other words, the existing structures have to be used as the basis for changing the structures of the organization and in this sense they determine the possibilities of change. Thus, if the existing communication structures became non-viable – due to whatever reasons – they could paralyze any communication processes; even those communication processes that could change these structures. As a result the entire communication system would be destroyed – in the sense of not being reproduced anymore. Thus, foreseeing future paralyzing situations at a time when the organization is still able to act (i.e., communicate) could be of vital importance for its survival.

The other argument is also both correct and incorrect. It is true that it is impossible to foresee events in the external environment and that Ansoff's idea of foresight in this respect is impossible. Nevertheless, foresight is not impossible with regard to the *constructions* of the environment. In other words, organizations might not be able to foresee developments in the environment, but they might be able to foresee the development of their own constructions of it. This is true, first of all, in a very simple sense: organizations possess structures (conceptualized as expectations) that determine what communication processes come about. Thus, structures *by definition* express expectations about future communications. However, foresight, as we will argue, is also possible in a more sophisticated way. Organizations cannot only foresee in terms of their own structures, but they can – under certain conditions – also foresee future failures of their own structures. In other words, they can know in advance that their own structures might become non-viable and have to be exchanged. Thus, in contrast to Ansoff's concept, foresight would not be conceptualized as knowledge about discontinuities in the external environment, but about (structural) discontinuities in the development of the internal communications (about it).

In the following we want to have a closer look at these internal discontinuities. Communication structures become non-viable, as we said above, if they do not fit into the network of other communications and communication structures. Such inconsistencies can exist between a structure and a concrete communication or between one structure and another structure. In the first case for example, a plan (i.e. structure) to increase the market share by lowering the price for one's products might be inconsistent with the feedback from the marketing department that their figures show a drop in market share since the introduction of that measure. This inconsistency might just be ignored – which is often the case – or the plan might be changed to remove the inconsistency. In the second case, for example, the plan to increase the market share through pricing policy might be inconsistent with the quality management policy. This inconsistency might be ignored, for example, by selectively highlighting one of the structures in a concrete situation; or the structure(s) might simply be changed.

Inconsistencies in organizations are nothing extraordinary and removing them is part of their daily business. There are however, as we noted above, inconsistencies of different degrees. Some inconsistencies are more or less insignificant and might be easily removed or even safely ignored. Other ones again might be substantial in that they might lead to paralysis and in this way threaten the survival of the organization. These major inconsistencies resemble very much Ansoff's "strategic" discontinuities. Such inconsistencies cannot just be removed by changing one of the structures, but rather require a readjustment of the *entire* system. For example, a company that (communicatively) describes itself as specialized in producing and selling record players cannot react to the report that it has no customers – as records are not being produced anymore – by simply changing its pricing policy. The organization rather has to readjust the entire system. This type of overall change has been described in the literature as second-order change or double-loop learning (Argyris, 1992; Argyris and Schön, 1978; Bateson, 1972; Grinyer and Spender, 1979; Watzlawick et al., 1974). In this sense, a strategic inconsistency could be conceptualized as one that requires second-order change or double-loop learning. For the organization, conceptualized as a system of communications, this means the organization has to communicate about the coherence of its structuring and realign itself. Such fundamental change, however, might not be possible anymore when the inconsistency finally has been openly experienced, as we argued above. In order to avert the threat of such inconsistencies, organizations might thus have to try to foresee them.

Based on the above arguments, foresight would have to be conceptualized as the communication about strategic inconsistencies already before they have become so prominent that they threaten to paralyze the organizational communication processes. In analogy to Ansoff's original idea one could argue that there might be some weak signals that could point at the strategic inconsistency. But what could they be? Ultimately these weak signals would have to be conceptualized themselves as inconsistencies. They would be inconsistencies that, first, appear fairly insignificant, in the sense that they could easily be removed or even ignored without direct consequences; and which, second, have something to do with structures or relations of structures that might lead to the experience of a strategic inconsistency. In other words, while the initial inconsistencies themselves just call for a "local" readjustment of structures, a proper analysis of the inconsistencies would lead to a reconsideration of the structuring of the system as a whole.

Analogously to our analysis in the first section, we can distinguish two reasons for the weakness of the signal. First, it could either be the case that the initial inconsistency is only weakly linked to a later strategic inconsistency – in the sense that the strategic inconsistency *might* follow, but *does not necessarily* follow. For example, the initial non-strategic inconsistency could indicate that *if* similar situations took place, the same inconsistency might be experienced again, which then might not so easily be removable. In other words, the initial inconsistency is only weakly linked, as it is not certain that a similar situation will recur, where first-order change is not enough. For example, an inconsistency between the production plan and the sales figures (as two communications) might initially be solvable by a change of the pricing policy (as another communication). If the inconsistency, however, is experienced repeatedly the pricing policy might not solve the inconsistency any more. Instead the organization might have to reconsider its entire business model.

A foresightful reaction to any experience of inconsistency would be the reflection on the structuring of the organization as a whole. The organization would have to analyze how likely it is that the same situation arises again and how likely it is that single-order change would not be enough. Analogously to Ansoff's idea of environmental scanning and monitoring, the experience of the initial inconsistency would have to lead to a scanning and monitoring of the *organizational communications* for similar situations. If the organization, for example, finds out that the same inconsistency is repeatedly experienced, it is a strong signal that at some point the inconsistency might require second-order change. This would give the organization the chance to start the second order change initiative in time. In our example of the producer of record players, we could imagine that in one part of the organization one might experience an inconsistency between the production plan for a particular type of record player and the falling sales figures. This inconsistency might lead to first-order change efforts; for example, change of price or quality policies. The same inconsistencies might, however, also turn up with regard to other types of record players. At some point these inconsistencies would not be solvable with first-order change, but would require a review of the entire business model. As a result the organization might change from a producer of record players, for example, to a producer of CD players. The earlier the organization registered the recurrence of the same inconsistency, the earlier it could reconsider its general business model.

A second reason for the weakness of the signal might be that the connection between the initial inconsistency and a later strategic inconsistency might be strong but is just not seen as such. This might be the case if the initially experienced inconsistency was the result of another more fundamental inconsistency that is not clearly seen. For example, there might be a contradiction in the corporate strategy which – in modified form – is experienced in a concrete situation as fairly insignificant inconsistency. As the real (source of the) inconsistency is not clearly seen, the organization would normally either ignore the inconsistency or react with merely first-order change, leaving the "real" inconsistency in place. This inconsistency might then pop up at some later stage, where it is openly experienced as *strategic* inconsistency, forcing the organization to second-order change. In this case the organization would be foresightful if it was able to analyze the initial inconsistency properly and so understood its strategic nature. An example for such a situation can be found in Osborn and Ashforth (1990). They describe a nuclear power plant that exhibited two inconsistent self-descriptions, or two inherently different logics (structures) of communication: on the one hand, as "efficient provider" and, on the other, as "safe provider." The inherent inconsistency between the two structures surfaced in different decision situations, but its strategic relevance was not seen. The reaction to it was a "glossing over" of the inconsistency. This, of course, did not remove the inconsistency. Rather, one could expect it to become manifest again at a later stage, where it will force a reconsideration of the overall identity. By taking the inconsistency seriously in the first place, the necessity of a second-order change could have been foreseen.

Ultimately, foresight in both cases of weak signals requires an analysis of experienced inconsistencies against the background of the structuring of the organization as a whole. In other words, an organization is foresightful to the extent that "local" inconsistencies are reflected in their relevance for the structuring of the organization as a whole and are not merely dealt with in the context of the requirements of the immediate situation only. However, in order to become foresightful, it is not enough to deal with the inconsistencies that have been experienced, it might be necessary to actively search for the inconsistencies in the first place. In other words, one would have to stimulate situations in which potential inconsistencies might surface. In analogy to the environmental scanning described above, this could be described as scanning of the organization for inconsistencies.

## Examples of Foresightful Structuring

In the following we want to describe some exemplary[9] organizational characteristics that increase an organization's ability of foresight by increasing the chance for "local" inconsistencies to be reflected as potential weak signals for strategic inconsistencies. They all increase foresight by increasing the ability for second-order learning. The first point that we want to look at is the way that strategic decisions are made and evaluated. We want to argue that the higher the degree of participation, the more foresightful the organization is. The reasoning behind that is a simple one: strategy reviews and the like are instances in which the structuring of the organization as a whole is (communicatively) reflected (cf. Dietel and Seidl, 2003). Everything communicated in such reviews will be reflected with regard to its relevance for the organization as a whole. Whether a locally experienced inconsistency makes its way into the review process depends on the participants (inter alia); i.e. on whether there is anybody who "knows" about the inconsistency. Thus, the greater and the more diverse the participants are, the greater is the chance for relevant inconsistencies to be (communicatively) reflected there, and the greater is the chance for connections to a strategic inconsistency to be seen. More generally, however, taking part in discussions about the organization's strategies raises the awareness for the (structuring of the) organization as a whole. This increases the chances for experienced inconsistencies to be interpreted not only in the context of the immediate, "local" situation, but also in the context of the organization as a whole. That is to say, the members are more likely to notice weak signals. In addition to that, strategy reviews with a high level of participation raise the chance of seeing *connections* also between inconsistencies that initially were experienced at different locations. The strategy review in this sense might provide the opportunity for members from different parts of the organization to communicate and find out about similarities in the inconsistencies they experience. This increases the chances of perceiving the recurrence of particular inconsistencies. Taking our example from above, the more members of different departments of the record player producer meet at the strategy review, the greater is the chance that the recurrence of the same inconsistency is perceived and that the need for second-order change is understood.

Another relevant point is the internal transparency of the organization. The less transparent the structuring of the organization is, the more likely it is that inconsistencies are interpreted merely in the context of the immediate situation and the more likely that their potential strategic relevance is missed. For example, if the overall goals of an organization are not known, the relevance of inconsistencies for the goals cannot be analyzed. Thus, the ability of foresight can be increased by making it easier to get a "picture" of the structuring of the organization as a whole, against whose background inconsistencies can be interpreted. This can be achieved in several ways. The organization could provide support for understanding the existing structuring of the organization. In other words, the organization could provide a self-description (cf. Seidl, 2003a; b); or, metaphorically speaking, a map of itself.[10] Another way of increasing the transparency is to change the structuring itself, so that it is easier to (communicatively) conceptualize the organization as a whole. The organizational structures in this sense could be simplified. Possibilities for this have variously been discussed under the label "lean management" or "lean organization." Another possibility is to structure the different parts of the organization in a self-similar way. This type of structuring has been discussed under such labels as "holographic organization" (see e.g. Morgan, 1997) or "fractal organization" (Warnecke, 1993). If the different parts of the organization are structured in a self-similar way, one would know the organization as a whole, even if very complex, by knowing just one part of it. Thus, if an inconsistency was experienced in one part of the organization, its relevance for the organization as a whole could fairly easily be reflected.

## Summary and Conclusion

In this chapter we revisited Ansoff's concept of weak signals and tried to show that it is still of relevance – although not in its original form. We started with a review of the original texts and the research it sparked (particularly in Germany). All the literature rested on a simple idea: in advance of a strategic discontinuity there usually are some events that are (directly or indirectly) causally linked to it. In order to foresee the strategic discontinuity, organizations, thus, would only have to register the preceding events and understand their relation. In this sense, these events constitute signals for the discontinuity. Often, however, these signals are only weak, because either the connection is weak or because the organization can only see a weak link. With regard to these cases organizations would be more or less foresightful depending on their ability to deal with the weakness. While this idea at first glance seems very reasonable, we argued in the second part that it is problematic, as it rested on a naive representationalist epistemology. Nevertheless, we went on to show that despite its problematic epistemological assumptions the original concept of weak signals, if slightly modified, is still of value. In this vein we re-described the original concept in the constructivist framework of Luhmann's systems theory. We argued that one has to focus entirely on the internal communication processes, since organizations have no access to any reality beyond their own communications. Consequently, strategic discontinuities and weak signals have to be conceptualized as communicational phenomena: *strategic discontinuities* should be perceived as inconsistencies in the communication structures that require a readjustment of the entire structuring of the organization; and *weak signals* should be perceived as inconsistencies in the communications that – while themselves fairly insignificant and removable by first-order change – in some way or other are linked to (later) strategic discontinuities. Analogously to the original concept, organizations would be foresightful to the extent that they notice such "local" inconsistencies and understand their link to (potential) strategic inconsistencies. Thus, we reversed the direction of the original concept from the environment to the organization itself. *From a concept for observing the environment it has become a concept for self-observation.* However, since the constructivist framework assumes that *all* observation (even observation of the environment) is merely self-observation, the difference between the original concept and our re-description is not that great. In fact, even where the original concept is practically used in the *illusion* of observing the environment – where in reality one is observing one's own communicative constructions – the result is often fairly similar. Nevertheless, our re-description, if taken seriously, might heighten the awareness for one's own responsibility regarding one's development.

## NOTES

1   There were of course precursors e.g. Aguilar (1967) and Bright (1970; 1973).

2   In the sense, for example, of possessing a common cause.

3   Liebl (1994, p. 376) distinguishes between three aspects of the weakness of a signal: incompleteness, vagueness, and uncertainty.

4   There are different theories that have been used for explaining the emergence of strategic discontinuities – in particular chaos theory and the theory of "third variables" by Galtung (1978) (see Kirsch, 1997a, p. 51 Müller, 1981).

5   Ansoff et al. (1982) argue that such ambiguities have to be made explicit.

6   According to Luhmann (1995) social systems are also clearly differentiated against psychic systems. Psychic operations cannot become part of social processes and vice versa. In this sense psychic systems and social systems constitute environment for each other.

7   Luhmann (2003), in fact, conceptualizes organizations as systems reproducing themselves entirely on the basis of decision communications; other communications do not take part in the reproduction. For our argument, however, this point is relevant.

8   Luhmann (1989) famously argued that the destruction of our natural environment has no relevance for a social system unless it communicates about it; and the way it communicates about it is determined by the specific communicative structures of that system.

9   The aim of this section is not to develop a particularly foresightful organizational design or even management system – this goes beyond the scope of this chapter. Neither can we reconsider the management systems suggested in the traditional literature (see e.g. Albach, 1979; Ansoff, 1980; Ansoff et al., 1982; Calori, 1989; Krystek and Müller-Stewens, 1993; Liebl, 1991; Narchal et al., 1987; Reinhardt, 1984). Rather, we merely want to give two examples as an illustration of our above arguments.

10   However, such self-descriptions sometimes also impede second-order change, if they become too strong (cf. Brown and Starkey, 2000).

## REFERENCES

Aguilar, F. J. (1967) *Scanning the Business Environment*, New York: Macmillan.

Albach, H. (ed.) (1979) *Frühwarnsysteme*, Wiesbaden: Gabler.

Ansoff, H. I. (1975) Managing strategic surprise by response to weak signals, *California Management Review*, 18, 21–33.

Ansoff, H. I. (1976) Managing surprise and discontinuity – strategic response to weak signals, *Zeitschrift für betriebswirtschaftliche Forschung*, 28, 129–52.

Ansoff, H. I. (1980) Strategic issue management, *Strategic Management Journal*, 1, 131–48.

Ansoff, H. I. (1984) *Implanting Strategic Management*, Englewood Cliffs, NJ: Prentice-Hall.

Ansoff, H. I., Kirsch, W. and Roventa, P. (1982) Dispersed positioning in portfolio analysis, *Industrial Marketing Management*, 11, 237–52.

Argyris, C. (1992) *On Organizational Learning*, Oxford: Blackwell.

Argyris, C. and Schön, D. A. (1978) *Organizational Learning*, Reading, MA: Addison Wesley.

Bateson, G. (1972) *Steps to an Ecology of Mind*, New York: Ballantine.

Berg, C. (1979) Theoretische Grundlagen und praktische Ansatzpunkte zum Aufbau von Frühwarnsystemen im Bereich der Materialwirtschaft, *Zeitschrift für Betriebswirtschaft*, 2 (special issue), 135–47.

Bright, J. R. (1970) Evaluating signals of technological change, *Harvard Business Review*, 48, 62–70.

Bright, J. R. (1973) Forecasting by monitoring signals of technological change. In J. R. Bright and M. E. Schoeman (eds.), *A Guide to Practical Technological Forecasting*, Englewood Cliffs, NJ: Prentice-Hall, 238–56.

Brown, A. and Starkey, K. (2000) Organizational identity and learning: A psychodynamic perspective, *Academy of Management Review*, 25, 102–20.

Calori, R. (1989) Designing a business scanning system, *Long Range Planning*, 22, 69–82.

Churchman, C. W. (1971) *The Design of Inquiring Systems: Basic Concepts of Systems and Organization*, New York and London: Basic Books.

Courtney, J. F. (2001) Decision making and knowledge management in inquiring organizations: Toward a new decision-making paradigm for DSS, *Decision Support Systems*, 31, 17–38.

Courtney, J., Croasdell, D., and Paradice, D. (1998) Inquiring organizations, *Australian Journal of Information Systems*, 6, 3–15.

Dietel, B. and Seidl, D. (2003) Überlegungen zu einem allgemeinen Strategiebegriff. In M. Ringelstetter, H. Henzler, and M. Mirow (eds.) *Perspektiven der Strategischen Unternehmensführung: Theorien – Konzepte – Anwendungen*, Wiesbaden: Gabler, pp. 25–42.

Galtung, J. (1978) *Methodologie und Ideologie*, Frankfurt a.M.: Suhrkamp.

Grinyer, P. H. and Spender, J.-C. (1979) Recipes, crises, and adaptation in mature businesses, *International Studies of Management and Organization*. 9, 113–33.

Kirsch, W. (1997a) *Strategisches Management: Die geplante Evolution von Unternehmen*, Herrsching: Kirsch.

Kirsch, W. (1997b) *Wegweiser zur Konstruktion einer evolutionären Theorie der strategischen Führung*, Herrsching: Kirsch.

Kirsch, W. and Klein, H. K. (1977) *Management-Informationssysteme II*, Stuttgart: Kohlhammer.

Kirsch, W. and Trux, W. (1979) Strategische Frühaufklärung und Portfolio-Analyse, *Zeitschrift für Betriebswirtschaft*, 49 (special issue), 47–69.

Kirsch, W. and Trux, W. (1983) Strategische Frühaufklärung. In W. Kirsch and P. Roventa (eds.), *Bausteine eines strategischen Managements: Dialoge zwischen Wissenschaft und Praxis*, Berlin and New York: de Gruyter, pp. 225–36.

Krystek, U. and Müller-Stewens, G. (1993) *Frühaufklärung für Unternehmen. Identifikation und Handhabung zukünftiger Chancen und Bedrohungen*, Stuttgart: Schäfer-Poeschel.

Liebl, F. (1991) *Schwache Signale und künstliche Intelligenz im strategischen Issue Management*, Franfurt et al.: Peter Lang.

Liebl, F. (1994) Issue management, *Zeitschrift für Betriebswirtschaft*, 64, 359–83.

Luhmann, N. (1986) The autopoiesis of social systems. In F. Geyer and J. Van der Zeuwen (eds.), *Sociocybernetic Paradoxes: Observation, Control and Evolution of Self-Steering Systems*, London: Sage, pp. 172–92.

Luhmann, N. (1989) *Ecological Communications*, Cambridge: Polity.

Luhmann, N. (1990a) Meaning as sociology's basic concept. In N. Luhmann (ed.), *Essays on Self-Reference*, New York: Columbia University Press, pp. 21–79.

Luhmann, N. (1990b) The cognitive program of constructivism and a reality that remains unknown, In W. Krohn et al. (eds.), *Selforganization: Portrait of a Scientific Revolution*. Dordrecht: Klüwer, pp. 64–85.

Luhmann, N. (1991) Wie lassen sich latente Strukturen beobachten?. In P. Watzlawick and P. Krieg (eds.), *Das Auge Des Betrachters: Beiträge zum Konstruktivismus*, München: Piper, pp. 61–74.

Luhmann, N. (1993) *Soziologische Aufklärung 5. Konstruktivistische Perspektiven*, Opladen: Westdeutscher Verlag.

Luhmann, N. (1995) *Social Systems*, Stanford. Stanford University Press.

Luhmann, N. (2000) *Organisation und Entscheidung*, Opladen: Westdeutscher Verlag.

Luhmann, N. (2003) Organization. In T. Hernes and T. Bakken (eds.), *Autopoietic Organization Theory. Drawing on Niklas Luhmann's Social System Perspective*, Copenhagen: Copenhagen Business School Press.

Mason, R. O. (1969) A dialectical approach to strategic planning, *Management Science*, 15, 403–14.

Mason, R. O. and Mitroff, I. I. (1981) *Challenging Strategic Planning Assumtions: Theory, Cases, and Techniques*, New York: John Wiley & Sons.

Maturana, H. and Varela, F. (1980) *Autopoiesis and Cognition: The Realization of the Living*, Dordrecht: Reidel.

Maturana, H. and Varela, F. (1992). *The Tree of Knowledge: The Biological Roots of Understanding*, Boston: Shambhala.

Morgan, G. (1997) *Images of Organization*, Thousand Oaks, CA: Sage.

Müller, G. (1981) *Strategische Frühaufklärung*. München, Kirsch.

Narchal, R. M., Kittappa, K., and Bhattacharya, P. (1987) An environmental scanning system for business planning, *Long Range Planning* 20, 96–05.

Orton, J. D. and Weick, K. E. (1990) Loosely coupled systems: A reconceptualisation, *Academy of Management Review*, 15, 203–23.

Osborn, R. N. and Ashforth, B. E. (1990) Investigating the challenges to senior leadership in complex, high-risk technologies, *Leadership Quarterly*, 1, 147–63.

Reinhardt, W. A. (1984) An early warning system for strategic planning, *Long Range Planning*, 17, 25–34.

Rorty, R. (1989) *Contingency, Irony, and Solidarity*, Cambridge: Cambridge University Press.

Rorty, R. (1991) *Objectivism, Relativism and Truth*, Cambridge: Cambridge University Press.

Seidl, D. (2003a) Metaphorical self-descriptions of organizations. In A. Müller, and A. Kieser (eds.) *Communication in Organizations*. New York et al.: Peter Lang, pp. 165–82.

Seidl, D. (2003b) Organisational identity in Luhmann's Theory of Social Systems. In T. Hernes, and T. Bakken, (eds.), *Autopoietic Organization Theory. Drawing on Niklas Luhmann's Social System Perspective*. Copenhagen: Copenhagen Business School Press.

Tsoukas, H. (2000) False dilemmas in organization theory: realism or social constructivism, *Organization*, 7, 531–5.

Von Foerster, H. (1981) *Observing Systems*, Seaside, CA: Intersystems.

Von Foerster, H. (1985) *Sicht und Einsicht*. Wiesbaden: Viehweg.

Von Foerster, H. (1993) Für Niklas Luhmann: Wie rekursiv ist Kommunikation?, *Teoria Sociologica*, 2, 61–88.

Von Krogh, G., Roos, J. and Slocum, K. (1994) An essay on corporate epistemology, *Strategic Management Journal*, 15, 53–71.

Von Krogh, G., and Roos, J. (1995) *Organizational Epistemology*, Basingstoke: Macmillan.

Warnecke, H.-J. (1993) *The Fractal Company. A Revolution in Corporate Culture*. Berlin. New York: Springer.

Watzlawick, P., Weakland, J. H., Fisch, R. (1974) *Change: Principles of Problem Formation and Problem Resolution*, New York: Horten.

Wilensky, H. L. (1967) *Organizational Intelligence, Knowledge and Policy in Government and Industry*. New York: Basic Books.

# Chapter Ten

# Meta-rules for Entrepreneurial Foresight

*Ted Fuller, Paul Argyle, and Paul Moran*

## Introduction

Schumpeter's insight that some people have "the capacity of seeing things in a way which afterwards proves to be true, even if it cannot be established at the moment" (Schumpeter, 1934, p. 85), is an accolade for the entrepreneur which may not be justified. In this chapter we explore this "foresight" capacity in the context of the entrepreneurial firm from various methodological perspectives. Can entrepreneurs "see ahead," can entrepreneurial firms anticipate their futures, and if so how do they do that?

We make links between foresight as an interpretative process, i.e. personal competence in an entrepreneurial context and the sustainability of the enterprise, i.e. the organizational ability to maintain or improve fitness in a changing landscape, and hence survive or grow. Previous literature that offers different accounts of entrepreneurial and small business foresight is reviewed. This leads to the proposition that enterprises are emergent and contingent on the meaning of their relationships with the environment.

The case of Flight Directors is then narrated by one of the co-authors of this chapter. The theoretical insight provided by an analysis of this case study is that entrepreneurial foresight exists as a commitment to a particular identity, albeit changing reflexively, and that this commitment takes the enterprise through times when its normal behavior patterns are disrupted by external or internal events.

Organizationally, foresight is theorized as a series of experiments whose success becomes the temporary dominant logic, or organizing domain, of the business. Both the personal and the organizational perspective need to be understood if useful models of entrepreneurial foresight are to be developed. The chapter concludes with suggestions for such a model, which is agent-based in its conception.

## Foresight in Entrepreneurial Contexts

The empirical domain used in this chapter is that of smaller firms, i.e. owner managed and with fewer than 250 employees. Entrepreneurs are not a single homogeneous phenomenon (Chell et al., 1991; Dunkelberg and Cooper, 1982; Miner, 1997; Scase and Goffee, 1987; Smith, 1967). Shane and Venkataraman (2000) consider small business as a context, and that entrepreneurship is a process of discovery, evaluation, and exploitation of opportunities that may occur in many contexts.

The centrality of the business owner to the outcomes of a particular small business has been extensively delineated (Carland et al., 1984, p. 356; Hornaday, 1990). Explanations of differences in the outcome of any particular small business include differences in owner manager motivation (e.g. McClelland, 1987), personality (e.g. Chell et al., 1991), capability (e.g. Penrose, 1959) and intentionality (e.g. Bird, 1988). However, the future of a particular firm is unlikely to be the result of a single entrepreneurial decision or act. Each firm exists within a context of stakeholder relationships, competitive forces, regulatory frameworks, and other structures. In order to theorize about what foresight is in the context of entrepreneurial firms, linkages between the owner, as key decision-maker, the firm itself, and the structures (environment) within which the firm operates must be considered, preferably in some integrated way.

The literature on the subject of foresight and entrepreneurship is relatively sparse. Gibb and Scott (1985) suggest that one way of describing the orientation of owner managers to the future is "Strategic Awareness." This, they suggest, is a mixture of being forward-looking in order to anticipate problems and being able to comprehend the fit between the business idea or model and the external environment.

> Strategic Awareness implies the ability to make an assessment of the total impact of any particular change. This means not only awareness of the immediate impact of any new development but also reflections on longer-term repercussions.... Failing to think in that way will not mean that the owner manager is unable to cope. Almost certainly, however, the evidence suggests that he would have more problems because he has failed to anticipate. The essence of small company planning is its ability to project into the future the consequences of its present actions and think strategically about these. (Gibb and Scott, 1985, p. 619)

This definition constructs foresight as a competence in strategic awareness, which is similar to the approach taken by Slaughter (1995a, p. 48), i.e. foresight as an attribute, or a competence; "[a] process that attempts to broaden the boundaries of perception in four ways:

- by assessing the implications of present actions, decisions, etc. (consequent assessment);
- by detecting and avoiding problems before they occur (early warning and guidance);

- by considering the present implications of possible future events (proactive strategy formulation); [and]
- by envisioning aspects of desired futures (normative scenarios)."

A competence-based view of strategy is that competitive advantage accrues from a firm's competencies, i.e. "the collective learning in the organization, especially how to co-ordinate diverse production skills and integrate multiple streams of technologies" (Prahalad and Hamel, 1990, p. 80). Hamel and Prahalad (1994) have since asserted that the competence of Strategic Intent, which requires a "highly visible vision of the future," creates competitive advantage for the firm.

Major et al. (2001) identify the core competence of Pathfinding suggested by Turner and Crawford (1994) as congruent with ideas of foresight in organizations:

[Pathfinding] is the corporate competence to identify, crystallize and articulate achievable new directions for the firm. Part of the competence stems from an outward and future orientation of the firm's members and the intelligent use of systems and processes that empower this. Environmental scanning systems; strategic planning exercises; processes which collect competitor and market information in a systematic and disciplined way; involvement in trade and research groupings that are concerned with corporate or national development; all foster widespread involvement in opportunity seeking and the crystallization of informed views about new directions. Forums for discussions, with different and sometimes overlapping membership, help to sustain this competence.

Pathfinding involves a mixture of search and creativity. It also depends on self-knowledge and an understanding of the transformability of the firm's own assets, i.e. the degree to which it can practically apply or mould them to other uses. The paths that search reveals are only relevant to the extent that the organization is able to exploit them. This, in turn, depends to some degree on creativity in finding ways to exploit or reconfigure possibilities. This competence impacts on future performance. (Turner and Crawford, 1994, p. 253)

Major's empirical work (Major and Cordey-Hayes, 2000) identifies the pathfinding practises of 49 small firms, and their comparative use of external information sources. Only five firms looked well outside their normal transactional sphere, to research institutions, business advisors and "personal networks," a further ten firms indicated intermediate knowledge of foresight concepts and use of external sources of information, and networks. Major draws the conclusion that the individuals within the firm and the people and organizations with a close relationship to the firm are a key feature of the process of interpretation of "external" views about the future into "internal" usable knowledge (or "wisdom") and action by the firm.

Fuller and Lewis (2003) also study the significance to the future of current relationships between the owner or entrepreneur and their close stakeholders, such as customers and suppliers. The majority of small firms examined in their study had an orientation to particular regular relationships, rather than looking outside their everyday networks. In each of the 35 cases studies, the owner manager talked in terms of having a long-term strategy for building relationships with customers and suppliers. Through such strategies, Fuller and Lewis claim, the meaning of environmental change and customer expectations were reflexively interpreted (Beck et al., 1994). Moreover, there was evidence that these relationship strategies could change, resulting in reinterpretations of meaning and practice. They found evidence that such changes caused considerable unanticipated discontinuities throughout the business.

Small firms have little power to create structural changes in markets, and so the idea that foresight can be teleological, i.e. that the firm has the power to achieve a particular stated goal, is unlikely. The landscape for the small firms in Fuller and Lewis's study was, on the whole, the sets of existing relationships they had developed. An explanation for this is found in social network theory (Boissevain and Mitchell, 1973; Janowitz, 1976; Leifer and White, 1986), i.e. that the development of trust, empathy, and reciprocity creates interdependencies and forms of power which are not market or hierarchical.

The above research illustrates a range of interpretations of what foresight competence means in the small business context; from a rational logical process to a more unconsciously reflexive process, and from wide scanning and interpretation of the environment to a responsive interaction with close stakeholders. What is not clear from the above are the processes by which individuals' interpretations of the environment are managed organizationally, i.e. what the nature of organizational foresight is in entrepreneurial firms.

Greater insights into the way that new knowledge is assimilated into the enterprise, and the processes by which change is triggered by the orientation of the entrepreneur comes from a study by Lichtenstein (2000). In each of four high technology business start-ups the business model had to be changed several times before becoming stable, not because a particular pattern was unstable per se, but because it was designed relative to an unstable and unpredictable environment. The reshaped behavior pattern of the enterprise is, according to Lichtenstein, an "emergence from a process of self-organizing" that created repeating and amplified behaviors around the "dominant logic." Lichtenstein notes how various critical points are reached in the short history of the organizations, which triggered new behavior based on new "dominant logic," and claims from the cases that successful transformation is both incremental and evolutionary.

Brown and Eisenhardt (1997, p. 1) offer some observations about possible "rules" for reorganizing dominant logic in corporate organizations:

- Successful innovation blends limited structure around responsibilities with extensive communication and design freedom to create improvisation.
- Successful firms rely on a wide variety of low-cost probes into the future.
- Successful firms link the present and future together through rhythmic, time-paced transition processes.

Their thesis is that organizational change does not occur as punctuated equilibrium (i.e. step change) but is continuous. They offer the ideas of Semistructures, Links in Time, and Sequenced Steps to "crystallize the key properties of these continuously changing organizations." Lichtenstein's perspective of entrepreneurial situations is evolutionary but less poetic, less rational, less formal, and more related to individuals.

Both accounts give the sense of particular repeating models of operations, rules or patterns of behavior, being broken, reshaped, and reformed with varying degrees of difficulty.

Whatever the mechanisms for anticipating and maintaining an organization's fitness with the environment, their enactment implies the existence of a motivational force or posture (Covin and Slevin, 1991) that both creates impetus for change and enables the nature of required change to be understood, i.e. an ongoing coherence of meaning. This motivational force is interpreted by Gibb and Scott (1985), and Flores and Gray (2000) as personal commitment, which the latter suggest is commitment to a problem-solving activity or the development of particular practise. This commitment is a "constitutive element of entrepreneurial life," central to the identity of the entrepreneur, so much so that [entrepreneurs] become "authors of a continuous life story."

Foresight in an entrepreneurial small business context would thus appear to be linked to the personal competences and commitment of the owner manager. These are constitutive of their reflexive interpretations of the environment and its meaning for the firm. Reflexivity acts as a mechanism for triggering change, such that the firm is reorganized to behave in novel ways, which become a recursive pattern that is coherent with its intentions, giving rise to a de facto business model.

Fuller and Moran (2001) provide a schematic model for the relationships between the individual, the firm, and the environment, conceived as a process of emergence, i.e. that the firm, what it does, and how it does it, is an emergent property of its relationships with its stakeholders. The model, shown in Figure 10.1 suggests

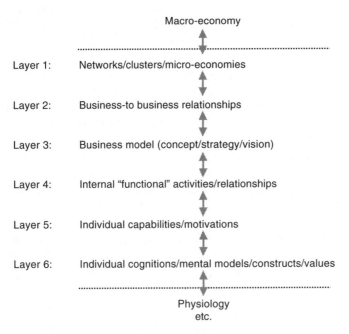

**Figure 10.1** An ontologically layered model of the small firm domain
*Source: (Fuller and Moran 2001) used with permission*

candidate emergent ontological layers in the small firm domain. Fuller and Moran suggest that each layer influences the properties of its neighboring layers, i.e. an interdependent reflexive formation of emergent properties. The figure is schematic, grounded in a classification of small business literature.

The process of emergence, or the establishment of "emergent properties," gives a sense of being both time and context dependent, i.e. that emergence is a process of "becoming" (Prigogine, 1980) from pre-existing conditions. The question of how foresight, some notion of a time or conditions yet to come, engages with a process of emergence, is problematic. The question is explored below through the case study and the discussion that follows. Throughout the case study it is possible to identify instances where the owners of the business formed anticipations with regard to its future, and to note how closely these anticipations are aligned in the (self)-narrative with the changing self-identity of the narrator. It is also possible to detect the nature of the organizing and re-organizing patterns that occurred.

### Case Study: Historical Turns and the Evolution of Flight Directors Limited

## *Analytical Framework*

Flight Directors Limited (FD) is a UK business set up in 1984 originally with two directors who were "best" friends. The chief executive and major shareholder for the whole of its life has been Paul Argyle. He recently produced an account of the development of the business over that period (Argyle, 2000) using his own recollections, interviews with a number of key staff, and company records. The analytical framework was informed by concepts from complexity theory, i.e.:

- bifurcation, used as a description of turning points or discontinuities and also as the production of diversity;
- ontological layers, after Harvey and Reed (1996), drawing on Fuller and Moran (2001) to model emergent properties and to map rules or processes. Argyle articulated patterns of behavior that linked these levels in his own firm at each point of "bifurcation"; and
- adaptive tension, after McKelvey (1999) to identify motivations. McKelvey seeks to identify what triggers organizations to maintain fitness. Using the Bénard cell (Prigogine and Stengers, 1984) as a model McKelvey defines adaptive tension as the product of (i) the difference between a firm's or agent's current state and a different, more desirable state relevant to the firm or agent; multiplied by (ii) the intrinsic or extrinsic motivation of the agent to respond." This point is a critical value.

In the written account, as at September 2000, Argyle also puts forward alternative scenarios for the future of the business. In 2002, Argyle added a note to update the history and make a retrospective analysis of the nature of forward thinking at each of the bifurcation points (Argyle, 2002). Throughout the case study, Argyle reflects on his own, and others' perspectives as they remember them at the time, the narrative uses the metaphors from complexity theory as literate explanatory models.

The case is presented with two voices, the narrative voice of the co-authors of this chapter setting out the story and reflecting on the original author's own narrative and the voice of the original narrator (Argyle) giving an account and a reflection on events using a complexity perspective. Argyle's personal accounts are indented in the text.

## The Case: Bifurcation Points in the History of Flight Directors Limited

FD was set up on July 1, 1984. The 29-year-old founder had a passion for the air industry. At 18 he had been offered but failed to complete a pilot training scholarship with British Airways. Then he became a junior shareholder in an air-brokering business. When he left after an "acrimonious" falling out with the majority share-holder, he set up FD with two colleagues. The three founding members of FD operated as brokers between the growing holiday companies and the aircraft operators. However, over the next three years the industry became more concentrated in the hands of a couple of major tour operators and most of FD's customers closed down or were taken over. The company faced closure, or as Paul Argyle (2000) writes from his interviews:

### Bifurcation A 1987

"We only had one customer left, so we decided to concentrate on him . . . " (J.P. (Co-director) interviewed July 2000)

What was it that motivated the firm to continue at this point, when it would have been quite possible for the three people involved to find employment with the new large-scale tour operators? To what extent was there "foresight", i.e. either an expectation of the future or a "vision" that compelled continuity?

Bifurcation A was a critical value change point. There was a conscious decision to continue the company and grow. I, as owner/manager, and being immersed in the market place, could sense opportunity despite the downturn in current business. Internal conditions were right for future growth (cash in bank, small close knit team of friends, little current business to administrate). This change (vision) was easily (simply?) communicable to the close friends with whom I shared the business.

In McKelvey's terms there was a big difference in the current and desirable states and the personal motivation to respond was high.

There was a particular day when I took time away from the day-to-day business issues and took time out to consider my future and the future of the organization.

The two alternative trajectories were either to continue or to stop. The decision to continue meant that the organization had to change from a three man company, with the business being generated solely by the owner manager, into a larger organization with other individuals acting as revenue generators and the owner manager moving towards a more managerial role.

The vision of this future was initially one of a team of brokers backed by a strong functionally focused team of supporters.

I could think it – act it – share it – achieve it (it = vision of the future) with little complexity to get in the way.

Argyle believed that the business needed to get bigger in order to fit with the increasing sizes of the main players in the industry. He had a desire for it to grow, which effectively was "foresight" at this stage. He carried support from his colleagues and from an ambitious bank manager. The overall business mood was optimistic, since 1987 was also a time of economic prosperity.

The business prospered from this point, developing in much the way that Argyle envisaged. The scope of the business then expanded.

The evolution of the vision for the business was generated through repeated discussions between the three founders of the organization over the years between A & B.

The evolution of the business was largely based on one strong relationship with a tour operator that grew from having a few hundred passengers annually to be market leader with over a million passengers in 1992. Being wary of overdependence on this relationship the business used its increased profits to diversify. By 1993 the firm had established four separate business units, none of which reflected the charter brokering "niche" that identified the firm in 1987, but all of which were related to booking air passengers and airlines.

**Bifurcation B 1993** In 1993, European Union deregulation created significant changes in the structure of the industry, which meant that the current business model was not effective in this new environment. Or as one employee put it to Paul in his interview:

"Everything was beginning to unravel, there were so many things we should have done . . . " (LB, Financial Director interview July 2000.)

It took the company, which by 1993 had about 60 employees, about six months to respond to a worsening outlook. As Argyle puts it:

The organization by this time had a Board of Directors who met to discuss the performance of the organization and its future strategy. The consensus at a number of Board meetings, and as discussed openly within the company, was that sooner or later the organization needed to radically review its future strategy if it was going to survive. The decision to do this was not reached for six months.

The point Argyle makes about this situation is that it is quite different from the earlier Bifurcation A.

In the Bernoulli's cell [sic] experiment – the direction of the movement of molecules changes as externally supplied energy increases. The Bifurcation points chosen (for this case analysis) can be compared to either the point where the direction changed (i.e. critical value) or the point where the external energy source changed (i.e. heat was applied). Bifurcation point A is seen as reaching a critical value, whereas point B, as described, is analogous to the heat being removed (i.e. a reduction in resources or energy).

The implication of this is that, in his interpretation, nothing happens internally until a critical value is reached. The directors' "desired state" was the one they had, and were reluctant to give up despite market pressure. The subsequent reshaping of the business, therefore, happened gradually. As Argyle notes:

> The vision for the business gradually shifted from one of perceived continual growth and success to one determined to survive . . . the difference between the current state and a new more desirable state was between the over extended current organization and a vastly slimmed down business with fewer people, fewer types of transaction, less office space, less management. The motivation was supplied by a need to respond or risk losing everything. (I can't help feeling that in the BC experiment analogy someone had switched off the heat!)[sic]

Argyle made a "painful" decision to focus on two streams of business and make 30 percent of the workforce redundant. This "vision," as he calls it, enabled him and the other directors to "retrench" and implement difficult decisions to survive.

The difficulty with retrenching was that "FD did not have a strong organizational self-identity around which the company could regroup, accordingly it was cut to shreds." Individual brokers left to work for competitors and customers and suppliers went elsewhere. So, although there was "foresight" in the sense of retrenchment, there was no coherence in the business.

Gradually the business reshaped around what Argyle calls an "internal attractor" of one particular business unit, and a new relationship with a new entrant, a Spanish charter airline. For the next three years the firm stabilized revenues and continued trading with low profitability, in an opportunistic way. Meanwhile, the industry changes continued at a pace. FD new competitor was taken over in this process, and one very capable broker (Michael) who had left FD to join them returned to FD.

### Bifurcation C 1996

> "Most people had left or were trying to leave; not many people were doing very much then Michael re-joined at about the lowest point . . . " (S F., employee interview July, 2000)

This point seems to represent a reinvention of the business and a (self) reinvention of the identity of the Chief Executive (CEO). If there was any "foresight" at this point, it was Argyle's "perverse optimism starting from the realization that the organization had survived a very difficult period." A more structural identity began to emerge for the CEO. New opportunities arising from new niche markets were evident, though these were diverse, and different from the original nature of the business. The opportunities were being created by the activities and motivations of specific individuals, not directly by the CEO.

Throughout the history of the business, the founders had provided conditions for opportunities to be created, for example investing early in new technologies. By 1996, as well as providing technical and cultural supporting conditions, the remaining two founders began to experiment with managerial conditions, to create a Group.

> This time the anticipations took even longer to shape. The gradual return of corporate confidence took the form of problems being solved through allocation of personal responsibilities within the management team, the return of Michael to head up the charter team and the emergence of Melanie as a strong leader for the Scheduled Services team. Returning to profitability and growth owed more to the internal mood rather than to any exterior event or trend.
>
> The turnaround can be seen as directly attributable to the organization hooking into new market opportunities, identified and pursued by key members of the organization. The power to greatly influence the direction of the organization shifted from the hands of the two founders into a team of four. The founder is now removed from day to day business generation and focussed instead on developing relationships with key stakeholders (bankers, accountants etc.).

The first strategy meeting of Flight Directors Group was on September 1, 1999. The Group consisted of Aviation (FDA Ltd) and Scheduled Services (FDSS Ltd). The two teams "formulated and explained their three years plans each of which contained a new major project to be initiated within the next twelve months."

Those plans were:

> The Scheduled service team decided to build a new call centre business alongside its existing strands of business. The Aviation team decided to commit to leasing their own aircraft capacity, becoming a principal rather than merely an intermediary. By the 1st September 2000 both of these ideas had become realities with the call centre handling in excess of 60,000 calls per month for three major carriers and, from separate premises, an exclusive aircraft flying under the brand name, Sunbird Airlines.

## Scenarios Post-2000

As well as providing a historical analysis of the life of the business, Argyle produced some scenarios of possible futures, as at September 2000. These scenarios were produced from:

> The personal research and reflection necessary to produce the historic analysis.
> - The participation in the interview process and sharing of the analysis with the other founding partner.
> - A period of personal reflection.

- A brainstorming session with the founding partner from which emerged three themes.
- The building of three scenarios per business unit by both personal reflection and conversation with the founding partner.

I think it's fair to say that the scenarios were not shaped by just looking at the organization as a single entity (agent?) and then trying to identify its capabilities and fitting these to perceived trends in the airline industry. The process was much more complex and looked at the current characteristics of the organization through use of the layered model [Cf. (Fuller and Moran, 2001)] and tried to project forward in time how current characteristics of individual layers may develop and which may become dominant factors in determining likely trajectories for the organization. This process started from a deep understanding of the history of the organization; of the key characters within the organization (their roles and personalities) and the state of the industry. The idea of "attractors" from complexity science was used as a framework on which to develop these ideas.

Three scenarios were developed for each business, all following a similar pattern. Argyle used the idea of an attractor around which patterns of behavior form to create alternative scenarios, after Fuller (1999). He noted that after the various crises, the business had reformed in different patterns around a particular attractor. At critical point A (1987), it was a personal commitment and a coherent practice (of brokerage) that seems to formed the patterns. This pattern was later amplified through their relationship with a major tour operator.

At point B (1993), although the need to change was clear, there was no clear pattern. Again, the attractor pattern was, he says, established by Argyle's own commitment to retrenchment. Those who stayed with the firm persevered with a number of experiments, i.e. different business models, until one began to pay off from a new business relationship. In this period Argyle noted that the patterns tended to be built around individual people, i.e. leaders, so it followed naturally that this became a stronger focus.

Thus at point C (1996), when again the company faced a discontinuity of business, Argyle turned to individual leaders within the firm as a way of creating internal attractors, i.e. consistency and value in particular patterns of behavior (business units). This attractor pattern was entrenched by formal social processes of business plans, titles, de facto management positions and physical location. However, these patterns were sustained in their early stages by what Argyle calls an "optimistic mood."

In the scenarios created in 2000, the alternative futures depended on the relative strengths of (i) individuals, (ii) internal projects or business opportunities and (iii) adverse external industry/market changes. Each main "attractor" produced significantly different scenarios, and in particular illustrated the nature of what decisions the owners would have to make in these differing conditions. Consistent "rules" for the adaptive tension of each main business area were made explicit and applied in these different scenarios, i.e.:

For Aviation, [FDA Ltd] Adaptive Tension is created by the need to survive in a constantly changing market place and dissipated by a mechanism which drives the organization to seek out better solutions to the aviation problems of its existing and potential clients.

For Scheduled Services, [FDSS Ltd.] Adaptive Tension is also created by the need to survive in a constantly changing market place, however, the mechanisms for dissipation is the identification and fulfilment of new market opportunities where existing skill bases can be utilized.

Implicit in these rules is the CEO's perspective – the imperative of survival (at this point in the firms history, survival was a key issue), and different conceptions of the business units. The first, a more flexible approach to problem solving through aviation expertise, the second a more explicit resource-based strategy finding new customers for the systems already established. Thus different external conditions create the need for different business models, rules or organizing domains.

The scenarios that were developed from these rules ran to several pages with quite detailed descriptions of possible dynamics over the next three years. The meaning of these was largely resonant only with Argyle, who had created them.

The personal experience of exploring the bifurcation points [A (1987), B (1993) and C (1996)], specifically by trying to understand the causes of the change and the characteristics of each post bifurcation trajectory, provided a major building block in the development of the scenarios.

The potential value of these scenarios was evident in the response by one Director upon his exposure to them. Because of the story-like descriptions coupled implicit and explicit causal messages his response was to immediately explore personally different alternative scenarios and also discuss what current decisions needed to taken in light of this new "understanding" of the future.

These scenarios were the direct result of the information and understanding of the organization derived from the preceding research being combined with the perspective created by the language and metaphors of complexity. In the context of this research their value is limited to their impact upon the interpretative capability of the author as Chief Executive.

## September 11, 2001

By April 2001 it was clear from the firm's financial information and other indicators that the Aviation business (FDA) was unsatisfactory. Two of the September 2000 scenarios had pointed to the potential for this situation, so they were mentally prepared for this eventuality.

The hijacking and deliberate crashing of civil aircraft on civilian targets in New York and Washington on September 11, 2001 had, *inter alia*, a huge effect on the air industry. The industry was already over supplied and going through significant changes. That event accelerated the changes. Overnight FD Group moved from a slow recovery to the brink of collapse. The next two months were spent in frantic negotiations with creditors and on the day before the firm was to be placed in liquidation, deals were struck by the CEO with creditors that meant survival for the Scheduled Services business (FDSS Ltd) as the only remaining subsidiary of the group.

In the first quarter of 2002 the overflow booking business grew again and as at June 2002, the firm employed 120 people, including many part time staff. The two founders remain, as does the central identity of being in the airline business. Other than these features, the business is completely different from how it was in its early years.

## Analysis and Discussion: What Does Foresight Mean in This Case Study?

If foresight is an idealized conception of the anticipation of particular events, or of being aware of significant changes in the environment before they occur, then at first reading, FD does not have foresight. Its history appears to be entirely composed of the disruptive effects of environmental changes to their contemporary way of doing business. A phenomenon Argyle recently called "enforced agility."

How do notions of foresight relate to this case? The firm, or the directors, do not appear to have the cognitive prescience that Schumpeter or Whitehead ascribe to successful organizations. It cannot be said that the business exemplifies pathfinding (Turner and Crawford, 1994) competences in its everyday approach to business. It does not routinely or explicitly undertake the foresight activities suggested by Slaughter (Slaughter, 1995b), it cannot assess the "total impact of any particular change" that strategic awareness assumes (Gibb and Scott, 1985). Nor is there evidence of the "highly visible vision of the future" that Hamel and Prahalad (1994) associate with Strategic Intent.

However, we suggest that the evidence does show how the firm interprets external information (Major and Cordey-Hayes, 2000). It creates usable knowledge and action not as explicit wisdom as Major et al. (2001) suggest but as new initiatives or projects, some of which survive to become distinct businesses and some of which do not. In time, some of FD's experiments have become the "future" business, though it was not known at the time when they were established.

As written, the history of the business with a focus on critical points of failure or regeneration, fails to identify the creation of the seeds of the future successful projects. Throughout the history of the business, growth and profitability have come from strong co-evolutionary relationships with other players. In the profitable periods additional investment has been made in experiments i.e. new operating models. The nature and choice of these experiments have not been fully revealed because of lack of evidence, but further investigation of this creative process may reveal clues to the nature of the evolution of the firm.

However, such instances do not fully explain the sustainability of the firm. That sustainability is, we suggest, more bound up in the commitment of the founder, in an existential way, to an ongoing interwoven life story of Flight Directors and Paul Argyle. The close identity of Argyle, and his fellow founder, to the airline industry has maintained the business when it might otherwise have ceased. The motivation to survive and maintain this identity has outstripped the huge environmental or systemic changes. This is not to suggest that sustainability has been achieved through pure opportunism. While particular business units have been created on the basis of opportunities, the meaning of these opportunities has been interpreted within the overall coherent direction of the founders, which is to be independent and part of the airline industry.

It could be argued that this strong identity has manifested itself in the orientation, culture, and language of the directors with respect to themselves, each other, and their employees, and that this has meant survival. This reflects the sense and power of strategic intent described by Leidtka (1998), and the way in which this deeply held identity is communicated (Baum et al., 1998). The self-identity of the founders has, to some extent, changed over time. For example Argyle sees himself now as CEO, rather than salesmen or MD. This has brought with it changes in the patterns of the business, i.e. changes in the organizing domains (Lichtenstein, 2000), for example, the way that operational responsibilities have been delegated.

## Conclusions: Entrepreneurial Foresight?

This chapter contributes to understanding the nature of the relationships between entrepreneurs and the future. How do entrepreneurial businesses survive? If entrepreneurial firms are agile, i.e. do change and survive, then to what extent does their forward view (foresight) play a part in this, and how is this manifest?

The evidence from this case study shows that the forward view of the firm does not exist as a set of clearly articulated and maintained scenarios that explicitly shape the policies and plans of the organization. It is questionable as to whether the strong ambitions of the founders and their very clear sense of identity, could be comfortably labelled as strategic intent. That identity appears more intuitive and personal, and reflexive in Beck's (1994, p. 170) sense of "unintentional self-dissolution, self-endangerment," which is a non-conscious process.

This development of a reflexive identity seems closer to the notions of becoming (Deleuze, 1994; Grosz, 1999; Prigogine, 1980) than a rational teleological sense implied by strategic intent or pathfinding. The process of becoming appears to be both cognitive and internal to the founders (agent) and manifest in the operational patterns, language, and relationships (structures) of the firm.

Nor does it appear that foresight is a structured process of planning or of the "rhythmic, time-paced transition processes" suggested by Brown and Eisenhardt (1997). The evidence suggests that becoming is a process of experiments, that are designed according to the environment or context they take place in. The experiments are projections from existing patterns or models and create new patterns. They are created because of an anticipated need from the close stakeholders, i.e. co-evolutionary in their foundation. Some experiments work and some do not, that is some enhance the relationships and gain rents or resources from these relationships, and some fail to do this.

The sustainability of the overall business appears to depend on the existence of these experiments and the ability of the overall business to change its "organizing domains" in resonance with the changing landscape, both internal and external to the firm. Organizing domains are not however, just a matter of patterns of procedures. They involve in themselves changes in self-identity by the people involved. The inability to reshape identity puts the future at risk for the firm. This does *not* mean that firms are chameleon-like, and able or willing to change their more fundamental values. Paradoxically, it is the underlying strength of their basic values and self-identity that has sustained FD.

What does this particular case, which is probably unique in its analytical mode, i.e. self-analysis from a complexity theory perspective, which is then subject to a deconstruction, contribute theoretically and pragmatically to organizational or entrepreneurial foresight?

Entrepreneurs and entrepreneurial firms do not think and act uniformly. The way we theorize about entrepreneurial firms has to acknowledge the nature of differences produced from voluntaristic action, (Astley and Van de Ven, 1983) i.e. the very nature of agency that entrepreneurship produces. Approaches to understanding voluntaristic action are, we suggest, more likely to be found in constructionist methodologies e.g. (Berger and Luckmann, 1967; Gergen, 1985), which seek to find explanations in how people meaningfully regard their actions, and how their identities and interpretations of the external world are constructed and reconstructed from their continuing experiences of that world i.e. reflexivity (Garfinkel, 1967). We would suggest that the way in which commitments to the future (Flores and Gray, 2000) are implicated in the social constructions of entrepreneurs is a fruitful area for further research.

One pragmatic implication of this case analysis is that agility; the ability to maintain systemic fitness, is a function of (i) the quality of reflexivity (the way that the dynamic internal model is able to transcend external systemic changes), (ii) the number and quality of experiments that deal with "weak signals" of opportunities, (iii) the sensitivity to changes in conditions, and (iv) the capacity to restructure patterns of behavior and self-image, i.e. the organizing domains. This suggests to us a model of entrepreneurial foresight that allows for voluntaristic action. This perspective is that of the entrepreneurial firm as "agent based" model (McKelvey, 2003). The main attributes of such a model are:

- the reflexive construction of identity; operationalized as motivations, learning processes and re-identification of behavioural imperatives;
- experiments; operationalized as a range of diverse behaviors (projects) at any one time by the agent;
- sensitivity to conditions; operationalized in terms of the threshold of environmental change that triggers change in the agent and the length of time before change occurs; and
- organizing domains; operationalized as the speed at which a change is constituted as consistent and sustainable (energy attracting) patterns of behavior.

## Summary

There is little research evidence on the presence of foresight activities in small firms through such formal or rational methods as scenarios or environmental scanning. Nor is there adequate theory or empirical evidence of the futures orientation of entrepreneurs. This chapter has addressed the issue of foresight for sustainability in an enterprise through an in-depth analysis of a historical account by an entrepreneur of various turning points in his business and the way in which anticipations played a part in the directions taken. The evidence, and previous research, indicates that foresight has a personal and reflexive characteristic but needs organizational agility to be effective in affording sustainability. This chapter proposes some candidate attributes for investigating models of foresight for enterprise sustainability.

## REFERENCES

Argyle, P. (2000) *Through the Looking Glass of Complexity: A Single Case Study*, MA dissertation, Durham, UK: University of Durham: Business School.

Argyle, P. (2002) Notes on Flight Directors since September 2000, personal communication.

Astley, G. W. and Van de Ven, A. H. (1983) Central perspectives and debates in organizational theory, *Administrative Science Quarterly*, 28, 245–73.

Baum, J. R., Locke, E. A., and Kirkpatrick, S. A. (1998) A longitudinal study of the relation of vision and vision communication to venture growth in entrepreneurial firms, *Journal of Applied Psychology*, 83(1), 43–54.

Beck, U., Giddens, A., and Lash, S. (1994) *Reflexive Modernisation; Politics, Tradition and Aesthetics in the Modern Social Order*, Cambridge: Polity Press.

Berger, P. L. and Luckmann, T. (1967) *The Social Construction of Reality*, London: Penguin.

Bird, B. (1988) Implementing entrepreneurial ideas: The case of intention, *Academy of Management Review*, 13(3), 442–53.

Boissevain, J. and Mitchell, J. C. (eds.) (1973) *Network Analysis Studies in Human Interaction*, The Hague: Mowton.

Brown, S. L. and Eisenhardt, K. M. (1997) The art of continuous change: Linking complexity theory and time-paced evolution in relentlessly shifting organizations, *Administrative Science Quarterly*, 42(1), 1–34.

Carland, J. W., Hoy, F., Boulton, W. R. and Carland, J. A. C. (1984) Differentiating entrepreneurs from owner managers, *Academy of Management Review*, 9(2), 354–9.

Chell, E., Haworth, J., and Brearley, S. (1991) *The Entrepreneurial Personality*, London: Routledge.

Covin, J. G. and Slevin, D. P. (1991) A conceptual model of entrepreneurship as firm behavior, *Entrepreneurship: Theory & Practice*, 16(1), 7.

Deleuze, G. (1994) *Difference and Repetition*, New York: Columbia University Press.

Dunkelberg, W. C. and Cooper, A. C. (1982) Entrepreneurial typologies: An empirical study. In K. H. Vesper (ed.), *Frontiers of Entrepreneurial Research*, Wellesley, MA: Babson College, Center for Entrepreneurial Studies, pp. 1–15.

Flores, F. and Gray, J. (2000) *Entrepreneurship and the Wired Life*, London: Demos.

Fuller, T. (1999) Complexity metaphors and the process of small business foresighting. In M. Lissack and H. Guntz (eds.), *Managing the Complex*, Boston, MA: Quorum Books, pp. 336–51.

Fuller, T. and Lewis, J. (2003) Relationships mean everything, *British Journal of Management*, 13(4), 317–36.

Fuller, T. and Moran, P. (2001) Small enterprises as complex adaptive systems: A methodological question?, *Entrepreneurship and Regional Development*, 13(1), 47–63.

Garfinkel, H. (1967) *Studies in Ethnomethodology*, Englewood Cliffs, NJ: Prentice Hall.

Gergen, K. J. (1985) The social constructionist movement in modern psychology, *American Psychologist*, 49(3), 266–75.

Gibb, A. A. and Scott, M. G. (1985) Strategic awareness, personal commitment and the process of planning in the small business, *Journal of Management Studies*, 22(6), 597–625.

Grosz, E. A. (ed.) (1999) *Becomings : Explorations in Time, Memory and Futures*, Ithaca, Cornell University Press.

Hamel, G. and Prahalad, C. K. (1994) *Competing for the Future*, Boston, MA: Harvard Business School Press.

Harvey, D. L. and M. Reed (1996) Social science as the study of complex systems. In L. D. Kiel and E. Elliot (eds.), *Chaos Theory in the Social Sciences*, Ann Arbor: University of Michigan Press, pp. 295–323.

Hornaday, R. W. (1990) Dropping the e-words from small business research' *Journal of Small Business Management*, 28(4), 22–33.

Janowitz, M. (1976) *The Social Control of the Welfare State*, New York: Elsevier.

Leidtka, J. M. (1998) Linking strategic thinking with strategic planning, *Strategy and Leadership*, 26(4), 30–6.

Leifer, E. M. and White, H. C. (1986) Wheeling and annealing: Federal and multidivisional control. In J. F. Short (ed.), *The Social Fabric: Dimensions and Issues*, Beverly Hills, CA: Sage, pp. 223–42.

Lichtenstein, B. M. B. (2000) Emergence as a process of self-organizing – New assumptions and insights from the study of non-linear dynamic systems, *Journal of Organizational Change Management*, 13(6), 526–44.

Major, E. J. and Cordey-Hayes, M. (2000) Engaging the business support network to give SMEs the benefit of foresight, *Technovation*, 20(11), 589–603.

Major, E., Asch, D., and Cordey-Hayes, M. (2001) Foresight as a core competence, *Futures*, 33(2), 91–107.

McClelland, D. C. (1987) Characteristics of successful entrepreneurs, *Journal of Creative Behavior*, 21(3), 219–33.

McKelvey, B. (1999) Self-organization, complexity catastrophe, and microstate models at the edge of chaos. In J. A. C. Baum and B. McKelvey (eds.), *Variations in Organization Science – In Honor of Donald T. Campbell, J. A. C. Baum and Bill McKelvey (eds.)*, Thousand Oaks, CA: Sage, chapter 15.

McKelvey, B. (2003, forthcoming) Towards a complexity theory of entrepreneurship, *Journal of Business Venturing*.

Miner, J. (1997) Psychological typology and relationship to entrepreneurial success, *Entrepreneurship and Regional Development*, 9, 319–44.

Penrose, E. T. (1959) *The Theory of the Growth of the Firm*, Oxford: Blackwell.

Prahalad, C. K. and Hamel, G. (1990) The core competence of the corporation, *Harvard Business Review*, May–June, 79–91.

Prigogine, I. (1980) *From Being to Becoming: Time and Complexity in the Physical Sciences*, San Francisco: W H Freeman & Co.

Prigogine, I. and Stengers, I. (1984) *Order Out of Chaos: Man's New Dialogue with Nature*, New York: Bantam.

Scase, R. and Goffee, R. (1987) *The Real World of the Small Business Owner*, London and New York: Routledge.

Schumpeter, J. A. (1934) *The Theory of Economic Development: An Inquiry into Profits, Capital, Credit, Interest and the Business Cycle*, Cambridge, MA: Harvard University Press.

Shane, S. and Venkataraman, S. (2000) The promise of entrepreneurship as a field of research, *Academy of Management Review*, 25(1), 217–26.

Slaughter, R. A. (1995a) *The Foresight Principle; Cultural Recovery in the 21st Century*, London: Adamantine Press.

Slaughter, R. A. (1995b) *Futures Tools and Techniques*, Melbourne, Australia: Futures Study Centre.

Smith, N. R. (1967) *The Entrepreneur and His Firm: The Relationship Between Type of Man and Type of Company*, East Lansing: Michigan State University, Bureau of Business and Economic Research.

Turner, D. and Crawford, M. (1994) Managing current and future competitive performance: The role of competence. In G. Hamel and A. Heene (eds.), *Competence Based Competition*, Chichester: John Wiley and Sons.

# Chapter Eleven

# Autopoietic Limitations of Probing the Future

*Deborah A. Blackman and Steven Henderson*

## Introduction

Foresight, according to Slaughter (1995, p. 1) is "a human attribute that allows us to weigh up pros and cons, to evaluate different courses of actions and to invest possible futures on every level with enough reality and meaning to use them as decision making aids . . . The simplest possible definition is: opening to the future with every means at our disposal, developing views of future options, and then choosing between them." This indicates that foresight is about processes and behaviours that will enable the firm to undertake more proactive behaviors in developing its future. Accurate foresight is considered to be an important part of organizational strategic development as it should, if done well, enable successful strategic decisions and actions.

However, for such developments to be successful, firms must be open and discrete systems that can understand both themselves and the environment in which they exist. A theory that challenges the openness of organizations and raises doubts about the ability of the firm to understand itself is autopoiesis (Maturana and Varela, 1980). This chapter intends to consider what the impacts of autopoietic tendencies within a firm would be upon foresight development, and tries to show that any foresight developed can be associated with severely dysfunctional organizational dynamics. It will be argued that the implication of autopoietic analysis is that probing the future necessarily produces an inexact and incomplete picture of the organization's present that is projected onto the future, extending a narrative based around conservation rather than change, adaptation, and transformation.

The chapter begins with a brief introduction to the notion of autopoiesis. The key ideas will then be illustrated using Mellahi et al.'s (2002) recent case study on the decline of Marks & Spencer. Subsequently, the organizational behaviors identified as necessary to produce foresight are evaluated from an autopoietic perspective. This discussion will show that appropriate behaviors are not possible for a firm that resembles an autopoietic system. Further, although observers may still be able to identify foresight and foresight processes, their descriptions of it are themselves a function of autopoietic processes rather than examples of insightful, accurate foresight.

## The Theory of Autopoiesis

Autopoiesis has its origins in debates about the nature of living systems (Maturana, 1999) but its principles have been extended into social and managerial systems (Keane et al., 1999; Maula, 2000 von Krogh and Roos, 1995; von Krogh et al., 1994). It is a theory of conservation, of how a system maintains its integrity by conserving some components of itself, in spite of environmental disturbances (called perturbations in autopoietic literature) while changing other parts of its structure. A system is defined in terms of what it conserves, (its organization) not what it changes. Thus a living system is autopoietic when the components and relations that make up the structure are constituted so as to maintain itself (Cull, 1999, Maturana and Varela, 1980; Varela et al., 1974).

In autopoiesis a living system does not exist in an external environment, as such, rather it maintains itself by self-referential (predetermined) interactions with other systems. Morgan (1986) gives the example of a bee. The bee only survives through its interactions with other bees in the hive system. The hive only survives through its interactions with local fauna. The local fauna is itself maintained by the actions of the bees in the hive. Morgan might also have pointed out that the internal organs of the bee exist in similar relationships to each other and the bee. Thus, to change the bees is to change the hive and the fauna, and vice versa. The bee is a point on a lattice of circular, self-referencing systems; it is misleading to think of it as a complete entity that exists in an independent environment. Morgan concludes (1986, p. 254), "a system's interaction with its 'environment' is really a reflection and part of its own organization."

In order to maintain the self-referential systems the living organism closes in upon itself and, as a result, the components and relations of the structure become operationally closed. It remains open only in two senses. First, it will take in elements necessary to ensure its survival: food, air, sunlight, and so on, which it transforms into itself. Second, it will be open to environmental perturbations, which may lead to a need for change in order to survive. However, adaptation to such perturbations will be the result of possibilities, limitations, and filters imposed by existing structural patterns, not the perturbation itself or any cognitive processing. This may mean that, where perturbations to the environmental system are not perceived by the autopoietic system of an organism within it, organizational closure and the limitations of accepted behaviors will prevent survival long term.

For example, both foxes and turtles interact with parts of the environment that are perturbed by urbanization. The fox does not "understand" urbanization but experiences the demise of hunting territory and the growth of fast food detritus. A fox's structure enables it to both hunt and scavenge but the balance of these behaviors will now determine the survival of each fox. The structure of a turtle does not permit behavioral changes in the face of similar environmental perturbations. Upon hatching, its structure and permitted behaviors drive it towards the strongest light source in its vision, taking it to the ocean in the normal course of events, but to a car park in an urban landscape. There is nothing in a turtle's structure to create awareness of this perturbation before the turtle's death.

In an autopoietic analysis, one creature has survived because adaptation to perturbations in the environment caused by urbanization is consistent with the range of behaviors permitted by its structure. The other creature does not have such width within its structure, and is less likely to survive. Neither has foreseen the changes and developed appropriate behaviors in advance. The fox may demonstrate some new behaviors, but only those permitted by its structure. Humans have adapted their behavior in response – many now habitually leave food to encourage these migrants.

This section indicated that the self-referential and interdependent systems posited by the theory of autopoiesis are very different to an open systems model of strategy. The autopoietic relationships between the firm and the environment might be so different from traditional representations as to explain why companies, apparently following appropriate strategic development processes, fail to develop effective foresight and, in many cases, try to learn from inadequate hindsight too.

## Elements of an Autopoietic System

In the following section we examine how autopoietic tendencies within a large UK retailer prevented the development of foresight that might have helped it avoid the problems that caused it great damage. Marks & Spencer (M&S) is a leading retailer in the UK (and, for a period, globally), which had a legendary and almost iconic status. It was often held up as an example of how effective businesses should be run and was "recognized as one of the best managed companies in Europe" (Tse, 1985, p. 1). However, since 1997 the situation has been very different, "M&S is experiencing unprecedented troubles. The company has seen its sales stagnate, profits collapse and market share fall. Its reputation is much reduced both home and abroad, where, for example it has been fined by the French courts and severely criticized for its attitude and its behaviour towards its workers" (Mellahi et al., 2002, p. 15). At one stage it appeared that M&S would even lose its independent status and be taken over. The appointment of Luc Vandevelde as managing director has rejuvenated the look and styles of the shops, and closed some branches. Profits rose throughout 2002 and the firm appears to be recovering. Of interest within this chapter, however, is the question of why M&S could not foresee or (re)cognize their problems.

An analysis of the events will be made using terms utilized by autopoietic theory. Explanations of the terms will be given, along with examples of how this applied to M&S. It is not argued that M&S was an autopoietic company, but what can be seen is that it demonstrated autopoietic behaviors, which could have been the reason why its foresight behaviors were ineffective. Autopoietic analysis can be confusing as two of the most important terms, organization and structure, are also used in the management literature to mean different things. In order to promote clarity in this chapter we will use the terms "firm" and "hierarchy" when we are writing about companies and not autopoiesis.

*Organization* refers to elements that the firm must conserve to be recognizable as a discrete, autopoietic system. In the case of M&S this appears to have been a paradigm, constructed over many successful years around core beliefs and values, about the efficacy of certain business processes, in particular:

- merchandising on the basis of quality and value, rather than marketing or image management;
- offering very high standards of customer care;
- promoting management from within the firm;
- tight links with integrated UK firms; and
- branding of products around the St. Michael's label.

It was not M&S's failure to adjust this paradigm, and its commensurate behaviors, quickly or effectively that caused their problems, but that all levels actively resisted acceptance of the need for change: "M&S's past, characterized by long and continuous success, led to an overwhelming belief in the company's management paradigm.... Change was not welcomed and viewed as unjustifiable, given past performance" (Mellahi et al., 2002, p. 23).

When the paradigm is conserved, an autopoietic firm also conserves the way that it makes distinctions and thus generates knowledge in autopoietic terms. This can be observed in the persistence of ideal types over time (Lawrence and Lorsch, 1967; Miles and Snow, 1978). It is possible to characterize these types in terms of the different distinctions the knowledge trees will make, that is to say that the internal structure of the firm will determine what it learns, and the future it sees, rather than any external properties of the environment.

An autopoietic analysis would find this entirely predictable, as the firm is actively seeking to conserve its current organization. However, firms and other autopoietic systems are not completely inflexible; those elements that it will change, in order to preserve the organization and no other purpose, are known as its structure.

*Structure* refers to elements of the autopoietic system that can be changed, in order to maintain and conserve the organization. In the case of M&S, its structure would have included changes in personnel, minor adjustments to hierarchy (particularly increasing specialization) and the products themselves, providing that each change was consistent with, and referred to, the organization. Such changes occur as a result of the system reacting to perturbations within its environment. When an autopoietic system interacts with its environment in a systematic way it is said to be structurally coupled.

*Structural Coupling* means that a change in the environment will automatically lead to a reaction by the system. In the case of M&S, where there were problems in its environment it almost always reacted by adapting its structure in such a way as to save costs. Such reoccurring structural coupling between systems creates a consensual domain.

*Consensual Domain*: this describes the range of acceptable behaviours between structurally coupled systems, such as M&S, its suppliers, customers, and other stakeholders. According to Mellahi et al. (2002) in the case of M&S, the basis of the consensual domain was trust – in particular with suppliers. This had given the firm a competitive advantage over retailers that relied on more adversarial, contract-based supply chains. Relationships that depend upon consideration of the aims of both systems (in this case the suppliers as well as M&S's) are termed "loving" in autopoietic jargon, and are thought quite exceptional between firms. The paradigm at M&S led it to believe that customers would try new products and lines because of their trust in the brand; obviating the need for market research, product launches, advertising, sales support, or foresight. In autopoietic terms it seemed to believe that there was a consensual domain between itself and its consumers such that the provided products would be appreciated and bought. It also meant that the M&S system would assume that that such coupling would work both ways and that M&S would experience the perturbations from the customer's system which would drive the required adaptations to the M&S system.

*Adaptation* is the adjustment of an autopoietic system's structure to perturbations in the environment through the structural coupling. Where such adaptation is successful, that is the organization is conserved, the autopoietic system is said to have "learned." The behavior of making descriptions about the changes in behavior (i.e. the learning) is called cognition. If the descriptions include the descriptions about those making the descriptions, the system is self-aware. It should be stressed that these descriptions are not descriptions of truth, and learning does not mean that there will be new, useful knowledge.

However, an observer might erroneously ascribe a degree of computation and information gathering to those behaviors in the consensual domain. Maturana (1999, p. 158) refers to this error as semantic coupling, "intrinsically inadequate and fallacious." The autopoietic firm does not make objective studies, distinctions, and descriptions about its environment, as described above; it is incapable of doing so. Observations of the environment are inevitably interpreted according to the organization. This can be seen clearly when observing chameleons who, when moved to a different coloured part of the environment automatically change to that colour. An observer may assume that chameleons know what they are standing on and what colour it is. In fact a set of structural triggers automatically react and nothing is, in fact, learnt or known about its current setting.

In the case of M&S the management paradigm led to adaptations but real learning did not occur: "signals were ignored, denied, or in particular, rationalized" (Mellahi et al., 2002, p. 25). Rather, the distinctions and descriptions the firm made about their environment, and their consequent actions, were functions of the self-referentiality within the firm not results from new knowledge gained.

*Self-Referentiality* according to Maturana and Varela (1980) is the way in which relations are set up within the systems. Morgan (1986, p. 236), explained it as:

> living systems strive to maintain an identity by subordinating all changes to the maintenance of their own organization as a given set of relations. They do so by engaging in circular patterns of interaction whereby change in one element of the system is coupled with changes elsewhere, setting up continuous patterns of interaction that are always self-referential. They are self-referential because a system cannot enter into interactions that

are not specified in the pattern of relationships that define its organization. *Thus a system's interaction with its "environment" is really a reflection and part of its own organization.* (emphasis added)

Therefore, all apparently cognitive developments will, in fact, be the result of some already existing structure. An autopoietic system responds to environmental triggers (and is therefore open). However, the way it responds is not determined by the environment, but by pre-existing structural properties already present within the system that act as filters and limitations thus closing the system.

The internal factors that led to problems for M&S result directly from self-referential properties inherent in any autopoietic system. The centralized management structures were focused upon decision-making processes and internal customers, rather than consumers and competitors. Individual executives refused to take actions that would lead to a loss in status for their own functions and specialist operations, particularly as these had been set up as a consequence of success in the past.

Recruitment and promotion were based on conformity to the M&S management paradigm. Thus actions were inevitably focused upon making existing paradigms work more effectively, and reasserting such tried solutions as reducing marginal cost (Mellahi et al., 2002, p. 24), as any predisposition to question the paradigm, or experiment outside it would have challenged the self-referentiality of the system and would, therefore, have been filtered out by senior levels. Managers were not only unwilling to consider change, they did not have the means to think about it or act upon it as there were no processes or discussions in place that could lead to change engendered by real foresight.

*Conversation* is said to consist of two elements, emotioning and languaging (Maturana and Bunnell, 1997). Emotioning refers to the compulsion of the autopoietic system to preserve its organization. Languaging is a means for coordinating actions within the consensual domain between structurally coupled systems. Conversation is thus an interaction between two autopoietic systems in which both use languaging to preserve their emotionally determined states. As Maturana (1988, p.79) puts it, "We human beings are not rational animals; we are emotional, languaging animals that use the operational coherences of language, through the constitution of rational systems, to explain and justify our actions, while in the process, and without realizing it, we blind ourselves about the emotional grounding of all the rational domains that we bring forth." Thus it follows that within autopoiesis conversation is not a means for communicating truth, rationality or knowledge independent of action. As a result it can not be expected that conversations between managers will lead to insights that will challenge the dominant worldviews where these have been internalized to become the object of an individual's emotioning.

Disagreement (via conversation) about strategy and marketing did arise within M&S but this was filtered out by infighting and the expulsion of dissenting managers. As the remaining managers were appointed from within the system, the self-referential nature of the knowledge held within the firm merely led to a restatement of the original management paradigm and a demonizing of change.

The criteria for accepting knowledge is socially constructed by a community of observers that share a common praxis. Maturana (1988) remarks that such inter-actions occur within the praxis of living in language, and divergent explanations are resolved by reference to operational coherence, not by reference to the experience that gave rise to the distinction in the first place. In the case of M&S, the coherence of the paradigm prevented counter narratives that could lead to changes in behavior. A firm can only adapt according to the plasticity of its operational coherences. Adaptation becomes less likely as operational coherences gain strength and embed themselves in the language that is used by individuals in the firm to describe themselves and their actions.

*Observation:* Autopoietic systems are described by an external observer. Observers make descriptions and distinctions about what they observe. An observer can ordin-arily see the boundaries of an autopoietic system, rather than its internal workings, and the way that it appears to interact with its environment. With a business firm, the boundary might be the distinction between those employed by the company, and those who are not. The behaviours, artifacts, and ideofacts held within the firm can be described as the workings of the autopoietic system. In a self-aware system internal observers can also make descriptions about internal workings, however, it is import-ant to note that the descriptions about what the observer sees are not necessarily true in any objective sense.

In this case, Mellahi et al. (2002) have relied on the descriptions of internal and external observers, and tried to cross-reference these to identify the facts. This is acceptable, even rather good scholarship, but suspect from an autopoietic perspective – the facts are not to be found in consistencies between the descriptions and distinc-tions made by several observers. Some parts of the actual relationships within the firm and between the firm and its environment can only been seen by one (or perhaps none) of the observers, thus limiting what can cross-referenced. Further, the obser-vers themselves are autopoietic systems, and their descriptions are a function of their own structures, rather than the facts as such. Thus, this chapter has applied an autopoietic analysis to a description of the crisis at M&S; no greater epistemological claim can be made for it, or any similar analyses.

## Autopoiesis and Marks & Spencer

Taken individually and together the processes identified imply that, within M&S, what was being conserved was the management paradigm. The analysis suggests that the conservation of a successful paradigm can encourage autopoietic tendencies that make further adaptation difficult. This result is consistent with studies into strategic change (Johnson, 1988; Miller, 1990; Miller and Frieson, 1980; Sherman and Schultz, 1999). At M&S, there was no internally generated dynamic that bought the problems to an end. Such foresight as they had were extensions of the existing paradigm and their resulting behaviors (such as continuing to purchase and open new stores with city centre locations) appear foolish in hindsight. Only when the crisis worsened, going beyond the behaviors permitted by consensual domain of the structural coupling with financial investors and institutions, was an outsider (the new managing director) appointed to change the company by breaking the self-referentiality.

So far we have shown that autopoietic theory can be applied to create a description of the dynamics that led to a period of failure at M&S. However, success or failure is not caused by autopoiesis. These terms are judgments, distinctions, made by an external observer about the performance of the system from an external perspective. The organization, the paradigm, was successfully conserved at M&S until the structure no longer supported it in its environment, at which point it began to disintegrate. Disintegration was avoided by the intervention of other autopoietic systems with which it was structurally coupled in this case. In other instances, interacting autopoietic systems may better preserve their organization by allowing the firm to disintegrate, perhaps feeding on its carcass.

What can be seen during the autopoietic analysis is that the processes and behaviors being undertaken within the system failed to deliver foresight or its subsequent strategic advantage. In the next section we review the behaviors required for effective foresight, before considering these from an autopoietic viewpoint.

## Foresighting as a Behavior

Foresight is the knowledge obtained by a process. It is not whimsical to say that it is a learning process with the future as its object. Major et al.'s (2001) study of foresight practises in 49 companies (henceforward called foresighting) verified those described as "pathfinding" by Turner and Crawford (1994) and concur that these resemble a core competence (Prahalad and Hamel, 1990). The competence is recognized by a superior *identification*, *crystallization*, and *articulation* of new directions for the firm and is based upon the integration of a range of complex behaviors which include:

- environmental scanning;
- strategic planning;
- gathering information concerning competitors and customers;
- involvement in national development groups and forums,
- empowerment of outward and future orientated systems and processes; and
- self-knowledge, particularly regarding the transformability of assets.

Horton (1999) groups similar behaviors into three process stages that are similar to those of Major et al.'s competence (2001). These are:

1 collection, collation and summarization (identification);
2 translation and interpretation (crystallization); and
3 assimilation and evaluation to produce commitment to action (articulation).

Clearly, for both Major et al. (2001) and Horton (1999), foresighting revolves around the transition of information into knowledge and then knowledge into action.

It can be inferred, therefore, that the success of foresighting will depend upon the ability of the system to undertake these behaviors in such a way as to acquire, interpret, and utilize the information in a meaningful way.

## Identification and Autopoiesis

The identification stage of foresighting consists chiefly of information searching and processing. As indicated above the descriptions and distinctions made by the observer will be crucial to what foresight is developed. There are several issues that effect the descriptions that observers can make. First, there is the question of what the observer can see. Second, there is an issue of how firms deal with the unknown. Third, the location of the observer – internal or external – affects both what can be seen and the type of descriptions that will be made about the firm.

The part of the environment that the autopoietic system inhabits is referred to as its niche. The niche is experienced through structural couplings, and moderated through the systems structure. In this way, the firm "learns" through its own structure and structural coupling and gains its knowledge, which is not a direct representation of the environment. Whitaker (1996, p. 3) asserts that "A cognizing system engages the 'world' only in terms of the perturbations in its nervous system, which is 'operationally closed' (i.e., its transformations occur within its bounds). To the extent that the nervous system recursively interconnects its components (as in our brains), the organism is capable of generating, maintaining and re-engaging its own states as if they were literal re-presentations of external phenomena." Observers can, therefore, only describe within the niche.

The parts of the niche that are not structurally coupled will not trigger the creation of information that could be used for foresighting. It is possible for the searching firm to become aware of this lack – Hoerem et al. (1996, p.121) use the term "scarce knowledge" in this case. Scarce knowledge is knowing that there is a lack of knowledge about something (in this case a clear understanding of the current environment and the future) within the system. The question would be how a firm would go about trying to create descriptions to fill this gap. It is not possible for an external observer to see the niche in its entirety, unless the autopoietic system moves away from it (Maturana and Bunnell, 1997) in which case the description is one of hindsight, not foresight. Further, the niche cannot be understood independently of the firm's behavior. An external observer cannot make observations about what is internal to the system. The observer is forced to make inferences based on the behavior of the firm. These behaviors include making descriptions about itself, in the form of publicity, corporate image management, stories, and conversations. These behaviors will be interpreted according to the past experience of the observers themselves.

An internal observer, someone within the firm, is allowed the possibility of observing and reflecting upon himself or herself as though he or she were an external observer (Maturana, 1978), although this does not help us as much as we might think. The internal observer remains governed by the same limitations of his or her own structure. If the unit of analysis is the firm, that is the firm is considered to be an autopoietic system, then the behavior of individuals, including observation, is governed by the structure of the firm. The stronger the organization, the less likelihood there is of any adaptations that are not merely structural changes that conserve the original way of thinking and seeing as was seen in the M&S case. To refer back to M&S's relationship with their customers as an example, they were sure they knew what their customers required. They made very little effort to find out their requirements and when they did inquire they would ask in such a way as to gain information and "learn" new things that supported what they already knew.

This occurs because as managers are part of the consensual domain they can only respond to perturbations through structural coupling, as determined by existing structure. Information systems, knowledge management systems, scenario planning, and environmental scanning may enable managers to make ever fuller descriptions and finer distinctions, but this does not overcome the descriptive fallacies resulting from self-referentiality or semantic coupling. In short, by observing and describing, an autopoietic firm is likely to have demonstrated the social processes that develop descriptions about the future and imply foresighting behavior. However, these descriptions are reflections of the firm's internal structures and organization, they are not particularly related to external changes or enlightened insights about the future. As Maturana (1978, p. 45) puts it:

> Any description of learning in terms of the acquisition of a representation of the environment is, therefore, merely metaphorical and carries no explanatory value. Furthermore, such a description is necessarily misleading, because it implies a system in which instructive interactions would take place, and such a system is, epistemologically, out of the question.

## *Crystallization and Autopoiesis*

In the crystallization stage, the information strands are drawn together into coherent views about the future and the firm's possible position within it. Maturana and Bunnell (1997, p. 29) state that: "We tend to think of learning as the acquisition of information, this is not what it is. It is a transformation in living together, it is a transformation of doings in a process of doing things together with others." This transformation can only be brought about by conversations leading to an operating consensus between executives, and these conversations must be able to develop knowledge that is outside the current system if there is to be change.

We have already seen that autopoiesis does not invest conversations with meaning, but with languaging and emotioning that enables a sharing of ideas but not necessarily useful knowledge. A useful example of meaningless languaging can be found in von Krogh et al. (1996), who observed conversations between a number of vice presidents concerned with human resource management on such issues as core competence, competitive advantage, and so on. As the researchers put it, "The words seemed to change meaning, and different words, which at one point seemed to complement each other, were at other times used as synonyms" (von Krogh et al.,

1996, p. 102). That is to say, that the conversations were not communicating shared values, meaning, or observations, but nonetheless participants were not reported as bothered by this. This may be because participants assumed a shared meaning, or that those in the conversation were simply not listening to each other but filtering according to expectations (Fiumara, 1990). One assumes that despite the lack of clarity (or meaning), such conversations would be the source of coordinating behaviors, and even behavior changes. Shared values based in ambiguity rather than clarity or meaning, may help the firm to retain plasticity within its coordinating behaviors (languaging). The lack of clarity may even confer an advantage if it makes successful behaviors difficult for a rival to replicate (Peteraf, 1993). But again, these advantages fall short of a meaningful crystallization of foresight.

What emerges is that the translation and interpretation of the ideas being shared is unlikely to challenge the current system. All adaptations will be designed to conserve the organization and so the crystallization will reconfirm what is to be conserved and strengthen the organization.

## Articulation and Autopoiesis

This stage requires that the information and shared beliefs about the firm, its environment, and the future are developed into actions about how the firm should be in future. However, the ability of autopoietic systems to deliberately transform themselves is circumscribed: "If a human being can observe the social system that he creates with his behaviour, he may dislike it and reject it, and thus become a source of change, but if he can only undergo interactions specified by the social system that he integrates, he cannot be an observer of it and his behaviour can only confirm it" (Maturana, 1978, p. 62). We interpret this as offering qualified support to the notion that individuals in a firm can choose to change their behavior if they believe that current or foreseen states are undesirable. However, undesirable can only mean that the organization – the parts of the structure that must be conserved – is perceived as under threat. Consequently, the foresight and actions articulated can only relate to the organization. This requires us to think about what a firm might attempt to conserve with its articulated foresight.

The name of the firm, or ownership of the firm, are possibilities for conservation, particularly in family businesses. However, the visions about the future that such conservation brings are entirely self-referential, that is the future is defined by whether or not the firm will be in it, and what the firm will be called, and who will own it. It is difficult to see how conserving such things could lead to prescient ideas about what the future would be like, or the range of roles that could be undertaken.

Another suggestion is that a firm must conserve its supply of resources (Maturana and Bunnell, 1997), particularly finance and people. These might be regarded as the energy of the system. Failure to secure these undoubtedly brings the firm to an end. However, the resource base of an autopoietic system is created by its history of adaptation, referred to as ontogeny in the biological literature, and similarly defined in the resource base view of strategy (Barney, 1995). The point is that the resource base is a function of past adaptation, rather an object of conservation. The individuals in the firm may wish to conserve type of products made or particular relationships with customers as sources of energy, but these are survival-orientated relationships of the present (von Krogh et al., 1994) rather than foresight about future possibilities. Studies into relationship-based marketing have also identified the limitations in terms of adaptation and foresight (Clancey, 1992; Major et al., 2001).

Foresight would require the conservation to be centered upon the firm itself; some identity or sense of purpose that could project a vision or visions about the future and the firm's place within it. Mission statements and other text that the firm generates about itself might be taken as a statement of the values, or purposes that the firm wishes to conserve within its behaviors and aspirations. However, Maturana and Bunnell (1997) reject such a possibility, arguing that systems do not behave with a purpose, but according to their internal coherences. Even if the system was designed for a purpose, or an external observer sees a purpose, the system nonetheless operates according to its structure and organization. In the M&S case above, the paradigm was not created by its purpose, but by its history – it references the firm's past not its future. The managerial paradigm was conserved, creating mission statements and a range of consistent operational procedures and rules, not the other way around. In the more general case, the mission and descriptions generated might not be a particularly accurate reflection of how the firm actually behaves or what it conserves (Campbell and Yeung, 1991).

Further confinement of activities within a vision or long-term objective has the effect of reducing the intelligence of the system (Maturana and Bunnell, 1997). This curious effect is derived from the definition of intelligence within autopoietic theory, as the plasticity of the system's structural coupling. A clear, shared vision of the future can be achieved by languaging, but this makes the firm more likely to create blind spots in its perception of the environment as the more concrete the shared ideas the less plasticity there will be (plasticity in autopoietic theory refers to the ability to change behavior within a structural coupling in order to adapt and preserve the organization and the coupling). The M&S case shows how such blindness is sustained by the self-referentiality of the system. Consequently a clear vision of the future, whether accurate or not, may have the paradoxical effect of reducing the firm's ability to adapt to environmental changes.

The conserved aspects of the system thus have little if anything to do with generating foresight. This should not surprise us. Organization is developed from the autopoietic system's history of adapting for survival, it is not orientated to the future, nor could it be so. Behaviors, including foresighting, are inevitably self-referential and conservative.

## Observation of Foresight

Foresighting is a behavior that can be observed. It generates descriptions about the future, which can also be observed. Such studies as Major et al. (2001) are even able to a calibrate degrees of foresight and its foresighting and assign firms into categories of their own devising which indicate which firms are effective at achieving useful foresight and thus strategic advantage. Under autopoiesis, these can be conveniently described as semantic couplings of no great importance. However, we would rather examine the descriptions and review the autopoietic features embodied in them. The description offered by Major et al. (2001) is examined since it purports to be based on empirical observations of foresight. Whitehead's (1933) description is also reviewed, since it claims to be based, in part at least, on the socio-biological basis of social systems.

Major et al. (2001) examined the foresighting processes of 49 firms in two different industries associated with the UK Foresight Programme. The study enables a comparison of behaviors between "strategic" companies, where foresight was high and "reactive" companies where little foresight was developed. The study tended to focus on identification stages of the process.

It is striking that the features of reactive companies; reliance on homogeneous supply chains and intermediaries for information sources maps quite closely to the descriptions of M&S discussed earlier. Conversely, the strategic companies actively sought foresight from a large number of heterogeneous sources. Autopoiesis thus offers easy explanations for reactive companies. However, strategic companies may be explainable in autopoietic terms as well:

- The foresight developing in the identification stage does not challenge the operational coherence of the firm. An observer will see foresighting behaviors and can assume subsequent stages will lead to foresight and strategic change. It is also possible that the crystallization and articulation stages of the foresighting process could create autopoietic traits that shut down future or corrective foresighting behaviors.
- Foresighting is behavior consistent with the firm's operation coherence. Kets de Vries and Miller's (1989) "paranoid" firms are driven to scan the environment and create hostile mental models of it by the underlying fearfulness of top management. It is worth noting that in this case, remedial behavior does not generally follow from the foresight developed.
- The firms were not sufficiently operationally coherent for a single autopoietic system to emerge, and the firm is merely the medium in which competing autopoietic systems seek to preserve their organization as in the "schizoid" firms described by Kets de Vries and Miller (1989). The heterogeneous and externally focused identification behavior described is mistakenly attributed to a single authority by the observer.
- The firms are not autopoietic systems nor are they developing autopoietic traits.

This section suggests that observed foresighting behavior can have its origins in autopoietic behavior. As such, there is no particular reason to suppose that it confers any competitive advantage to its actors as these behaviors allow many dysfunctional organizational dynamics.

Whitehead (1933) argues that foresight is a human antidote to the dysfunctional outcomes of efficient, complex social routines. While such routines provide a stability upon which foresight can be based, they also reduce the intelligence present within the system because, although a system is created by intelligence, "when the adequate routine is established, intelligence vanishes, and the system is maintained by a co-ordination of conditioned reflexes" (Whitehead, 1933, p. 114). Without foresight, complex social behavior cannot develop, and resembles insect societies in their rigidity. Such a description of the firm as intrinsically routinized justifies the application of autopoiesis to his description of foresight.

Foresighting behavior is possible when the grounds for routines are understood – by "unflinching rationality" – in terms of both their social purpose and human nature. Such an understanding is developed by practical experience – since only with first-hand practical experience can anything useful be gained – and generalized training; particularly in the philosophical skill of generalizing from particulars and turning qualitative observation into quantitative estimates. The process of creating such quantitative estimates and, thus, foresight involves, according to Whitehead (1933, p. 111) "collecting and selecting the facts relevant to the particular types of forecast which we wish to make." Whitehead (1933) continues by stating that it is the selection of the relevant details from the welter of available information that proves to be particularly problematic, since only by understanding the past and the present accurately can the future be predicted.

However, an autopoietic analysis of Whitehead's work indicates several potential flaws and reasons why foresight may be much harder to achieve than is indicated.

- The problems with identification and crystallization of information into useful foresight have already been identified earlier in the chapter. Because those choosing the information are already experienced with the problems and issues it is likely that the choice of qualitative data will be self-reflexive. The future defined will be related to current models of the world. In short, foresighting will become routinized.
- The conditioned reflexes set up within the routines are likely to be structural couplings where reaction and adaptation occur without intelligence. This supposition is supported by Whitehead's view (1933, p. 114) that "No one ... need understand the system as a whole."
- Whitehead argues that the way out of the routinization of the firm is to develop foresight behaviors that will emerge from understanding the routines, through experience and approved philosophical training. Under autopoiesis this understanding must meet the criteria for accepting knowledge; it will be socially constructed by a community of observers that share a common praxis. Because emotioning and languaging will develop the "new" understandings, there is no reason why they should be accurate representations, if there is a strong desire for conservation within the system.
- For there to be real accuracy there will need to be an effective subject/object split present when new knowledge is being created. Autopoiesis, however, owing to its self-referentiality will always have a monist perspective and the objective, quantitative knowledge needed for foresight (in Whitehead's terms) is explicitly ruled out (Maturana, 1978).

- Whitehead argues that the future is encoded in the facts of the present. However, if the present consists of structurally coupled autopoietic systems, then these facts are not discernible. Moreover, changes made by one system, perhaps as a result of its foresight, will reverberate through the structural couplings in unforeseeable ways.

From these points, we suggest that foresighting behaviors will not lead to the kind of foresight that Whitehead describes. In Whitehead's terms, foresighting routines will merely become behaviors that satisfy human and social needs, such as articulating a sense of purpose.

## Concluding Thoughts

Foresight is a view about what might happen in the future. An autopoietic system has no means of discerning any such thing since adaptive behavior is modified via perturbations experienced through the structural coupling. Given that the future, by definition, is not in the present, it cannot be structurally coupled to the firm and the firm cannot adapt to it.

In strategic management terms foresight can be defined as being the result of "advancement activities" such as "developing distinctions and norms, ensuring knowledge connectivity, self referencing and languaging" (von Krogh et al., 1996, p. 172). However, we have shown that where there are autopoietic tendencies within an organization such activities are unlikely to lead to greater foresight and, paradoxically, undertaking foresighting behavior may encourage autopoietic routines to emerge.

Observers may describe foresighting routines, and even declare some of them successful or unsuccessful. However, these observations will not capture the autopoietic relationships that determined the outcomes described, but will necessarily be partial accounts of it constructed retrospectively. This may lead to a false sense of security as the firm believes it can see the future and is prepared for it.

In this chapter it has been demonstrated that an autopoietic firm cannot achieve foresight. Moreover, it has been shown that a firm does not have to be a completely autopoietic system to be affected by these concerns – behaviors that are considered necessary to achieve successful foresighting are less effective if there are any autopoietic tendencies within the firm, and such tendencies may well be present in firms that, on the face of it, would seem to be open, well-managed systems.

## REFERENCES

Barney, J. B. (1995) Looking inside for competitive advantage, *The Academy of Management Executive*, 9(4), 49–62.

Campbell, A. and Yeung, S. (1991) Creating a sense of mission, *Long Range Planning*, 24(4), 10–20.

Clancey, K. (1992) The dangers of death wish marketing, *Planning Review*, 20(5), 53–5.

Cull, J. (1999) *Living Systems: An Introductory Guide*, unpublished book available from the author via http://members.ozemail.com.au/~jcull/

Fiumara, G. C. (1990) *The Other Side of Language: A Philosophy of Listening*, London: Routledge.

Hoerem, T., von Krogh, G., and Roos, J. (1996) Knowledge-based strategic change. In G. von Krogh and J. Roos (eds.), *Managing Knowledge: Perspectives on Cooperation and Competition*, London: Sage.

Horton, A. M. (1999) A simple guide to successful foresight, *Foresight*, 1(1), 5–9.

Johnson, G. (1988) Rethinking incrementalism, *Strategic Management Journal*, 9(8), 75–91.

Keane, J. F., Taylor, W. A., Trueman, M., and Wright, G. (1999) Autopoiesis in Disneyland: Reassuring consumers via autopoietic brand management, *International Journal of Advertising*, 18, 519–36.

Kets de Vries, M. R. and Miller, D. (1989) *The Neurotic Organisation*, San Francisco: Jossey-Bass.

Lawrence, P. and Lorsch, J. (1967) *Organisation and Environment*, Boston, MA: Harvard Business School.

Major, E., Asch, D., and Cordey-Hayes, M. (2001) Foresight as a core competence, *Futures*, 33(2), 91–107.

Maturana, H. R. (1978) Biology of language: The epistemology of reality. In G. Miller and E. Lenneberg (eds.), *Psychology and Biology of Language and Thought*, New York: Academic Press.

Maturana, H. R. (1988) Reality: The search for objectivity or the quest for a compelling argument, *The Irish Journal of Psychology*, 9(1), 25–82.

Maturana, H. R. (1999) The organization of the living: A theory of the living organization, *International Journal of Human-Computer Studies*, 51, 149–68.

Maturana, H. R. and Bunnell, P. (1997) Biosphere, homosphere, and robosphere: What has that to do with business?, SOL, online at: www.sol-ne.org/res/wp/maturana/

Maturana, H. R. and Varela, F. J. (1980) *Autopoiesis and Cognition* (Boston Studies in Philosophy of Science, vol. 42), Boston, MA: D. Reidal Publishing Company.

Maula, M. (2000) The senses and memory of a firm -Implications of autopoiesis theory for knowledge management, *Journal of Knowledge Management*, 4(2), 157–61.

Mellahi, K., Jackson, P., and Sparks, L. (2002) An exploratory study into failure in successful organizations: The case of Marks and Spencer, *British Journal of Management*, 13(1), 15–30.

Miller, D. (1990) *The Icarus Paradox*, New York: Harper Business.

Miller, D. and Friesen, P. H. (1980) Momentum and revolution in organisational adaptation, *Academy of Management Journal*, 23(4), 591–614.

Miles, R. and Snow, C. (1978) *Organisational Strategy, Structure and Process*, New York: McGraw Hill.

Morgan, G. (1986) *Images of Organization*, London: Sage.

Peteraf, M. A. (1993) The cornerstones of competitive advantage: A resource-based view, *Strategic Management Journal*, 14, 179–91.

Prahalad, C. and Hamel, G. (1990) The core competence of the corporation, *Harvard Business Review*, 68(3), 79–91.

Slaughter, R. A. (1995) *The Foresight Principle: Cultural Recovery in the 21$^{st}$ Century*, London: Adamantine.

Sherman, H. and Schultz, R. (1999) Questions they never asked, *Across the Board*, 36(1), 13–14.

Tse, K. K. (1985) *Marks and Spencer – Anatomy of Britain's Most Efficiently Managed Company*, Oxford: Pergamon.

Turner, D. and Crawford, M. (1994) Managing current and future competitive performance: The role of competence. In G. Hamel and A. Heene (eds.), *Competence Based Competition*, Chichester: Wiley.

Varela, F. G., Maturana, H. R., and Uribe, R. (1974) Autopoiesis: The organization of living systems, its characterization and a model, *BioSystems*, 5, 187–96.

von Krogh, G. and Roos, J. (1995) *Organizational Epistemology*, Basingstoke: Macmillan Press.

von Krogh, G., Roos, J., and Slocum, K. (1994) An essay on corporate epistemology, *Strategic Management Journal*, 15, 53–71.

von Krogh, G., Roos, J., and Slocum, K. (1996) Corporate epistemology. In G. von Krogh and J. Roos (eds.), *Managing Knowledge: Perspectives on Cooperation and Competition*, London: Sage.

Whitaker, R. (1996) Tutorial on autopoiesis, The Observer Web, online at: www.informatik. umu.se/~rwhit/Tutorial.htm

Whitehead, A. N. (1933) *Adventure of Ideas*, Cambridge: Cambridge University Press.

# Afterword: Insights into Foresight

*Kees van der Heijden*

### Introduction

This book contains numerous examples of foresight projects. Indeed, it can be said that foresight methodology is enjoying a boom period. There is a growing stream of publications on case-based success stories. Inevitably we are also hearing an increasing number of reports of failure. In Strathclyde's Centre for Scenario Planning and Future Studies we monitor these developments, in an attempt to work out how to understand success and failure.

Our observation is that there is considerable confusion about what foresight approaches are and what they can achieve. Apparently, a distinctive foresight competence would be so valuable that people are prepared to have a go and hope for the best. Precise reasons why particular approaches are selected are mostly poorly articulated. We believe that this confusion causes an increasing number of perceived failures. Reasons for engaging in foresight approaches have many degrees of freedom, varying from the general, such as promoting a future-oriented thinking style, to detailed methodological aims, and from quick half-day workshops to projects spreading over a number of years with many diverse activities. The territory is so large that without clarity on what is to be achieved the process cannot be purposefully designed. Without clear purpose it is not altogether surprising that disappointment is the result.

This book makes a significant contribution towards mapping out this territory. A number of distinctions and categories are introduced that are helpful in articulating a meaningful discussion about purpose. Understanding relevant categories will prove to be helpful in strategic conversation aimed at increasing foresight. In this concluding chapter we will first highlight some of the more powerful distinctions that have emerged from the chapters in this book, and then discuss how these can be used to bring clarity to foresight projects.

## Emerging Distinctions

### *Events, Trends, and Structures*

The first powerful distinction emerging from this book is between events, trends, and structures. Foresight is about the future. It implies we can say something useful about it. The fact we are interested in it implies that we believe that there is at least something that is predictable, even if most aspects of the future are subject to overwhelming uncertainty. The distinction between events, trends, and structure is helpful in mapping out views about uncertainties.

Events are what can be seen and perceived around us. As emphasized in various places in this book, events exist only after we as observers have interpreted signals received through our appreciative system, and have organized these mentally into events. If we share a significant part of our appreciative system, for example in an organization, then we will tend to share the same events, and ignore others that are seen by other people with different perspectives. However, even if we largely create our own events, they also require signals to be read. We experience events not in our mind's eye but outside ourselves in the world around us. It is often referred to as the visible part above the water of the foresight "iceberg."

This situation is different with trends and structures. These are the invisible part of the iceberg under the waterline. A trend is a pattern that we read in a series of events. The human mind is a great pattern recognizer; we see trends everywhere around us. Some variables seem to be on the way up, and others down, others are steady. There seems to be some consistency here. This is the starting point of human foresight. If a trend is persistent we believe we can extrapolate it and make some prediction about the future. This leads to the discipline of forecasting, without which society could not function. For example, if we find what we need in the supermarket, this is because someone has done some successful forecasting.

But even if forecasting works most of the time, we also know that it frequently fails, often when we need it most. We call these situations trend breaks. Indeed, in an infinite world all trends can be argued to break at some time. The way we deal with this is through observing patterns among trends. We notice that some always move together, or show similar behavior if shifted over time. And we start asking ourselves questions of the nature: "why does A always go up?", "why do A and B always move together?" or "why is A always followed by B?" We call these relationships "cues of causality." We impute from such observations causal relationships between variables, and turn the world around us into a mesh of interrelated causes and effects. This is the underlying structure that explains the trends we see and which, in turn, explains why we see certain events taking place. If we want to understand breaks in trends as part of our interest in foresight we need to figure out this structure.

For example, if it rains in the Himalayas today we can predict that the Ganges will overflow its banks downstream in a few days time. How do we know this? First of all this has happened in a consistent manner many times in the past. We know the pattern and assume we can make extrapolations. But we know more. We also understand the causal laws of hydrodynamics, which explain how the two events are causally related over time. This makes us into very confident forecasters; our structural knowledge tells us that there will not be a break in trend this time. We can't have that degree of confidence about a similar relationship between war in the Middle East and the price of oil. In human affairs causal relationships are less firm and enduring.

Foresight is about saying something about the future. Making the distinction between events, trends, and structure helps practitioners to become aware of the sources of their effectiveness. For example, a popular foresight tool, scenarios, are essentially stories about the future. They relate a series of events that the writer believes develop in a plausible sequence, under certain assumptions. But what is logical for one person may not be all that obvious for another. How can the writer make the coupling with his/her readers more effective? The first requirement is for the stories to reflect the trends and patterns that readers expect, based on their own experience. So scenarios must be grounded in history, and be a logical extrapolation of it. But the scenario writer cannot stop there. Just extrapolation of the past may not be what is required from effective foresight. It may be that the purpose of the foresight project is to get some feel for the breaks in trends that could occur in the future. Here, the scenario writer has to delve into the underlying structure of the situation, and develop a mental model of the causal relations that give rise to the trends and patterns seen in history. The next step involves querying this model to find where causality could force trends into a new direction.

Once again, making the distinction between event, trend, and structure identifies important requirements of the foresight project, which, when heeded by the practitioners, help them become more effective in delivering what is expected of the project.

## The "Future of Desire" and the "Future of Fate"

An important distinction to be made in conversations about foresight is between the "future of desire" and the "future of fate." Desmond Bernal who first articulated this distinction in 1929 added: "man's reason has never learned to separate them properly." (Brand, 2000, p. 113) But understanding this distinction can be a matter of crucial importance in deciding what to do. For example, consider Tolstoy's analysis in *War and Peace* of Napoleon's debacle in Russia: "while Napoleon thought he was in control of events, the Russian general Kutuzov knew that neither of them were, and so he made fewer mistakes." (Tolstoy, 1982)

Many chapters in this book refer to this distinction, even if the language used differs sometimes. Under the heading of "future of desire" belong ideas such as "giving shape to the future," "foresight as invention," "transformative foresight," "normative scenarios," "strategic narratives," "entrepreneurial foresight as a commitment to a particular identity." Under the heading of "future of fate" belong ideas such as "probing the future," "foresight as prediction/navigation," "sensemaking foresight," "exploratory scenarios," "foresight as time travel," "entrepreneurial foresight as learning and adaptation." The distinction can be summarized in Table 12.1.

Why is it important to make this distinction? Consider a closely related issue: the common thinking flaw known as the "illusion of control," developed in an earlier chapter. In the future of desire, our commitment to a particular identity brings with it the danger of losing contact with reality, and loosening of our structural coupling with the environment. In the future of fate, our commitment to learning and adaptation brings the danger of paralysis in the face of complexity and uncertainty.

In our daily decision making we are dealing with both sides of this distinction at the same time. The potential contribution of foresight is to clarify what in our mental processes belongs to one side or the other. This will help us to address two important questions, (i) whether we have invested sufficiently in exploration and sensemaking, and (ii) whether our perceived strategic options are a fair reflection of our (always limited) sovereignty over the decision making situation. By making this distinction clear, foresight can surface these questions resulting in significant potential "process gain." But how can this be done? The next distinction that emerges from the writings in this book can be a powerful tool for the strategist in this respect.

## The "Contextual," "Transactional," and "Organizational" Environments

In order to minimize the dangers of the "illusion of control," it seems useful to mentally break up our environment in three parts, depending on the degree of control we believe we have. The first category is the contextual environment. This is the part of the world where we do not have any control or influence over the situation. In all foresight work it seems useful to try to be specific on the boundary of the territory where our influence ends. We are all subject to irreducible uncertainty, and identifying this puts the question of the illusion of control squarely on the table for us to address.

It is important to make a clear distinction between influence and "stake" in the situation. For example, if we are planning an outing tomorrow we may have a "stake" in the weather, but absolutely no influence over it. People often find it difficult to

**Table 12.1** Possible futures

| *Future of desire* | *Future of fate* |
| --- | --- |
| Giving shape to the future | Probing the future |
| Foresight as invention | Foresight as prediction/navigation |
| Transformative foresight | Sensemaking |
| Normative scenarios | Exploratory scenarios |
| Foresight as strategic narratives | Foresight as time travel |
| Commitment to a particular identity | Learning and adaptation |

accept their inability to influence situations that have a significant impact on them. However, sound foresight logic requires clarity on this issue. In the question of the boundary between the contextual and the transactional environments, it is important to consciously remove the consideration of "stake." In this distinction we are interested only in (potential) influence.

Does this mean there is nothing to be done in the contextual environment? On the contrary. A crucial contribution from foresight is to help us appreciate what is going on there. It involves linking history with perception, self-definition, and making sense of external signals, historical and current, and searching for internal inconsistencies in the resulting mental models. This is important because it will lead us towards understanding of some of the underlying causal relationships that any foresight project implicitly assumes as capable of extrapolation into the future. The foresight activity of appreciating the contextual environment is important in enhancing our understanding of the degree of influence we have in the transactional environment. In the transactional environment we (as a person or as an organization) are one of the players – i.e. we can influence the outcome of the game being played on this "playing field." But the shape and condition of the playing field is being determined in the contextual environment. Appreciating the contextual environment tells us whether the field is skewed, and in whose direction. This understanding is crucial to designing the game we will play.

Designing our game requires knowledge about us as well as about the playing field. While the contextual environment can be appreciated, and the transactional environment influenced, we have significant control within our own organization. We can change it, strengthen some aspects and weaken others, and in that way shape the game and influence its outcome. This is "future of desire" territory where we pursue aspirations, such as winning the game, or even, at a higher conceptual level, "creating a better future." This is where foresight work becomes normative and transformational.

Making the distinction is useful in any foresight project, as it develops a clearer understanding about where sense-making ends, and the normative world begins. Some people may want to engage with foresight methods because they feel they have lost contact with what is happening in the contextual environment. They need a sense-making approach. Others may want to develop a better understanding on how to enhance the position of their own organization. This requires a more normative strategic approach. Knowing where you are helps in a more skilful choice of foresight objective and method.

## A Purpose Framework

The authors of this book agree that the future is a mental construct. It derives from the way we interpret the past and the present. The future also drives action. Our actions and those of our organizations are not like playing ping-pong, reacting in a one-on-one fashion to incoming signals. Instead, our cognitive systems intermediate, and the mental constructs that we call "futures" play an important part in this process.

Sir Geoffrey Vickers (1965) adopted the name "interpretative system" for this intermediation process. He suggested that this system essentially depends on arriving at three judgments, which he called the appreciative judgment, the instrumental judgment and the value judgment. The appreciative judgment creates a picture of the state of the environment, the instrumental judgment decides on what levers for action are available, and the value judgment decides on what is desirable or not. The criteria on which these judgments are made are the result of experience, based on our activities in the past, and how these were correlated with subsequent events.

We have emphasized the importance of applying certain distinctions in foresight situations to help in making foresight projects more purposeful and thereby more successful. It seems that Vickers' model maps closely to the categories developed in this book. On that basis we arrive at three basic purpose categories for foresight projects:

1  In the contextual environment → Appreciative foresight.
2  In the transactional environment → Instrumental foresight.
3  In the organizational environment → Value foresight.

The following three examples illustrate how foresight can be categorized in this way.

## Appreciative Foresight

The purpose is to explore an as yet unexplored problematic situation. Deciding an intervention is not part of this foresight project. Instead we aim for sensitizing, reframing, surfacing assumptions, making sense, "seeing," anticipating.

An example of an appreciative project was the now legendary first application of the scenario approach in business, carried out by Pierre Wack in the Shell Company in the 1960s. This led to a reframing of the perception of the oil market by, for the first time, seriously looking at it from the perspective of oil producing countries. Up till that time it was assumed that governments give out concessions and companies decide production levels. This was the "Business as usual" world, based on clearly defined and understood role-assumptions. Scenario exploration made the team ask a new and maverick question: "What would happen if governments of producing countries decided to use their potential power to take on a new role in influencing production levels?" The team found that in the market conditions of that time, such a change could create an unexpectedly dramatic trend break, putting into focus the real possibility of a major price crisis in the not too distant future. This insight allowed Shell to "see" its business environment in a new way, and made the company prepared for the unprecedented price explosion when it actually happened a few years later.

## Instrumental Foresight

The purpose is to set direction and help in decision-making. While appreciative foresight aims to open up, instrumental foresight works towards closure. It is about how we can best act on the "playing field" towards winning the game. This may involve mapping options for intervention, mapping uncertainty, testing the business idea, "wind tunneling" options, building confidence to act, and involving stakeholders in decisions. The instrumental use of scenarios is the most common in the organizational world, where scenario projects aim to develop test beds for considering the relative merits of optional strategic decisions. Typical examples are companies considering major investments and wanting to create a larger more solid platform for decisions than available through traditional "business as usual" forecasting.

In a recent example a large company, finding itself under pressure in one of its markets identified their main game options as "withdraw," "keep ticking over," "make only investments with quick pay-outs," and "invest for the long term." The next step was to map these in a matrix against four contrasting scenarios of the contextual environment in which the game would play out. Each scenario/option combination was carefully evaluated. Overviewing the whole matrix it became clear that one game was always inferior and, therefore, had to be rejected ("withdraw"), and that the choice between the other three games would be a trade-off between level of potential returns versus level of risk of a negative outcome. Instrumental foresight helps management to decide to what extent they wish to take on future commitments, and where they need to invest in flexibility to be able to deal with the fundamentally unpredictable.

## *Value Foresight*

The purpose of value foresight is to bring groups of people together in a process of consensus building on the "future of desire." Value foresight helps organizations by strengthening future orientation, challenging groupthink, team building and language creation, bridge building with others, increasing common ground, and culture change. An example of a value foresight project was the Mont Fleur project in South Africa in the early 1990s, at the time discussions between the parties on apartheid had just started. Many in the hitherto suppressed population started to realize that a role in government was becoming a possibility, and that it would be rather different from the resistance "warfare" role that had been their daily life until then. While the value of overcoming apartheid had been a strong binding force between them, such a common value was less obvious for the time when this had been achieved, and trade-offs would have to be made in the collective domain.

The project brought together a wide range of individuals who decided they wanted to align their values by thinking through possible futures for South Africa, depending on possible changes in the power structure, and how they, as new players, might define their role and approach to governance. Many Mont Fleur participants subsequently moved on into influential government roles, and the scenarios made a significant contribution to the smooth transition by introducing a common language in which the new governance issues could be discussed. (Nelson Mandela: "Explain to me how this proposal does not lead to Icarus." [Icarus is one of the Mont Fleur scenarios] (Internal communication Adam Kahane)).

## Conclusions from the Examples

The three examples are presented here as illustrations of the very different shapes of foresight projects, depending on the objectives. In practice few foresight projects we have studied start from a clearly defined set of objectives. As a result projects drift around for long periods of time until the aims start to emerge and the project becomes more purposeful. Many projects do not even reach that stage and are prematurely scuttled, due to perceived "lack of progress." A major step forwards can be made by using the distinctions developed in this book to define the objectives of the project in unequivocal terms, thereby making it more purposeful and increasing its chances for success.

### Aesthetics

So what is next in the field of foresight? At the end of our considerations of the current field of foresight we find another aspect emerging as clearly under-developed. This is the question of motivation. Why do people want to engage with the future, why does such a thing as the "future of desire" exist, why do we like some futures better than others? The question arises clearly when we discuss value-based foresight, but even in the most rationalist appreciative foresight projects we can recognize moments of "magic" when a new perspective reveals a new reality and the feeling of "we can see it now" breaks through. This "aha" experience is an aesthetic moment, when the beauty of seeing something new evokes feelings of deep engagement and satisfaction.

Motivation of people, groups, and organizations is a crucial aspect of foresight work and is as yet unexplored. Does the field of aesthetics have something to offer to the foresight fraternity?

### REFERENCES

Brand, S. (2000) *The Clock of the Long Now*, New York: Basic Books.
Tolstoy, L (1982) *War and Peace*, Harmondsworth: Penguin.
Vickers, G. (1965) *The Art of Judgement*, London: Harper and Row.

CHESTER COLLEGE WARRINGTON LIBRARY

# Index